ESTONIA

The Guide

John O´Brien

HUMA®
Tallinn 1993

ESTONIA – The Guide

by John O'Brien

In collaboration with:
Mihkel Tiks, Andres Tõnisson, Urmas Kaup, Anu Jõesaar, Arvi Paidla, Hans Salm, Toomas Kokovkin, Gunnar Isotamm, Heino Mägi, Mare Albri
Photos: Taavi Grepp, Hillar Uusi, Toomas Huik.
Maps: Anne Tõnisson, Olev Soans, Regio Ltd.
Design: Piret Niinepuu
Layout: Sverre Lasn

Publisher: Huma Publishing Ltd.
P. O. Box 41 EE 0090 Tallinn.
Fax 372 - 2 44 16 58

Printer: Tallinna Raamatutrükikoda

ISBN 9985 - 801 - 01 - 6

Things to do, places to go...

There are four main reasons to visit Estonia: a green and pleasant landscape, a sturdy people with an ancient culture, a history that's written in bold strokes across the country, and the thrill of a nation reawakening after more or less 700 years of slavery. But let's get more specific:

Remnants of history

Estonia has been relatively free two-and-a-half times: up until the 12th century as an ancient Scandinavian culture; during the previous time of independence (1919-40); and today in post-Soviet days. (For more detail, read the last chapter and Tallinn and Tartu chapters.) The rulers and their Estonian underlings have left their mark upon the land ...

Where hill-forts stood: Ancient Estonian villages clustered around earthen fortresses, often built on hills or deep in forests or bogs. The wooden buildings have disappeared but the hilltops and some ramparts have survived. Many have had further careers as sites for churches, crypts or stone fortresses ... after all, they had the best sites! Other ancient relics include stone barrows (graves), sacrificial stones, and sacred trees and springs.

Medieval ruins: The first invaders brought with them the knowledge of building in stone. The ruins of their fortresses represent the early days of feudalism, when the German knights and bishops divided the country up among them. Some fortresses have been restored (most famous are the bishop's castle on Saaremaa island, and Narva's fortress which today looks over a controversial border with Russia). Several churches were built in gothic style, though many have undergone reconstruction and show typically Lutheran restraint. Their lofty steeples stand over villages and plains.

Smart national costume – reviving tradition.

The masters: Even when the Russian czars ruled, the barons in this country were Germans. In villages the finest building is often the manor house with its subsidiary buildings and manor park. Hundreds are spread around the country, the showpiece being Palmse estate in Western Virumaa. Only a few are in good condition inside and out. Some have fine exteriors but have been completely reconstructed inside to serve as schools, museums or collective farm offices; others are in ruin. The descendants of many of the owners are claiming back the property taken from them by the Soviets in the 1940s, and will renovate the magnificent neoclassical buildings and stone stables.

The servants: Serfdom was only abolished in the Russian Empire in 1819. While the Baltic-Germans were lording it in their manors, the bulk of the people were leading harsh lives as serfs or peasants. They lived in traditional wood or stone houses and were closely linked to the land and the seasons. You can see peasant architecture all over the country. The protected village of Koguva on Muhu island, the open-air museum at Rocca al Mare in Tallinn and several other museums evoke the days of sleeping in the threshing room, smoking fish in the sauna, and tilling small plots of land. People in the south-east still live in traditional villages, and there's a fashion among city-dwellers to build peasant-style summer cottages. Vassals for centuries, the people still love the land. Indeed, the national flower is the cornflower and the national bird is the barn swallow.

The cornflower, Estonia's national flower, is modest, bright and rural.

Life in towns: Wooden private houses, health resorts and mud institutes, enormous blocks of flats, Hanseatic towns, towns famous for their university (Tartu), bars and beaches (Pärnu), oil-shale hills (Kohtla-Järve), ruins (Viljandi, Rakvere, Haapsalu) and rebuilt forts (Kuressaare, Narva), role in history (Viljandi, Võru), hedges (Türi), mud baths, factories, parks, town halls, festivals ... And of course there's that city in which it's all concentrated, good and bad, marvellous and horrid, Tallinn.

Soviet stuff: For 50 years the Soviets controlled Estonia, shaping the country as forcefully and as violently as any previous ruler. Equality for the masses seemed to mean a crazy economy based on decisions made in Moscow, shoddy factory products, queuing as a way of life, perishing concrete housing, and a low life expectancy despite the free health care. There are remnants of these times everywhere. But now ...

Shifting meanings in a changing land

The rule of the Soviets has ended – Estonians are retaking control of their land. The nation is waking up, blinking in the new light and wiping the sleep from its eyes. In August 1991 Estonia re-established its independence. In 1992 it introduced its own currency, the kroon ("crown", EEK), backed by gold reserves deposited in foreign banks 50 years before. Driven by economic pressures as much as anything else, the Soviet occupying force began to trickle away.

Visitors are coming to help or merely to witness the country being transformed from a command-led Soviet economy to a capitalist one, with all the joys and problems of traumatic transition. It's a fascinating time to be here. Change is happening swiftly, and we apologise for any inaccuracies caused by the rapid changes.

Right now Estonia is hunting out its own identity. How should it think of itself, as European, western, developing, or something else? Should it look eastwards to related peoples in Siberia? Should it retain its old traditions or create a new culture? There are plenty of hurdles, such as an economy in tatters, the mass consumption of everything western, rising unemployment and failing industry. Crime is on the up, though as a westerner you should be safe as long as you exercise reasonable caution.

Forests -- and forest fruits

If you don't like trees, don't leave Tallinn. There are more forests today than when the Red Army invaded at the end of World War II. You can discover rustling birch woods, stark, aromatic pinewoods, sacred oaks and oak groves, birch forests, limetree-lined lanes. Under the arbours dwell elks and roes, wild boars, wolves, lynxes and even bears. So far north, the seasons shape life. July is the warmest month (average temperature 17°C) and February the coldest (average temperature -5°C). Though spring is short, summer is long and fruitful and autumn an extended explosion of colour.

In May the rhubarb pies fill cafe shelves. In September mushrooms cover forest floors and grace meat dishes. And between the two, a cornucopia of forest, marsh and field fruits come in and out of season, and a trip into the woods isn't complete without the pleasure of picking berries and other fruits. After 5000 years here, the people have deep roots in the land, and the seasons are keenly felt on the menu.

If hunting's your thing, Estvitalis hunting club has offices in most counties ... or you can organise a hunting party through a private tourist firm. Elk season is 15 Sept-15 Dec, roedeer Sept-Nov, lynx Nov-Feb, wild geese and ducks Aug-Nov, and wild boars, wolves, raccoons and foxes all year round.

Hills, lakes, islands and bogs

Estonia's loveliest landscapes lie in the south-eastern corner -- in the Haanja highlands of Võru county, the hills around the Võrtsjärv lake, southern Põlva county and the Otepää area. Here be numerous small lakes, some buried deep in forests, others lying beside towns. The roads climb and curve around hillsides, and many hills have viewing towers. The most famous tower is on top of the highest peak in the Baltics, Suur Munamägi ("great egg hill", though it still hasn't hatched), a giant 318 m above sea level.

Most of Estonia is flat, relieved only by varied forests or the odd farmstead or collective farm. Bogs and marshes cover over a fifth of the land though you rarely see them from the road. Pure bog pools, cranberry fields, horseflies and mosquitoes ... Only in a few places do tracks cross the bogs; otherwise you should go with a guide or a knowledgable local, who can pull you out if you get caught.

More accessible are the islands, nowadays. There are 1500 islands: until a couple of years ago, almost all were part of the Soviet frontier zone, and therefore off-limits even to non-resident Estonians. Some were systematically depopulated. The islands have their own culture, dialects, food and wildlife. Ironically the Soviet restrictions helped preserve some unique ecosystems on Saaremaa and Hiiumaa islands and on many tiny islets.

Cemeteries and other monuments

Estonians take their cemeteries seriously. A grave of raked sand, a little seat, a juniper bush in each corner of the plot and a small pot of flowers seems more zen than Estonian, yet it's typical. Headstones tend to be small and restrained, and decorated with an inspirational relief. An old hand-pump often stands amid the graves and gets plenty of use. Every graveyard has its own personality: Kuusalu's, for example, is enormous, sparse, peaceful, and divided along national lines; while Viljandi's Riia St cemetery is an overgrown and heavily populated hill. Of course a forest hangs over the graves, which makes graveyards seasonal too (ah, autumn ...).

In churchyards, town squares, on hilltops and deep in swamps, monuments to the War of Independence (1918-20) have been proliferating recently. Every town has one. When the Red Army was closing in during World War II, Estonians rescued many of the statues and hid them in hearths and haylofts. Now they're back, exuding a 1930s heroic charm. You can also find busts of writers, statues of figures involved with the national awakening last century, and Soviet war memorials and worker monuments. You might even discover the odd Lenin or Stalin in a museum or in someone's basement.

Interesting places to eat and drink

One theory has it that what Estonian eating places lack in adventurous food, they make up for in atmosphere. If there's a medieval cellar, an old post-station, windmill or fortress tower, someone will stick in a bar or restaurant. And tales of Soviet cuisine are fast becoming legends and distant memories. You can still find those typical fatty meat and overcooked vegetable meals, especially in a canteen *(söökla)* or small-town restaurant. But seasonal fruits and vegetables, local breads and beers, pastries, soups and ice-creams can be choice. Many bars and restaurants have live music. Country groups are popular, and even the most uncoordinated Estonians will get up and dance, usually in couples.

Festivals

From May to September is festival time all over Estonia. Haapsalu's White Lady Festival, Türi's flower fair, Rock Summer in Tallinn, Pärnu's Fiesta, accordian festivals, jazz and country music festivals, folk festivals, Tartu's Dionysian days, Setu village wars, Kihnu weddings... Some are big events featuring international acts, but if you're lucky you might chance on a local celebration.

Then there's national party night! Estonians celebrate Midsummer Eve on the night of 23 June (one day later

Three things that dwell in Estonian hearts – the lakes, the sea and old homesteads.

on Muhu island), sitting round bonfires, singing, dancing, eating and wandering off with a lover in search of the elusive fern flower. They swing on their town swings - the "Estonian national sex symbol", as one artist has put it - and wear traditional costumes. This is Jaaniôhtu, the Eve of St John's Day, when dawn gives dusk the gentlest kiss, as the old story goes. There are numerous local legends tied to it, and if your name is John you may find yourself the centre of attention.

John O'Brien

Star sights

* *recommended*
** *highly recommended*
*** *very important and/or beautiful*

TALLINN

Population: 495 000 **Area: 182,4 km²**

HISTORY OF TALLINN

Linda's tears and Tallinn's names

As you approach from the sea, the medieval skyline of the Old Town of Tallinn rises above the busy ranks of harbour cranes. For centuries merchants and travellers have seen the same tall spires from their ships as they landed. Then they headed through the Great Coast Gate and followed a long street into the lower town to conduct their business. Most paid a visit to the Hall of the Great Guild on the way. But Tallinn was a divided city even in the Middle Ages. Above the bustling merchant centre there stood a mighty fortress on a great hill 50 m high: **Toompea.** Here the rulers lived, seemingly aloof from the dirty business of money. Here was the cathedral, as it still is today. And today Toompea remains a fortress, a symbol, the heart of the capital of Estonia.

According to the national epic poem, *Kalevipoeg*, Toompea is also a burial mound. When great king Kalev died it was left to his wife, Linda, to bury him. Afterwards she gathered huge boulders and began to build a tombstone. She worked diligently the entire day and that night the tremendous memorial was almost complete. As she forged uphill carrying the last boulder in her apron, the apron-string suddenly snapped and out rolled the boulder. The exhausted woman sat down and burst into tears. Linda cried for a long time, so long that her tears formed a lake. Today **Lake Ülemiste** is the main source of drinking water for Tallinners. It's not the world's cleanest: some genius planner in the 1930s built Tallinn Airport right next to it. **Lindakivi** ("Linda's stone"), the one that escaped from her apron, lies in the lake near the shore. So Toompea is a royal monument without the last stone.

Weeping Linda and proud Pikk Hermann.

(By the way, the lake is also the dwelling place of the mysterious Old Man of Ülemiste, who knocks at the city gate once a year and asks if the city is finished yet. The correct answer is no, since he's sworn to drown the city as soon as it's completed. And so the building of the

Tallinn's arms on the Great Coast Gate may have welcomed your great great great grandfather.

city continues feverishly even today, though about 1/3 of Estonia's inhabitants already live in Tallinn.)
You can see a sculpture of the mourning Linda on the slope of Toompea hill. She might have been weeping for Tallinn's future as well. The history of the city, like that of Estonia, is fraught with invasion and suppression ... something the city's several names bear witness to. When the Arab traveller al-Idrisi marked Tallinn on his map of the known world in 1154, he called it Kolyvan, which comes from the Old-Estonian word *kaleva* meaning strong and brave. But the Danes conquered Toompea and founded their fortress there, Castrum Danorum. Estonians translated this to *Tanin Lidna* ("Danish fortress") or later *Taani Linn* ("city of the Danes"). In the 17th century this was shortened to Tallinn. The Germans, who would rule Estonia for centuries, called Tallinn Reval, after the old Estonian district Rävala. To Russians it was Revel or Tallin with one "n" for a long time; but the spelling was so important to Estonians that the Russian authorities were forced to add the other "n". By now the passions revolving around the name have calmed down and Tallinn is only Tallinn, for everyone.

Trade

Trade makes cities, and **ancient Estonian Tallinn** was already an important trading centre. Some streets in the Old Town still follow the routes of the old inland tradeways; three of them – Lai, Pikk and Ratas-kaevu Sts – lead to the port. From the junction of Pikk and Lai Sts, Pikk jalg ("long leg") climbs up Toompea hill. All the tradeways met near the old market place, now Raekoja plats (Town Hall Square).
The city was based upon "three whales" – the fortress, the market place and the port. Warehouses, stores and sheds for nets and fishing boats surrounded the port. There were warehouses for merchants and houses for artisans near the market place as well. They may have only been used in summertime, since it seems that Estonians wintered elsewhere.

City of the Danes

In 1193 Pope Celestine III declared that the crusade against heathens was to be waged not only in Palestine, but in Northern Europe as well. There's some evidence that Estonians near the principal trade routes may already have been christianised – but Estonia, especially Tallinn, spelt trade and profit, so the army of Bishop Albert and the **German Knights of the Sword** invaded Estonia from the south. They fought bloody battles over 20 years (1208-27) before the heathens surrendered.

Once a medieval merchant's house ... but are the Three Sisters ready to marry for money in the new Estonia?

Toompea has never been taken by assault.

In 1219, while the Germans were taking the southern half of the land, their ally King Valdemar II of **Denmark** landed in Tallinn with 1500 ships. A bloody battle ensued. The heathens frightened the Danes and by the third day they were on the verge of flight. As a last resort, Archbishop Andres raised his eyes towards heaven, and (lo!) the heavens opened and a red flag with a white cross fell into his hands. The Danes gained courage and eventually won a resounding victory. This battle gave the Danes their national flag.

The alliance of Danes and Germans crumbled and in 1227 the Knights of the Sword took Toompea and built the first stone fortress there. In 1238 the Danes got it back. They would control the fortress for over a century ... long enough for the city to earn its name "Taani linn". But it was the Germans who sowed the seeds of greatness during their first brief reign when, in 1230, they invited 200 German merchant families to settle at the foot of the hill.

Tallinn port – the "window to Europe" as dreamed by Czar Peter I.

Hanseatic greatness

Fortified Niguliste kirik (St Nicholas church) became the German merchants' centre. By 1285 Tallinn was a member of the **Hanseatic League** of northern European trading cities. In medieval times Hanseatic towns were the trading hubs of Europe. They were glued together by a common trading language, German.

In 1346, three years after the Estonians' last-ditch attempt to retake their land in the St George's Night uprising, the Danes sold Tallinn and north Estonia to the Teutonic Order, who sold it on to the Livonian Order. **German nobles** again settled into Toompea. Wealth

A little village rose around Niguliste church ...

and population grew, and so did the frequency of fires. The citizens began to build larger houses out of limestone. Streets were paved with limestone slabs and cobbles. In 1360 the City Council ordered home-owners to sweep the streets in front of their doors on Saturdays, so that folk wouldn't spoil their clothes going to church on Sundays. The city executioner swept the streets on working days.

A wall-anchor is handsome (also holds the house together).

From the 13th century on, Tallinn was divided into two parts: the upper town, citadel of feudal power, and the lower town of merchants and artisans. Each party had its own interests and laws. Typically for a Hanseatic city, gentry and merchants were usually at loggerheads. For 700 years a high, thick wall with heavy gates locked at nightfall separated the upper town from the lower. The city pocketed the keys and thus Toompea, born as a geological island, remained a social one as well.
The Hanseatic times were Tallinn's heyday. The greatness of the Old Town today lies in the **sheer volume of medieval architecture** that's survived. Despite wars and fires, walls, towers, churches and medieval houses have been preserved in their original form.
So who built Tallinn? As you walk through the streets are you looking at

an Estonian city, a German city or what? Nowadays historians believe that "Hanseatic" is the best description. Ethnic Germans were the most powerful group and held all the important positions, but within Tallinn there were Swedish and Russian communities, and an Estonian community around Pühavaimu ("Holy Ghost") church, the poorest church. Nine out of ten stonemasons in the late Middle Ages were Estonian, but none were masters, and they were prohibited from joining the most powerful guilds. So it seems that Germans laid the plans while Estonian workers laid the bricks.

Tallinn became the main centre where goods from the west (salt, cloth, arms, wine, herring) were landed. From here they were sent on to the central Russian city of Novgorod. Russian goods (furs, hides, wax, honey, fish, fat, linen, hemp, tar) travelled the other way. The most important commodity was salt. A medieval saying had it that Tallinn was built on salt. By the 16th century, with almost 8000 inhabitants, Tallinn was one of the largest cities in Northern Europe. The flow of immigrants was large, especially runaway serfs. Any serf who remained unclaimed for a year and a day under town law was given freedom.

Tallinn's secret

By the 16th century the power of the Hanseatic League was diminishing, the trade in salt had dwindled. The **Russians** had barely escaped from the rule of the Tartars when Moscow felt a yen to obtain the Baltic countries. Tallinn ceased to be an economic power during the Livonian War (1558-83). The war coincided with years of plague, storms and bitterly cold winters that froze the harbour. From that time on, the city more and more resembled an impoverished nobleman who keeps patching his tatty dress coat and polishing his old decorations ...

Which explains why medieval Tallinn is so well-preserved: it was too poor to throw out anything! If something was demolished, it was only to repair a corner of wall, a pillar or a bay window. That's how Lennart Meri, writer, ethnographer and president of Estonia, explains the secret of Tallinn.

The war was long and cruel (and complicated). Ivan the Terrible repeatedly invaded Estonia over the course of the war. When the German Order suffered a devastating defeat at the Battle of Eremäe, both it and the citizens of the lower town offered the city and northern Estonia to the Swedish king, who was only too happy to take them up on the offer.

Ivan came back with a vengeance. In 1577 an ultimatum arrived ordering immediate surrender; otherwise every hut, shed and garden belonging to the people would be burned down. Panicky fortification began in the city. Where rose gardens had grown beside the town wall, a moat was dug. Tallinn was besieged for a total of 30 weeks before Ivan gave up. Tallinn and north Estonia were under **Swedish rule.** The Swedes then battled the Poles for south Estonia – by 1645 they controlled the whole country.

Under the Swedes

The plague of 1603 decimated the

In odd corners of the Old Town it's still the Middle Ages.

population. In 1684 a fire destroyed nearly all the buildings on Toompea. In 1695-97 Estonia was hit by a great famine. The rights of Tallinn were gradually diminished throughout the 17th century. Yet, despite it all, that era is recalled as the "good old Swedish days". The ages before and after were so much more dreadful.
For under his rule, Swedish King Gustav Adolf's education policy laid the basis for the development of a school system in Estonia. Primary schools were founded in towns, a teachers' seminary was set up, a grammar school was opened in Tallinn in 1631 and a university was founded in Tartu; these beginnings would thoroughly change the lives of Estonians. Russia began to deal with the problem of illiteracy only after 1917, while Estonia was one of the most literate countries in Europe by 1886.

From the czars to independence

The Swedes restricted the rights of the German gentry still ruling in their Estonian manors. Peasants were granted the right to own private property and even to sue their own masters. The barons began to work against the Swedes and favoured a new **Russian intervention.** In 1700 Peter I started the Northern War, attempting in his turn to gain access to the Baltic Sea – "to cut a window to Europe". Ten years later the Russian army reached Tallinn. Bombing and an outbreak of plague in the city forced the Swedish garrison, the Knighthood of Estonia and a meeting of Tallinn's citizens to surrender.

The cannons have rusted, and Paks Margareta ("fat Margaret") can be at peace.

This appeased the Russian authorities but not the plague: by the end of the year, less than 2000 of Tallinn's 10 000 inhabitants were left. By the end of the Northern War, the Russian general Sheremetyev could assure the Czar that "neither a dog's bark nor a rooster's crow can be heard in the land from Narva to Riga."
From 1721 the Baltic countries belonged to the czars. Tallinn became a provincial centre of the Russian Empire. The local elite remained the German gentry; any privileges that Sweden had restricted were restored. In Estonia serfdom would reign for another century.
Tallinn continued to struggle along until 1870, when the St Petersburg railway line opened, connecting it with Moscow and other parts of Russia. Tallinn swiftly became the third largest seaport in the Russian Empire after St Petersburg and Odessa. Industry developed, and the population of the city increased, for the factories needed workers. And workers – mainly Estonian peasants – needed training. The number of schools doubled. Estonia moved towards **national awakening.** The capital's second period of growth and building, lasting until today, began.
The national movement was centred in Tartu, but Estonians were active in Tallinn too, and in 1904 they managed to take control of the town council. In 1905 during the first Russian revolution, which failed, Estonian nationalists too rose up. It ended with the Czar's army units shooting at people in the centre of Tallinn and punitive expeditions rampaging through the countryside. The February Revolution of 1917 swept away the czarist empire. Yet

The sun, the sea, the towers.

an independent state of Estonia was only born after the October Revolution in Russia. It was followed in Estonia by short-lived Bolshevik power, proclamation of the **Republic of Estonia,** and the War of Independence against Russia and Baltic-German forces. The Red Army reached almost 20 km from Tallinn before the tide of war turned. Finally on 24 February 1919 Prime Minister Konstantin Päts could declare: the soil of Estonia is free of enemies!

Years of independence

For 20 years Tallinn enjoyed the status of capital of an independent state. The task of the young republic was to restore what had been destroyed by war and create a basis for economic development. A great part of Estonian industry was concentrated in Tallinn: at least seven large enterprises and a number of smaller ones. The rebuilt port regained its prominence, and traded directly with six foreign ports.

The look of the city changed. Peter's Square lost its statue of Peter the Great and became Vabaduse väljak ("freedom square"), surrounded by modernist buildings designed by Estonian architects. Parks were restored and new ones founded. The shabby and decaying provincial town was transformed into a proud and beautiful city.

Hit by war (again)

In 1940 the **Soviet Union** annexed the Baltic states. In 1941 the **German army** came. On the evening of 9 March 1944 Soviet planes bombed Tallinn. The bombing had no strategic value: it was a show of raw power. Hundreds were left homeless, districts of old wooden houses burned down, and buildings of historical value were destroyed. More than 50 years of **Soviet occupation** followed.

After 50 years as Tallinn 1st Secondary School, the Gustav Adolf High School, founded in 1631, has got its old name back.

The building of socialism

Soviet power saw unlimited possibilities to expand industry of every kind in Tallinn. New, large enterprises appeared by the dozens. Old businesses that made, for example, cars, were converted into single-product factories making, for example, one tank part. As the existing labour force did not suffice, unrestrained immigration from Russia began. In 1937 there were 175 000 inhabitants in Tallinn; today there are nearly half a million.

The new proletariat had to be housed somewhere. Unrestrained construction burgeoned, which continues today. More than 100 000 people live in one "concrete jungle" alone, the new housing district Lasnamäe. An earnest Estonian is said to have already cried out, "Hey, Old Man of Ülemiste, Lasnamäe is completed!"

The school remembers its royal Swedish founder.

New hopes

Gorbachev's **perestroika era** brought new hope for freedom and a better life. In the beginning, people believed in the "good czar" and "economic independence": the Baltic states would be the vanguard of the new revolution. The independence movement was unchained in 1988, uniting the whole nation. Hundreds of thousands of people from every corner of Estonia arrived at the Song

Festival Grounds to affirm their existence through song. National awakening, known as the **"Singing Revolution"**, began anew. Now Estonia, together with its capital, is attemtping to clean up the mess left by the Soviet Union.
And what a mess, as any visit to Tallinn will assure you! Tallinn hosts prestigious choral festivals, political gatherings and scientific conferences, but its inhabitants have to wait for years to get a telephone installed or to buy a car. The streets abound in attractively dressed people, but in Tallinn's slums you can see old women in shabby dresses dragging piles of peat briquette to heat stoves in small abodes that lack any modern conveniences. Tallinn takes pride in its rich history and national identity, yet there is almost no money available for maintaining its museums or restoring its great buildings. Over 50% of its population is non-Estonian. Although a third of Tallinn's territory is covered with parks and verdant areas, air pollution levels are enormous at busy traffic junctions. There's a wonderful sandy beach at Pirita, but on Tallinn's 45 km coastline you can hardly find clean water to swim in.
That's the current battle in a nutshell. And that's what you, a visitor, will witness: a beautiful, historic, cluttered town, full of contrasts, striving yet again to become a worthy centrepiece to a nation.

THE OLD TOWN

The Old Town is divided in two: Toompea was the mighty citadel and home of the rulers of Estonia; the thriving lower town is one of the best preserved medieval centres in Europe.

Getting there

Old Tallinn is best toured on foot. Its heart, **Town Hall Square,** is also the most popular meeting place and the easiest spot to find.
The most imposing way to Town Hall Square is **along Viru St,** which starts opposite the Viru Hotel and leads through the old outer Viru Gate right up to the town hall itself. The street leading **from the passenger terminal** is Sadama St, and a left from it into Mere pst *(puiestee =* "boulevard") skirts the Old Town for 500 m before reaching Viru St. Harju St on the north side of **Vabaduse väljak,** diagonally across from the Palace Hotel, goes straight to Town Hall Square. From the **Olümpia Hotel** head north-west along Lembitu St past the limestone Sakala Centre, round the Estonia Theatre and cross Pärnu mnt *(maantee =* "main road" or "highway"); several small streets lead into the centre from here. If you're coming from the **Balti jaam railway station,** take the pedestrian tunnel; the street between the parks, Nunne St, curves round to a junction of several streets; a left into Voorimehe St goes to Town Hall Square.

Orientation

From Town Hall Square, Niguliste church with its white tower and black turret is a little way to the south along Kullassepa/Harju St. Alleys on the north side lead to Pikk St and thence north past the towering spike of Oleviste church to the Great Coast Gate. Viru St leads eastwards to Narva mnt and from there 210 km to Narva.
To get from Town Hall Square to the upper town of Toompea, use Voorimehe St which goes to a

The last Estonian Republic was declared in this building (11 Estonia pst).

The Soviets renamed Vabaduse väljak ("freedom square") Victory Square. Now it's freedom again.

gateway at the foot of a steep, cobbled street, **Pikk jalg** ("long leg"). This most atmospheric way up to Toompea was for centuries the only entrance.

Don't worry too much about getting lost: this is a medieval city, it was designed so that 500 years later visitors *would* get lost and discover out-of-the-way crannies for themselves. If in doubt, head for the towers.

TOOMPEA

A fortress has stood on Toompea since ancient times. This is the citadel of nobles, the seat of power, the home of parliament and of the Lutheran and Orthodox cathedrals. Toompea has been much altered since medieval times. Only a few buildings survived a devastating fire in 1684.

Where the tricolour flies

Everybody who has ever ruled over Estonia has settled down at **Toompea*****. The fact that the upper town was the residence of the nobility, in contrast to the merchants and craftsmen in the lower town, is obvious even from the houses, which are grander on Toompea than those down below.

The most important building is **Toompea Castle*****. It was built in 1227-29 by the Knights of the Sword as a small fortress within the larger fortress of Toompea. Like Estonia itself, it's been enlarged, fortified, dismantled and rebuilt over the centuries. Today only the northern and western walls and three towers have been preserved in their 15th century form. The tallest tower, **Pikk Hermann** ("tall Hermann"), is the symbol of political power in Estonia; the flag at its top has always belonged to the masters of the land. Today, after a break of nearly 50 years, that flag is once again the Estonian blue, black and white tricolour. On the other hand, a Soviet monument on the base of the tower commemorates the 1905

uprising!
In the 1770s Russia tore down the eastern walls and built administrative buildings. As we went to press, visitors weren't allowed in to see the neoclassical interior, which is similar in places to Rägavere manor in Western Virumaa; the same man, Schultz, designed them both. Parliamentary sessions are held in the most recent addition, the **Riigikogu** ("parliament"), a pseudo-baroque wing from 1935 on the Pikk Hermann side of the castle complex.

Russian might

The first thing members of parliament see as they leave Toompea Castle is a piece of czarist Russia. Lossi plats ("castle place") was once much more spacious. There was a proposal in the 1890s to erect an enormous statue of Martin Luther here. But this was the high time of russification – Russian had just been made the sole language of education and officialdom, in a country which at that stage had hardly any Russians. So in the middle of the great old square the **Alexander Nevsky Orthodox church**** was completed in 1901. Money for the construction was collected throughout the Russian Empire and builders were brought in from Russia. The base of the huge building of limestone and bricks is Finnish granite. The most valuable piece in the cathedral is its **chime,** which includes the churchbell (about 3 m high and weighing 4.7 tonnes). The mosaic **icons** on the facade and many inside are also impressive.

Lasnamäe may one day be an open-air museum of Soviet architecture.

This is one of several overtly political churches built in Europe at the time: others include Sacre Coeur in Paris, and basilicas in Lyon, France, and Kaunas, Lithuania, all of which are similarly chunky. To bring the church closer to Estonians, the authorities made up a "legend". At the time of construction, an old man was said to have seen Kalev rise from an iron tomb under the basement of the church. The king of ancient Estonians was said to have promised to cast a spell on anybody who harmed the church. So in a sense the Nevsky cathedral is the final stone on Kalev's tomb.

The last barricades of Toompea? This was 1991.

In the 1930s there was a plan to relocate it. But the time to shift the church is now long past, even though in colour, style and political gall it clashes with Toompea's other buildings and almost overshadows the grey and modest, but venerable Toomkirik.

The cathedral

Toomkirik*** (St Mary's Cathedral) was first mentioned in records in 1223. Construction is believed to have begun as soon as the Danish army conquered Tallinn in 1219. In 1240 the church was consecrated and named the Main Church of Our Redeemer and Virgin Mary. Since then it has been the central church in Tallinn. Even today it's the hub from

which Toompea's streets radiate. The Estonian name, Toomkirik, comes from the German *domkirche,* which in turn gave the name to the citadel, named *Domberg* (in Estonian *Toompea)* by the Germans in 1486.
In 1684 a fire devastated Toompea and Toomkirik was rebuilt as a gothic basilica. The western tower in the late baroque style is younger, dating from the years 1778-79. After the fire, the ground on Toompea was covered with a layer of rubble a metre thick. The new church was built onto the surviving foundations of the old one, and that's why the cathedral seems to have sunk into the ground: its portal is low and you have to step downstairs to enter the church.
Toomkirik no longer looks as powerful as it did in the Middle Ages when it towered sinisterly and mysteriously above the houses of its vassals. But the **interior** is as impressive as ever with old wooden benches, memorial tablets and coats-of-arms on the walls and grave slabs worn smooth by the feet of dozens of generations of churchgoers. The renaissance grave monuments and sarcophagi, the baroque altar and pulpit, the triumphal arch group, and epitaphs in the form of coats-of-arms add colour to the sparse Lutheran interior. Only nobles and rich merchants had the right to be buried in the church. Among the important people interred here are Swedish general Pontus de la Gardie and his wife Sophie Gyllenhelm, daughter of King Johann III of Sweden, and the first Russian circumnavigator of the earth, Adam Johann Krusenstern.

Lord's-eye view of Tallinn

Some houses miraculously survived the fire in 1684: **21 Toomkooli** and **4 Rahukohtu** Sts both date from the 17th century. Most other important buildings are of later origin: the

Viru Gate, entryway to the Old Town.

Commandant's house at 1 Toompea St, the dwelling houses at 2 Kiriku plats ("church square"), and 1-7 Lossi plats were built in the 18th century.
More important than individual buildings though is the atmosphere that overwhelms you on Toompea, especially in the evening when the restorers and tourists have gone home and the cobbled streets echo with your footsteps. The home of nobles, rulers and ministries still seems cut off from the bustle in the lower town. It's a shame that so little has survived from the "Time of the Order". The folk of the more free-thinking lower town long regarded the German knights as cruel, pompous and sometimes even ridiculous, but they were an integral part of medieval life. The lords in their turn believed the free towns were "disgracing both divine and human laws". Although the Order had lost its power by 1560, it left behind a late feudal system of barons in manors and a fettered peasantry in the countryside.
Back to the city ... there's a surprise waiting for you at the end of some streets, when you chance upon one of the viewing points. The **view***** spreads before you of old and new Tallinn with its towers, tiled roofs, chimneystacks and factories, the more distant parts of the city, and, of course, the sea.

Towers and town wall

One attractive section of the town wall stretches along the southern part of Toompea. The squared tower is a legendary watering-hole for tourists and students, **Neitsitorn**** ("virgin's tower"). Its ironical name is said to date back to the Middle Ages, when it was used as a prison for prostitutes. Now it's a cafe and one entire face of the tower is a window looking over the Old Town. You don't get the view from the Germanic-decor basement; that's famous for mulled wine instead.
The mightiest cannon tower in Tallinn, **Kiek in de Kök*****, is 46 m high, its diameter is 20 m and its walls 4 m thick. It was built in the late 15th century, though it lacked a roof ... as did most of Tallinn's wall towers when they were first erected. In 1577, Russian troops poured their cannonpower against the tower, and finally succeeded in smashing a hole into the wall of the 4th floor big enough, according to one commentator, to drive a pair of oxen through. Iron cannonballs have been walled into the tower as a memento of the damage. You can see them from the outside. The tower lost defensive relevance in the 18th century. At the beginning of this century weightlifters and wrestlers trained here.
Nowadays the six-storey building is a museum, by far the best display of the town's fortifications. The size of a medieval town was determined by its **town wall*****. If the town expanded, the new district had to be surrounded by a new wall. Nothing remains of Tallinn's first wooden fortifications dating from the first half of the 13th century. A limestone town wall built by the Danes in 1310-35 determined the size of the lower town for centuries. The wall was 2.5 km long, over 2 m thick and 15-16 m high. In the 15th century the rise of firearms caused major renovations. The last time the walls were used for defensive purposes was during the Crimean War in 1854-55, when the British and French navies blockaded the harbour. Today the wall protects Tallinn even better by its historical and aesthetic value. You can see almost 2 km of it, plus 20 of the original 48 towers.
This one, Kiek in de Kök, hosts photo exhibitions in the basement and on the sixth floor (sometimes the same show separated by four high, cold, stone storeys). The name is German dialect for "peep into the kitchen". Standing on the roof the soldiers on watch really could peer down through the medieval chimneys into the kitchens of the city. Tallinn's children often wonder what kinds of interesting things went on in those kitchens that such a mighty tower had to be built in order to peep into them!

Toompea's splendour.

Long and short legs

Today several roads lead down from Toompea, but before the 17th century, **Pikk jalg**** ("long leg") was the only access to the upper town from the lower. This narrow and steep cobbled street passes between two high limestone walls, with which the disobedient lower town tried to protect itself from the arrogant lord of Toompea. Going up and down the steep slope was a real test for coachmen. The English writer Elizabeth Rigby, who visited Tallinn in the 19th century, writes in her travel notes about coachmen shouting at the top of their voices to announce they were coming down, and the gatekeeper adding his cry so vehicles in Pikk St could keep well out of the way. The present **Pikk jalg gate tower*** dates from the year 1380. The gate was closed at nine every evening and if there was danger, a strong oak trellis on iron chains was lowered as an additional precaution. Partway down Pikk jalg you'll see a wee alley to the right and beyond it another oak gate, another way down from Toompea. This is where **Lühike jalg*** ("short leg") begins. Descend-

Some time ago you couldn't even mention "it". Now you can see "it" fluttering on the most prominent place in town – the tower of Pikk Hermann.

Toompea castle, the house of parliament.

ing Lühike jalg, actually a stepped street 80 m long, you come to Niguliste church – and the lower town, Tallinn's masterpiece.

THE LOWER TOWN

The medieval lower town is one of Estonia's great splendours: a merchant town that shone brightly in the Middle Ages, much of it intact and evocative again today. The Town Hall, the churches, the old warehouses and dwellings, the guild halls, the town wall ...

Alexander Nevsky Orthodox Church Right smack dab in the middle of Toompea.

The **lower town***** with its trading and handicrafts, noise and bustle is the real Old Tallinn. During its long history, Tallinn has never permitted capture by force. Yet the one who gained possession of the key of the city of Tallinn was soon master of the country. The key exists in reality and is at present kept in the Town Museum. When the rulers changed, the town councillors received the new masters at the city gates, carrying the key on a velvet cushion. After festive speeches it was ceremoniously handed over as a symbol of obedience.

A walk in the southern part of the Old Town presents the town hall, St Nicholas church, a picturesque street beside the town wall and a Stalinist masterpiece.

The very heart of old Tallinn

Town Hall Square*** *(Raekoja plats)* is the ancient market square where the main streets meet. It dates back to at least the 12th century and is surrounded on all sides by stylish old houses that create a storybook atmosphere, particularly in the mild light of early morning and late afternoon. In the Middle Ages the square was a market place surrounded by tailors', shoemakers' and blacksmiths' shops.

Town Hall Square has been the scene of rough acts of punishment and merry wedding processions. It has been the site of carnivals and other festive occasions. The most spectacular of these was the annual Christmas-tree-raising party. Czar Peter the Great himself once attended. Executions rarely took place in the town limits, though once a priest named Panicke who'd killed a waitress with an axe after she'd brought him three inedible omelettes in a row was beheaded here – the spot is marked by a flagstone with the letter "L". An oval granite rock marks the site of a medieval well.

Time has not greatly altered Raekoja plats. A two-storey weighing house stood in the square from the 16th century, but it was destroyed in 1944.

The soul of Estonia is Toomkirik, Tallinn's cathedral.

The Pinguin ice-cream shop must have one of the world's best locations. Though no market is held here now, in early June the square hosts the Old Town Festival. And though the pillory with a wooden statue of Justice at the top has disappeared from the middle of the square, the metal collar is still chained to a column in the town hall arcade. At Christmas time a green fir tree decorates the square.

Toomkirik.

Medieval pharmacy

Worth looking at on the square are an old dwelling at 12 Raekoja plats, and a municipal office at 15 Raekoja plats. Shops in several buildings sell Estonian art and crafts.

The **Town Council Pharmacy*** (11 Raekoja plats) is the oldest pharmacy and medical institution in Tallinn – in 1422 it was already up to its third owner. In the Middle Ages a chemist sold more than just medicine. The shop managed a brisk business in playing cards, tobacco and gunpowder, and an apprentice offered customers "claret", a fruit wine flavoured with cloves and ginger. Among the valuable remedies on sale were fish-eye powder, sheep-wool extract, ground rubies, extract of black cat's piss, and dried frogs legs that were known to help against 27 diseases.

In 1580 the shop was taken over by Johann Burchart, a German born in Hungary. Until the beginning of the 20th century it would be managed by a dynasty of Johann Burcharts (the eldest son was always named Johann). The Burcharts grew so famous that when Peter the Great was lying on his deathbed in 1725, he sent for Johann Burchart of Tallinn. Unfortunately the chemist learnt of the czar's death while still en route. Another Johann Burchart founded a home museum, Mon faible ("my weakness"), in 1802. He also organised Tallinn's first art exhibitions in his shop.

Another angle on Toompea.

Civic centre

The most important and monumental building in the square is the **town hall*****, the only surviving gothic town hall in northern Europe. Dragonhead waterspouts and fortress-like battlements at the top of the facade demonstrate the power of the council. The front rests on arches which served as a trading place in the Middle Ages. One door in the arcade opens on a coffee shop.

Tallinn's old town hall stood in the same place from 1341. The current model was built in 1402-04. The baroque facade dates from the middle of the 17th century. The top of the spire, 65 m high, is also baroque and dates from 1681. At the very tip stands a medieval warrior called **Vana Toomas** (Old Thomas). Old Thomas is a weathervane and Tallinn's watchful town guard. The original Old Thomas, made in 1530, is on show inside the town hall.

The **interior**** is a journey into history – about 40 minutes of history when you take the tour; during the

Across the rooftops, the view from Toompea.

Pikk Jalg ("long leg") begins.

Old Town Festival the town hall is free for everyone. The ground floor was long a storeroom and winecellar. Now mannequins pose in the costumes of six centuries of merchants. Upstairs, the mayor has used the **Citizen's Hall** for centuries to welcome guests of the city. The columns are painted green and red (for wealth) and yellow and blue (Hanseatic ship flag-colours). If you don't take a tour, you can always see a concert in this hall.

A Latin motto over the door to the next room exhorts councillors to cast away "excitements of private life" that might impair their judgment. For this is the **Council Hall,** for centuries the place where Tallinn's future was decided. It too is only used now for official meetings with guests of the city. Bench-ends bear elaborate carvings of David and Goliath, Samson and the lion, suggesting that the men who managed the city must be strong. Carvings of Tristan and Isolde, and Samson and Delilah suggest they must not listen to the prattle of women. The baroque frieze on the wall was carved by Elert Thiele in 1667.

Other rooms are a kitchen and the treasurer's office, which contains gifts to the town. Paintings include Charles V of Spain and William of Orange.

Even merchants have souls

Dunkri and Voorimehe ("coachman") Sts lead from Town Hall Square to Rataskaevu ("wheel well") St, which gets its name from a **wheel well*** that's stood here since 1386. For a long time there was a superstition that an evil water goblin lived in the well, which would flood the town if it weren't brought sacrifices

Neitsitorn ("virgin's tower"). Nice place for a coffee.

Niguliste church.

sometimes. Though a great many alley cats, dead or alive, were thrown to the goblin and the water became undrinkable, it was only in the middle of last century that the well was finally capped. Where Rataskaevu becomes Rüütli St you reach the spiritual centre of the old merchant town.

In 1230 German merchants and craftsmen, invited by the Order, settled at the foot of Toompea. These sea-trading merchants built a church dedicated to St Nicholas, patron saint of seamen. **Niguliste church***** was the centre of their settlement. In the 13th century it was a blunt building without a steeple, serving as house of worship, storehouse and fortress. The steeple was added in 1514. When Soviet planes bombed Tallinn the church was gutted, but its **high altar,** made in Lübeck in 1481, survived. When the double wings of the huge board are opened, the altar is 7 m wide. Scenes from the lives of Sts Nicholas and Victor are depicted on it.

The spaciousness of the church is surprising given its heavy, fortified exterior. Today Niguliste is a museum and concert hall. At least part of the **altar for St Anthony's chapel** was painted by Michel Sittow, a Tallinn artist who during his long, widely travelled career painted in the Spanish, Dutch and English courts. He also designed the skeletal

On Rüütli ("knight") St you know you're in a Hanseatic city.

tombstone for Dr Ballivi on one wall. A 17th-century baptistry and several painted wooden epitaphs for nobles are other highlights.

Niguliste's most famous exhibit was painted in about 1490 by the German artist Bernt Notke: **Danse macabre** ("dance of death"). Death levels everyone: the king, the pope, the noble, the cardinal and the merchant ... Holding hands with Death (a cadaver with bagpipes) they obediently jig along the last road. Art historians believe this canvas is a 7.5 m fragment of a 25 m work. Notke is also responsible for the high altar in Tallinn's Pühavaimu church.

South of Niguliste stands Tallinn's oldest tree, the **Kelch lime tree*.** It grows on the grave of the chronicler Christian Kelch, who wrote in his *History of Livonia* in 1695: "Estonia is the landlord's heaven, the pastor's paradise, the stranger's goldmine, and the peasant's hell."

Beyond the limetree are ruins of a cinema and restaurant. They've been left that way as a memorial to the terrible night of 9 March 1944 when Soviet planes decimated Tallinn, destroying whole districts of wooden houses and many older places – 20 000 lost their homes. They also bombed Lake Ülemiste, thinking its iced-over surface was the airport.

Saunas and executioners

Going from the church along Rüütli ("knight") St you pass the medieval cellar and restaurant of Sub Monte. A monument is plastered to the wall of 22 Rüütli St, once the home of artist Michael Sittow. A bathhouse was chronicled at 44 Rüütli St in 1387. Even in pre-Christian times, Estonians had to go to saunas once a week come hell or high water. Besides washing and sitting in hot steam, it was in saunas that Estonian women gave birth to children and that the sick regained their health. When Christianity came the sauna was also supposedly a place of witchcraft. Tales have come down to us of water turning to blood on Saturdays after midnight; of devils and werewolves tormenting late sauna-goers.

One visitor wrote, "The people of the country have a custom of going to a hot vapoury sauna, then running out and jumping into cold water. In winter they run from the hot sauna directly into a snowdrift or a brook not yet covered with ice." Estonian men and women visited the sauna together. In 1716 a law was issued forbidding such a shameful practice; but even in 1807 the police had to be instructed about the punishment of

Behind the hoarding archaeologists are excavating.

men and women found together in a public sauna. There were several public saunas, one of them near the Viru Gates, where a street called Sauna St runs even today.
At the end of Rüütli St you come up against the town wall and a small, **inconspicuous house** standing against it. "God's mercy is new every morning as I raise my sword and help the sinner into eternal life," reads the inscription on the sword of its occupant, who earned his daily bread as the town's executioner. The sword is now on display in the Town Hall Museum. The executioner was paid well but shunned by the townsfolk: he had to wear a red coat so he could be recognised from afar, his children could not attend school with the town's other children, he and his wife couldn't go to public Mass but took communion alone in a chapel, and he was buried outside the graveyard. No Tallinner was ever hired for the task.
Following **Müürivahe St**** to the left from here, you pass the Theatre and Music Museum, the new Tallinn Business Centre and one of Tallinn's two great Stalinist buildings, the **Sõprus Cinema**** (*sõprus* = "friendship" in Estonian; it's a word that's become debased because of overuse by the loathed Soviet authorities). The other Stalinist milestone is a block of flats on Tartu mnt about 1 km to the south-east.
Müürivahe St crosses Viru St just by the **Viru Gate**** (photo opportunity of the Hotel Viru framed by these sweet little gate-towers). Viru Gate Hill became a garden at the end of the 19th century and soon acquired the name of **Musumägi** ("kissing hill"). Müürivahe continues along a picturesque section of town wall

Town Hall Square is a good place to meet.

through an old old old part of town. **Alleys** linking this street with Vene St are among the loveliest around. One courtyard finds its way into most books on Tallinn.

Heading back to Town Hall Square along Viru St you come to Vana turu kael ("old market neck") along one edge of the town hall. One fine house, (3 Vana turu kael, one wing of which is 18 Raekoja plats) is a **renaissance merchant's house**** with coloured reliefs of apostles on the sides. The gothic facade complete with porch, wall-anchors and, high up, hoists and old warehouse door, is beautifully preserved. The originals of the bas-relief sculptures of the apostles, made in 1597 by Arent Passer, have been moved inside the building. The **area around the town hall***** has several such old home-warehouses. On many, a symbol hangs, denoting the products traded: fish, wine, and so on. My favourites adorn the button and thread shops in Harju St.

The northern part of the Old Town includes guild halls, a park of wall towers, two gothic churches and a fat cannon-tower.

Gothic survivor

From Town Hall Square, a narrow alley called Saiakäik ("whitebread passage") runs beside the Town Council Pharmacy. A brisk trade in

Extract of frog's leg, anyone? Raeapteek ("town council pharmacy").

small croissant-shaped rolls and other doughy Estonian specialties went on here from the 14th century until 1896, when the market was removed from the square. The alley exits beside **Pühavaimu ("Holy Ghost") church*****. The bright face of Tallinn's **oldest public clock** adorns the outside wall. The clock has recently been restored. Though the spire is baroque, the bell in it is Estonia's oldest, cast in 1433 and inscribed: "I strike time correctly to maid and manservant, to mistress and master, and no one may reproach me for that."

Unlike most of Estonia's Lutheran churches, which were renovated in a sparing manner, **Pühavaimu's interior** is decorated with sculptures, paintings and carvings. Besides baroque paintings and epitaphs, the **choir railing** carved by Elert Thiele in the 17th century is rather eye-catching. The **altarpiece** is another masterpiece by Bernt Notke of Lübeck, made in 1483. Its doors would have been gradually opened during the service, until the sculpted Mary and Child inside were fully displayed.

Pühavaimu church served one of the poorest congregations in town, the Estonians. Its pastors have played a prominent part in Estonia's cultural and social life. One of them, Johann Koell, translated the Lutheran Catechism into Estonian, producing the oldest surviving publication in Estonian in 1535. A colleague of his, Balthasar Russow, wrote a *Chronicle of the Province of Livonia*, which for the first time drew attention to the poor lot of Estonian peasants and reproached the feudal lords for brutality.

Concerts are sometimes held here; be prepared for neck-craning if you attend one.

At the corner of Pühavaimu and Pikk Sts you'll find the recently restored **Maiasmokk** ("sweet tooth") Cafe. The building was also a cafe during the period of Estonian independence, when it was Georg Stude's Cafe.

The town hall is a baroque gothic moorish mixture. Also tall.

Guilds on a long street

Pikk*** ("long") St is one of the oldest streets in Tallinn. It starts at the Pikk jalg gate mentioned earlier and ends 800 m later at Suur Rannavärav ("Great Coast Gate"), not far from the harbour. That was pretty long by medieval standards and it takes a good few minutes on foot. Pikk St was the centre of social life for Tallinn merchants. It's lined with magnificent houses that once belonged to the cream of society. Keep your eyes peeled for fine facades.

Across the street from the Maiasmokk Cafe and Pühavaimu clock stands the stately **building of the Great Guild*****. The Great Guild was a mighty force in the public life of the town: only rich, married, local merchants could join. It built its superb gothic residence in 1410. The festive hall, which imitates the town hall's Citizens Hall, was used for meetings and feasts.

The most famous of these was the election of the May Count. A young wealthy man, crowned May Count for his athletic, equestrian and shooting prowess, chose a Countess from among eight young beauties in a rose garden. A festive procession followed, with decorated horses and the Count and the Countess riding in the first coach. Today the building houses an **Estonian History Museum***.

Further down Pikk St are the houses of three more craft guilds. **St Canute's Guild** admitted craftsmen, although only those of German descent. It was probably founded in the 13th century. Its last home (20 Pikk St) was built in 1863-64 in neogothic style. The **art gallery** next door is an architectural companion piece: some of the best modern buildings in Tallinn date from the first two decades of the 20th century, when Estonian control of the council coincided with the art nouveau movement.

The facade of the house of the **Brotherhood of Blackheads**** (26 Pikk St) is the only example of renaissance architecture in Tallinn. Rumour has it the front of the gothic building was done up because the Queen of Sweden was coming to visit; she never made it. The coats-of-arms of four Hanseatic cities – Bruges, Novgorod, London and Bergen – on the facade of the building bear witness to Tallinn's flourishing past. The **interior** is gothic and quite lovely.

The Brotherhood of Blackheads existed only in the Baltic states. Their patron was St Mauritius, an Ethiopian whose black skin gave the guild its name and an air of mystery. Aspiring young men (not Estonians, though) joined with a view to later joining the Great Guild. The brotherhood was responsible for the defence of the city, which can't have been pleasant in wartime. The building has kept its youthfulness in one way – today it houses a young people's culture centre.

The adjoining house of **St Olaf's Guild** is part of the same youth centre. The oldest guild in Tallinn, St Olaf's was founded in the 13th cen-

Through Saiakang ("bun arch") you enter Saiakäik ("bun passage").

tury and united craftsmen of non-German descent, including Estonians. Members of the guild were not permitted to wear silk, velvet or taffeta, expensive furs or gold jewellery, that right was being reserved for merchants of German descent.

How merchants lived (and Olev died)

Pikk St also offers examples of **dwelling houses from the 15th century,** the flowering period of medieval Tallinn. It was then that a new type of rich merchant's or craftsman's house was formed. It actually consisted of several buildings, each with a different function. The facade was a gable facing the street. A vaulted arch led to a longish yard with stables, servants' house, brewery and so on. Inside the main building, the most important part was the *diele*, or hall, which often filled the whole ground floor. The kitchen, located in one of its corners, had a large mantle chimney. Characteristic decorations were carved stone portals and porch marks with figures of lions.

You can see a splendid example of a medieval home at 71 Pikk St, the **"Three Sisters"****. There are more good ones **on Lai**** ("wide") St, which runs parallel to Pikk (23, 27 and 29 Lai St). The first of these is now occupied by the Youth Theatre, so that even if you have no intention of seeing a performance, it pays to mount the porch steps and take a look inside.

Just before you come to the Three Sisters you pass a building that was once thought to be the highest in the world. **Oleviste church**** (St Olaf's) was first chronicled in 1267. Its pointed steeple no longer reaches the height of 159 m as it did in 1500, but even at 124 m it's a conspicuous landmark on Tallinn's skyline. Both lightning and fire have tried to destroy St Olaf's, yet it stands to this day as a grand example of gothic architecture.

Legend has it that Tallinners had long wanted to build a church of unprecedented height, but had been

The Cafe Maiasmokk, recommended in two periods of freedom.

unable to find a building master willing to undertake the job. At last a young man named Olev measured up to the task. The building was almost completed and seemed to be reaching the sky when the young builder cast a look down at the tiny dots of people below, lost his balance and fell to his death. When Olev's body hit the ground, a toad and a snake came out of his mouth. Needless to say, the church was named after the unfortunate builder. The skeleton of the master with toad and snake are reproduced in relief on a wall of St Mary's chapel in the church (open for Sunday services).

The memorial stone on the outside by Pikk St was made in 1513-16, for one H Pavels.

The peasantry has risen. Anyone can visit the House of the Great Guild now.

Stout Margaret

Pikk St takes you as far as **the Great Coast Gate****, Suur Rannavärav, which in the Middle Ages was one of six gates into Tallinn. Beside it you'll notice a powerful cannon tower called **Paks Margareta***** ("stout Margaret"), her diameter at waist being 24 m and her skin 4 m thick. The tower was completed in 1529. Its creator was Gert Konigk from Westphalia. Besides protecting the town, Margaret has been a storehouse, barracks and prison. Herr Konigk also carved the small coat-of-arms of Tallinn above the arch of the Great Coast Gate.

Paks Margareta houses the **Maritime Museum****, currently perhaps the best small museum in Estonia, even without text in English. Estonia has had a long, long marriage to the sea, and this is the family album: from clinker boats to research ships, from fishing gear to famous old salts, it's all here. The **vista**** from the roof gives a camera-hungry low-level scan across the rooftops and a broadside view of Oleviste church.

Bastions to parks

From the Great Coast Gate you can circle the town in either direction, crossing on the way some of the green belt of parks around the Old Town. In the 17th century the Swedish government decided to surround Tallinn with a chain of grandiose bastions. Few were built, but these parks are evidence of the plan. **Tornide väljak**** ("towers' square") is to the left from the Great Coast Gate. Seven towers are on guard here, looking pretty good for their age. A small rivulet runs down a limestone precipice, and at its foot stands a bronze roe deer sculpted by Jaan Koort.

The moat in **Toompark** was only dug at the foot of Toompea at the end of the 18th century. It's the only section of moat still filled with water and has the odd name of **Snelli tiik** ("Snelli's pond"), after a local gardener. The **view**** of Toompea Castle from here is formidable.

There are three parks further round from Toompark. The "Swedish bastion" was greened up in 1862. After the bronze sculpture of weeping Linda was unveiled in 1920, it was renamed **Linda's hill.** Its neighbour **Harjumägi,** next to Kiek in de Kök, became a park in 1860. **Hirvepark** ("deer park") is on an old filled moat below Linda's hill. Some time ago

The Brotherhood of Blackheads invites you to balls and discos.

In this medieval tradesmen's house the Noorsooteater ("youth theatre") rehearses.

roe deer were kept here.

You can also head **back to the centre** of the Old Town along either of the streets running parallel to Pikk St – **Lai**** or **Vene**** Sts. Along Vene ("Russian") St you'll see the 19th-century Orthodox **Nikolai church** whose round dome was much wondered at by the townspeople. A little further along you pass what remains of an early 13th-century **Dominican monastery****, presently a branch of the Tallinn Town Museum and in summer an open-air stage of the Youth Theatre. The **Town Museum*** itself, at 17 Vene St, is another rich merchant's dwelling with a splendid staircase in the hall.

OUTSIDE THE OLD TOWN

Outside the ring of parks, boulevards – Toompuiestee, Kaarli pst, Estonia pst, Mere pst and Rannamäe tee – circle the Old Town. From there, major roads radiate out in various directions – Pärnu maantee, Endla St, Paldiski mnt, Narva mnt and Tartu mnt.

Ancient foyer of the youth theatre.

The highest spire in medieval Europe – St Olaf's.

TO THE EAST

In the east spreads green Kadriorg park, and beyond that lies the new misanthropic housing development of Lasnamäe. North-east are the resort area of Pirita and the district of private villas at Meriválja.

Yuck

A line of buildings just beyond Viru St represents the last days of Soviet Estonia. In 1980 when Moscow hosted the Olympics, the yachting events were held at Pirita in the north-east part of Tallinn. In honour of the event, frantic building went on. Relatively the best of the lot was the **Post office*** in Narva mnt. Across the street, the **Hotel Viru** was built earlier, in 1970, to a Finnish design using Finnish labour. It cost a fortune and although the human Soviet elements that used to haunt it have recently been cleaned out, you still feel the weight of the building pressing on you in its corridors. The other side of the hotel, the windows of the 1960 **Department Store** *(Kaubamaja)* windows always offered a decidedly brighter prospect than its interior. Nowadays it has a reasonable quota of both western and eastern products, but you can imagine the times when one half was a glittering hard currency store and the other seemed to sell empty shelves. Tall, fat **Olümpia Hotel**, standing as grey as an inspector asking for your ID, is another product of the Olympic rush.

Dedicated to Kadri

By order of Peter the Great, the building of a **palace***** was started in Tallinn in 1718, and a large **park**** was laid out around it. Both were designed by the Italian architect Niccolo Michetti in late baroque style. Everything, including the roads, trees, fountains, flowerbeds and ponds, was set symmetrically. Water was channelled from Lake Ülemiste along a canal made of stone slabs. More than 70 species of trees, many squirrels and innumerable birds enliven the park. Shady paths, monuments and sculptures are in abundance, and swans gliding on the pond make it a favourite place for Tallinners to relax. Not far from an old sundial there's a sculpture of Friedrich Reinhold Kreutzwald, author of the national epic poem, *Kalevipoeg*.

The Czar conceived the whole grandiose business for his wife Catherine and called the place Katharinenthal. Catherine, however, is nothing but an Estonian country girl's name, Kadri. As the palace and the park are situated in a valley near Lasnamäe, the local people called it Kadriorg ("Kadri's valley"). The palace now houses the **Art Museum*****, which since 1992 has been under restoration: it's due to open again in xxxx at the earliest. A younger building, the **President's Palace,** is next door; for a long time the Supreme Soviet held sessions here. Not far off is **"Peter's cottage",** the wing in which Peter the Great stayed when he visited Tallinn – Peter died before the palace was completed.

You can get to Kadriorg by buses 1 & 5 and trams 1 & 3.

On the seashore opposite Kadriorg park you can see one of Estonian

Tornide väljak ("towers square").

A piece of Tallinn's bulwark.

Interested in somebody's secret recipe? Kiek in de Kök ("peep into the kitchen").

sculptor Amandus Adamson's most romantic works, **Russalka***, an angel erected in memory of sailors who drowned on a Russian ship of the same name.

Singing, yachting

An embankment leads from Kadriorg to Pirita. Along the way, in a natural amphitheatre, you'll see the **Song Festival Ground****. The structure there now is quite extraordinary considering it was built in 1960. Every five years (1990, 1995 ...) the National Song Festival is held here. At its peak the festival has drawn every third Estonian to see tens of thousands singing on stage. In September 1988, at the culmination of the second national awakening of Estonians, more than 300 000 people from all over Estonia gathered at the Song Festival Ground to sing in protest – this was the zenith of the famous "Singing Revolution". To get to the Song Ground take a Kadriorg bus (not tram) and get off a couple of stops further on.

Maarjamäe Palace was built as a summer house for Adjutant-General Orlov-Davidov in 1874. It's a strange concatenation of bold 19th-century exterior, 1930s interior and the **Estonian History Museum****, a storehouse of much that is precious in Estonian History.

The tall pointy **monument** was built by the Soviets to commemorate their "liberation" of Estonia in 1944.

Located right on the seacoast, just before crossing the Pirita River, are the **yachting centre***, where the Olympic regatta was held in 1980, and Sport Hotel. Opposite this complex in a pine forest is a cycling track and a motor racing track.

Nuns, TV, graves

Just beyond Pirita bridge you'll see a high facade on your right. The abbey of the **Brigidine Convent**** (hence the placename, Pirita) was founded by wealthy merchants about 1400. Nuns and priests lived here in separate cloisters. They say that the two genders weren't allowed to speak to each other and communicated by an elaborate sign language. After the Reformation the convent became a school, and it was plundered and later ruined by Russians in the 16th century during the Livonian War. Make sure you climb the tower in the far right corner (key kept at ticket office) for a **view**** of the river, harbour and Old Tallinn. Open-air performances and concerts are held in the ruins in summer.

Pirita's main attraction lies in its 2 km white sand **beach.** With its pine forest, the jagged skyline of Tallinn across the water and yachts sailing on the bay, it's an idyllic place on a sunny summer's day.

The Dominican convent offers no shelter to the concert-goer.

Up to Toompea via the Patkuli stairs. These weren't here in medieval times.

A short distance inland from Pirita the **Tallinn TV tower** is "hidden" in pine forest. From the top you get an extensive **panorama**** of the town and its environs. There's a restaurant, too, the Galaxy.

Bus 34 goes through Pirita to **Metsakalmistu**** ("forest cemetery"), an example of the sparser sort of Estonian cemetery. At times you hardly know you're in a cemetery, so discreet are the headstones amid a pine forest on grassy dunes. Many great sons and daughters of the country are buried here: in one row near the road you'll find the simple graves of singer Georg Ots, writer Anton Hansen Tammsaare, chess grandmaster Paul Keres, poet Lydia Koidula and others. The family plot of former president Konstantin Päts is a subdued memorial to a strident nationalist. The graves of less famous artists and musicians nearby bear more interesting designs.

Further west lies a city-jungle of panel-houses, a huge stone "bedroom" for 100 000 – the new housing district of **Lasnamäe.**

SOUTH-EAST AND SOUTH-WEST

In the south and south-east, the Old Town adjoins the new "town centre" with its service, trade and cultural establishments. Beyond them are Lake Ülemiste and Tallinn Airport. South-west you'll find the garden suburb of Nõmme.

Freedom Square and beyond

In medieval times **Vabaduse väljak*** ("freedom square") was a field crossed by roads along which cattle arrived at the city; from here they were led through Karja ("herd") gate to the market. Once the Russians had

N
TALLINN
PALJASSAARE
Tallinna laht
Kopli laht
KOPLI
Paljassaare tee
Kopli
Vasara
Kopliranna
Pelguranna
Sõle
Tööstuse
Ristiku
Soo
Põhja pst
Sadama
2
Kolde pst
Merimetsa tee
PELGU-LINN
Telliskivi
3
Tehnika
Toompea
Rannamäe
5
VANALINN
Mere pst
Ahtri
Tuukri
Jõe
NARVA MNT
Uus-Sadama
J.Tombi
Pronksi
Estonia pst
Gonsori
Kaarli pst
PÄRNU MNT
Luise
Endla
PALDISKI MNT
Tulika
Liivalaia
TARTU MNT
Juhkentali
4
Rannamõisa tee
12
13
ÕISMÄE
VESKI-METSA
MUSTJÕE
Ehitajate tee
Harku järv
Õismäe tee
Järveotsa tee
VÄIKE-ÕISMÄE
Tedre
Sõpruse pst
Nõmme tee
Räägu
Linnu tee
Kadaka tee
Mustamäe tee
A.H.Tammsaare tee
Kotka
Veerenni
Järvevana tee
Tondi
Kõo
Ülemiste järv
Akadeemia tee
E.Vilde tee
Retke tee
Sütiste
Rahumäe tee
MUSTAMÄE
Tähetorni
Vääna
Raudtee
Valdeku
Hiiu
Pargi
NÕMME
HIIU
Vabaduse pst
Lootuse pst
Männiku tee
VILJANDI MNT
MÄNNIKU
Kadaka pst
PÄÄSKÜLA
LAAGRI
PÄRNU
Pääsküla jõgi
VILJANDI

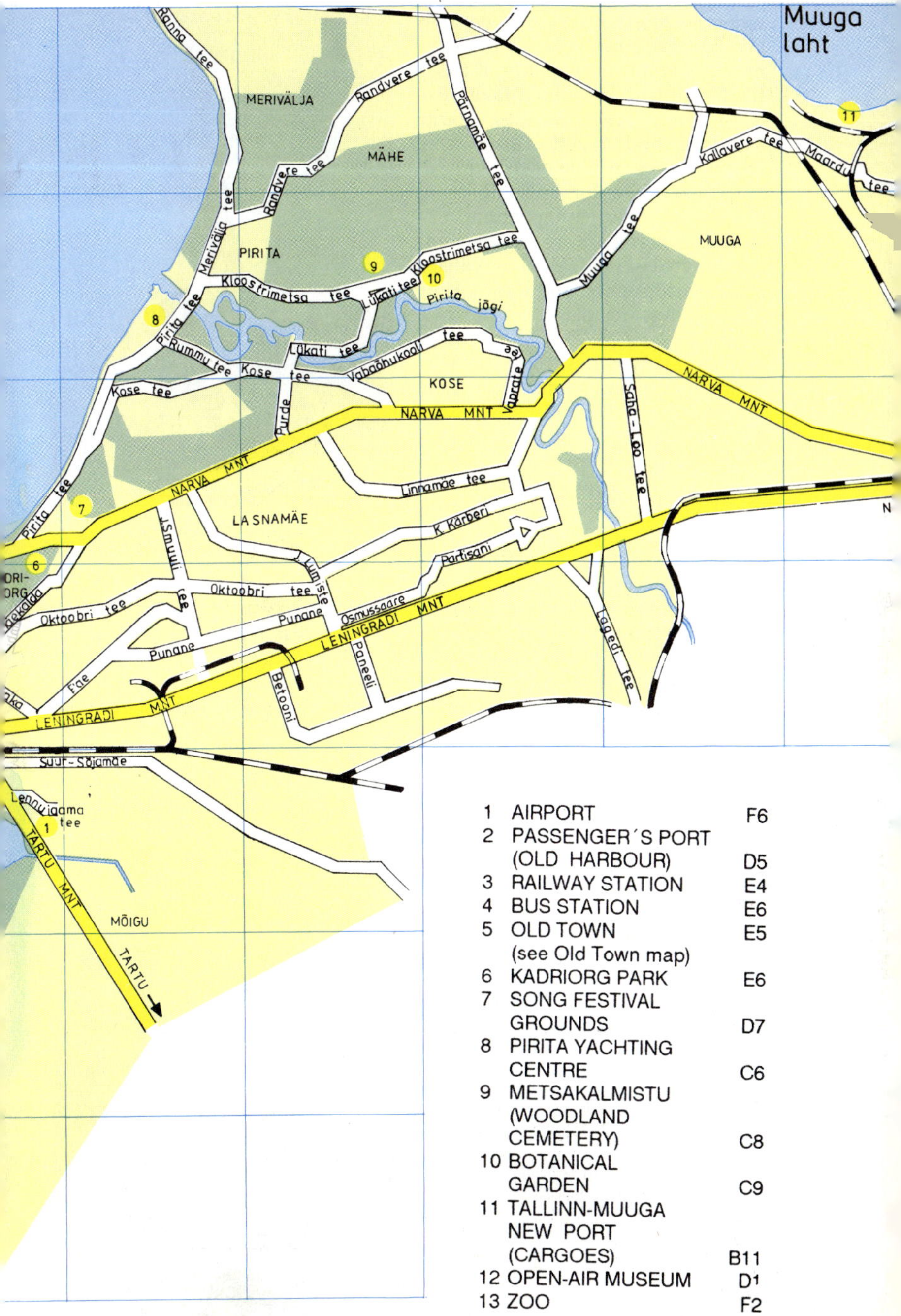

1 AIRPORT F6
2 PASSENGER´S PORT (OLD HARBOUR) D5
3 RAILWAY STATION E4
4 BUS STATION E6
5 OLD TOWN (see Old Town map) E5
6 KADRIORG PARK E6
7 SONG FESTIVAL GROUNDS D7
8 PIRITA YACHTING CENTRE C6
9 METSAKALMISTU (WOODLAND CEMETERY) C8
10 BOTANICAL GARDEN C9
11 TALLINN-MUUGA NEW PORT (CARGOES) B11
12 OPEN-AIR MUSEUM D1
13 ZOO F2

1 2 3 4 5 km

HUMA

won the Northern War it became Peetri plats ("Peter's place"). In 1910 a monumental bronze statue of Peter the Great, the czar who'd taken Estonia from the Swedes, built Kadriorg and razed Tartu, was erected in the middle of the square. He stood there for only 12 years before the new, independent Estonian government removed him. The square became Vabaduse väljak; Estonians designed and built a ring of buildings in place of the old wooden houses. When the Soviets took over they named the place Victory Square in honour of their "liberation" of Estonia. *(Võit*, "victory" is another word that leaves a sour taste in Estonian mouths.)

Now it's "freedom" again. The **modernist buildings*** bordering the square include the present offices of the Town Council, which are ornamented by sculptures by Jaan Koort. Next door at no 5, the crenellated **Russian Drama Theatre** was built as the Gloria Palace cinema in 1926. Its neighbour is now the Palace Hotel, one of the finest in the country. Across the way, art galleries and an artists' club occupy more 1930s buildings. Let's hope that some time in the future the cars will vacate the carpark and the square can be landscaped.

The Russalka statue watches for drowning sailors.

The goblin

South and east of here is the new "town centre". There's a little district of cultural buildings to the east. At 11 Estonia puistee, the Estonian Republic was declared in 1918. The memorable **Estonian Drama Theatre*** was built in 1910 as the German Theatre, to a design by Bubõr and Vassiliev. The co-winner in the same competition became the Small Vanemuine Theatre in Tartu. Across

The Estonia Theatre, a symbol of Estonian culture.

Palace of Kadriorg, temple of arts.

the road, the Ministry of Culture and Education is housed in a grand building from 1912 designed by Finnish architect Eliel Saarinen. Saarinen had plans for an entire rebuild of the Old Town – on his drawings only the churches and town hall appear to have survived the bulldozers. One such building is tremendous, a whole city might be a bit much.

On 9 March 1944, when the Soviet air force bombed Tallinn, the **Estonia Opera House and Concert Hall**** caught fire. At the time the troupe was performing the Estonian ballet *Kratt* ("goblin"). The festively dressed audience, firemen in uniforms and ballerinas in costumes escaped to the streets on an icy night, witnessing the ruin of a symbol of Estonian culture. The Estonia had been built at the beginning of the century with labour and money donated by Estonians. It was restored after the war, rather quickly, and a fresco of The Estonian People welcoming the Red Army as Liberators was splashed onto the ceiling of the opera hall.

In the park next to it you'll find a monument to one of Estonia's most important writers, Anton Hansen Tammsaare, whose masterwork *Truth and justice* is a fictional record of Estonian life during the national awakening and beyond.

The **Sakala Centre***, the large limestone thing behind the drama theatre, inspired awe and guffaws as the Political Education Centre not long ago. While it was being built it

Making friends in Kadriorg park.

Autumn in Kadriorg park.

acquired the nickname "Karl's Cathedral" because it looked so much like a church. Karl Vaino was the head of the Communist Party. Adjustments were made but the place still looks rather churchy.

Of limestone and Sovietskaya

There's a real Karl's church south-east of Vabaduse väljak. Lutherans are not great church builders and throughout the Soviet reign church-building was banned. One of Estonia's younger churches, 19th-century **Kaarli church***, is also one of only two in the country with two steeples. The brand new limestone building across the road is the **national library***. The library includes many English books in its collection; old guidebooks to Tallinn and Estonia can be a real treat. Estonian architects are returning to limestone, a traditional building material here for thousands of years. (And it ages well: even in polluted Tallinn a building like the fire station at the corner of Pronksi and Gonsiori Sts, dusted here and there with blackness, looks good.)

There's been much discussion lately on what to do about the old Soviet monuments. The dynamic one in

The Song Festival Ground holds over 100 000 people.

Pirita's past ...

front of the library has a particularly good spot. It celebrates not the bombing of 9 March but the arrival of the Red Army on 22 September 1944. The hill running up from the library, **Tõnismägi***, was for centuries the site of a little neighbouring village to Tallinn. At the end of last century it was discovered by the city elders and now sports a cool water-tower, the first one in Tallinn, among other things. The whole district is a service and administrative centre, with **pockets of old wooden homes**** scattered here and there. Estonians often seem blind to the value of these houses, even when they have gables, towers and "carpenter gothic" decorations. As representatives of a unique style of the last hundred years, they deserve preservation.

So does Tallinn's industrial masterpiece, the **Tallinn Cellulose and Paper Factory****, which you'll find along Tartu maantee just the other side of the bus station. A paper mill stood here back in 1664. This inspirational collection of industrial hardware, though, was assembled around the turn of the century and hardly altered since then. At one stage the factory used a third of all fresh water consumed in Tallinn.

Giant in a garden town

Another museum, although not officially designated so, is **Nõmme****, a few km to the south-west along the Pärnu highway. The name derives from the Estonian word *nõmm*, "heath". This is a garden town built on a sandy heath within a pine forest. You can walk for hours on end enjoying the attractive, modest villas in large gardens. Nõmme was an independent town under the Estonian Republic, and only incorporated into Tallinn in 1940. You can get there by buses 14 & 18. Better still, take a train from Baltijaam ("Baltic Station") to Rahumäe, Nõmme, Hiiu or Kivimäe stations.

... and Pirita's modern times.

If you stop at Hiiu station and head north you come to **Glehn's castle****. Nikolai von Glehn was an eccentric Baltic-German landowner at the turn of this century. He had a "castle" built on the edge of the sandy cliff, and people still talk about the plans he had for his manor and for Nõmme. Reputedly he planned to build a harbour, with a canal right up to the castle. An iron ring in the wall is waiting to tie up his boat. When his horse died he buried it on top of the hill and mounted an obelisk over it. When his wife died he had her buried in the marshy land at the bottom of the cliff. He invited all of Tallinn society to her funeral, and had masses of sand laid down so they wouldn't get their shoes wet. They got dirty anyway and were so cheesed off they left before the wake began.

Not far from the obelisk is Glehn's **Kalevipoeg*****. Estonia's hero of legend was never meant to look like this, and more than a few people called the statue "Glehn's devil" instead. Glehn tended to plaster his manor park with signs, gems of wisdom and so on. About this giant statue he wrote, "Kalevipoeg you are in name and soul, no matter how much the fools call you 'devil'." During World War I the Russians suspected an ulterior motive and tore Kalevipoeg down, searching for radio equipment. He was recently restored, and the remains of the original have been left, not far from a crocodile sculpture. The castle fell slowly into ruin after World War I when Glehn left Estonia, first for Germany and later Argentina. It was restored in 1975.

NORTH AND WEST

To the north of the Old Town lie the sea, the old port still working hard, and the suburbs of Kalamaja and Kopli. Due west, beyond the district of Pelgulinn, you'll find a new housing development, Õismäe, and directly north of it the green suburb of Rocca al Mare.

The whirl of a folk-dance ...

... and the lull of a farmhouse at Rocca al Mare.

Scrap and olden times

The cranes swivel and bend like slowed-down mosquitoes at the port. **Linnahall*** is a concert-hall, ice-skating rink and modernist monstrosity not far from the Great Coast Gate.

Even in medieval times there were warehouses and netsheds by the port for the fishermen of Tallinn. These were called *kalamajad* ("fish houses") and nowadays the district west of the port is **Kalamaja***. It's another area of old wooden houses that in any other country would be inhabited by yuppies. But it's not advisable to be out too late alone. The same goes for the neighbouring area of **Kopli,** a good place to practise your Russian during the day.

North of Kopli you'll find **Paljassaare peninsula,** which in the Middle Ages was an island. Now the water treatment plant is there and a former Soviet army base, and several scrap metal dealers. Through a couple of gaps in the wall and the wreckage you can get a miraculous **view*** of Tallinn.

Kolde St in the small suburb of **Pelgulinn** was a showcase of modern housing during the last time of independence. And Õismäe is a showcase of a different kind – a ring of panel-houses circles an artificial lake. Strangely, country music festivals are often held here.

On the shore of Kopli Bay a few kilometres from the centre is **Rocca al Mare**.** The Italian name ("rock by the sea"), was given to the place in 1863 by burgermeister and merchant Girard de Soucanton, who built his summer house on the high bank above the sea. There's another **view*** of the skyline of Old Tallinn across the bay.

Rocca al Mare is now best known for the **Open Air Museum**** where examples of rural architecture, at times hundreds of years old, have been gathered from all over Estonia. Buses

The garden suburb Nõmme.

21 & 45 will take you there. Homes, storehouses, watermills, smithies, fences, saunas, windmills and everything else a peasant needed for life are preserved here, as if the people had moved out yesterday. During Soviet times, it was customary to tell

In Nõmme live your wealthier Estonians.

Nõmme's own goblin guards Glehn park.

tourists from the east that this was the way of life Estonians practised before the Soviet "liberation". The museum is scattered over a large territory and you can stroll at your leisure, stopping from time to time in the yard of some homestead. Most Sundays the quiet museum hosts folk-dance and folk-music performances.

AND MORE ...

Between and betwixt all the places mentioned here there are others worth exploring. The best advice, particularly near the centre, is to lose your way. You never know what you'll find.

PRACTICAL DETAILS

HOTELS

PALACE 3 Vabaduse väljak, Tel. 44 34 61, the international 4-star hotel at the main square of Tallinn; 45 single, 41 double rooms and 5 suites with all mod cons, excellent service; business services; car rental; res. tennis courts.

VIRU 4 Viru väljak, Tel. 65 20 93 (9am-noon), 65 20 81, 21-storey modern hotel, a splendid view of the Old City.

OLYMPIA 33 Liivalaia, Tel. 60 56 66, 60 56 51, 60 24 34, 25-storey modern hotel, a superb view of the Old City.

RATASKAEVU, renovated cosy hotel in the Old City, primarily for Guest of State.

PIRITA 1 Regati, Tel. 23 85 98, Olympic Yachting Centre at Pirita, 3-storey hotel overlooking the bay, mainly for athletes.

TALLINN 27 Toompuiestee, Tel. 60 43 32, outdated but still rather comfortable 4-storey hotel.

KUNGLA 23 Kreutzwaldi, Tel. 42 14 60, 42 70 40 (9am-4pm), 7-storey unpretentious tourist hotel in the centre of the city.

KULLERVO 27/29 Tedre, Tel. 55 75 53, Fax. 52 72 12, 11 rooms accommodating 24 guests. Four de luxe suites with all mod cons and mini-bar. Transportation services offer a chauffeured car and a tourist coach seating 43.

SILVA, 14 Laulu, Tel. 51 49 90. 8 rooms and 2 luxury-rooms for families. 2 convention halls and sauna (with pool and cosy room with fireplace). Car rental (with, or without driver).

PEOLEO, 555 Pärnu maantee, Tel. 55 65 66. Hotel, brand new motor-hotel, two restaurants, gift shop, hair salon and more.

PEEDU PANSIONAAT, 22 Võrse, Tel/Fax (3722) 52 86 09. Mobil tel. (825) 24 82 48. Small cosy hotel with a restaurant and a bar.

KELLUKA, 11 Kelluka tee, Tel. 23 88 11, fax 23 73 98, small, cosy hotel not far from Pirita, sauna, bar.

MIHKLI, 23 Endla, Tel. 45 17 67. Unpretensious hotel in the centre of the city.

RANNA, 11 Tchaikovski, Tel. 49 52 19, 49 52 29. Unpretensious tourist hotel in the suburb Kopli.

ESTONIAN YOUTH HOSTELS is a chain of inexpensive accommodation places in Estonia. 2 Liivalaia, tel/fax 44 58 53.

FAMILY HOTEL SERVICE NETWORK has more than 300 family homes and separate apartments (with modern facilites, specially for longer stay) throughout Estonia. Most of them are in town centres.

Prices suit all budgets. The average price is US $ 10 per person per night. Tel/fax: +7 (3722) 44 11 87, address: Mere pst 6, EE 0001, Tallinn.

NOOBEL, 14b Tuvi, phone 444 889, 683 713.

RESTAURANTS

FIRST RATE RESTAURANTS

ASTORIA, 5 Vabaduse väljak, open 1pm-7pm; 9pm-2am. Restored luxurious a la carte restaurant seating 100 plus bar seating 25. In the evenings live music. Casino. Tickets can be booked from 1.30pm-3.30pm. Reservations Tel. 44 84 62.

CARINA, 26 Pirita tee, open Sun.-Thu. noon-midnight, Fri.-Sat. noon-6pm,8pm-2am. Tel. 23 74 75. Two halls seating 86 and 24 plus bar. Live music.

CORSO, 1 Roosikrantsi, open Mon.-Fri. 8am-3am. Sat. noon-3am, Sun. noon-11pm. Tel. 44 65 36. Newly opened restored restaurant at Vabaduse square. In the evenings live music. Fine place to take lunch or dinner.

EESLITALL, 4 Dunkri. Open noon-midnight; basement bar 4pm-4am. Tel. 44 80 33. Tallinn's most popular restaurant. An old restored restaurant in the Old Town. "The Order of the Donkey" club in the cellar bar.

GALAXY (Television Tower), 58A Kloostrimetsa tee, open 12.30pm-6.00pm; 8.00pm-2am. Tel. 23 82 50. Wonderful view over Tallinn and its suburbs. In the evening live music, seats 60.

MAHARAJA, 13 Raekoja plats, open noon-5pm; 7pm-11pm. Tel. 44 43 67, a la carte restaurant in an old restored vaulted cellar in the Raekoja plats serving traditional Indian cuisine, 50 seats. Also credit cards accepted.

LINDA, 3 Vabaduse väljak, Palace hotel restaurant - superb internation-

You can find cosy restaurants in the Old Town.

al cuisine; open noon-midnight, Tel. 44 34 61; payment also with credit cards.

SUB MONTE, 4 Rüütli, - á la carte restaurant in a medieval cellar in the Old Town, open noon-11pm, 50 seats, payment also with credit cards, res. tel. 66 68 71, international cuisine and traditional Estonian specialities.

TOOMKOOLI, 11 Toomkooli, on Toompea hill, close by the Dome church, tel. 44 66 13. One of Tallinn's most attractively sited restaurants. The menu offers an uncommonly large choice.

VANA SAKU, 555 Pärnu maantee, Tel. 55 65 66. At the "Peoleo" hotel, open every day 5pm-midnight. Live entertainment for dine and dance.

CABARET

GLORIA, 2 Müürivahe, open 12-6pm; 8pm-midnight (Fri. Sat. 12-6pm; 8pm-2am) Tel. 44 69 50. Large and respectable night-club restaurant. Variety show every day except Sun., Mon.; dance music; seats 145.

HOTEL TALLINN, 27 Toompuiestee, Tel. 60 44 46. A night-club restaurant at the Tallinn hotel. Hunters' Hall, Tea-bar, 2 cafés.

VIRU, 4 Viru väljak, night club of the Viru hotel, res. tel. 65 20 80, 65 07 76.

KUNGLA, 23 Kreutzwaldi, open noon-midnight, Tel. 42 45 41, 42 25 06. Hotel restaurant, Thur., Fri., Sat. variety show, dance music; seats 160. Night bar, open 3pm-3am, live music, dance band, cosy unique atmosphere.

OTHER RECOMMENDED RESTAURANTS

GNOOM, 2 Viru. Restaurant, grill and bar are open noon-11pm, Tel. 44 24 88; café 9am-9pm; Sun. noon-9pm, Tel. 44 27 55. A cosy place with a wonderful medieval interior where you have a choice of 4 dining rooms. Cellar restaurant with recorded music, seats 64; Grill with live music, seats 62; Bar with 24 seats; Café with 24 seats.

HUANGKONG, 24 Tartu maantee, open 11am-11pm, newly opened chinese restaurant, bar.

KARIKAS, 3 Kuninga, open 12-24, newly restored restaurant in the Old Town.

KULLASSEPA KELDER, 7/9/11 Kullassepa, open noon-midnight. Bar 11am-11pm. Tel. 44 22 40. A small intriguing restaurant in the stone-vaulted basement of an Old Town house. The main dish is grilled chicken. Recorded music, seats 48.

KÄNNU KUKK, 71 Vilde tee, in the Mustamäe district, trolly 2 or 3, open noon-5.30pm; 7.30pm-midnight. Tel. 52 32 43. Popular with Finnish tourists; seats 176, with a 90-seat banquet-hall, 35-seat café and a 36-seat pancake bar. In the evening there is dancing to an orchestra.

NORD, 3/5 Rataskaevu, on several storeys in an Old Town house. Restaurants open noon-11pm, Tel. 44 46 95. Rebaseurg (Fox Burrow), cocktail-bar, seats 44, in a vaulted cellar, open noon-6pm; 7pm-11pm. Tel. 44 85 91.

PIRITA, 5 Merivälja tee, open noon-5pm; 7pm-midnight (Fri.-Sat.-1am) Tel. 238 102; 238 108; 238 023. By the sea with a beautiful view and a nice

interior; seats 200, banquet-hall for 150; bar seats 40; dance band.
RAEKÖÖK, 5 Dunkri, open 12am-5pm; 6pm-midnight. Tel. 44 35 40. One of the few new buildings in the Old Town, still a cosy place with a Hanseatic atmosphere, dance band; seats 120, plus bar with 30 seats.
RATASKAEVU, 6 Dunkri, open noon-11pm. Tel. 44 84 26. A cosy little place in the Old Town, seats 64.
REEDER, 33 Vene, open noon-11pm. Tel. 44 65 18. In the Old Town; seats 36, beer cellar seats 30, 18-seats banquet-hall.
VANA TOOMAS, 8 Raekoja plats, open noon-5pm; 7pm-midnight (Fri. Sat.7pm-1am) Tel. 44 58 18. A cosy restaurant with Estonian dishes in Raekoja plats; Fri. Sat. Sun. dance band, seats 100, bar seats 20.

OTHER RESTAURANTS
KALINKA, 69 Kopli puiestee. Trams 1, 2; Kino Rahu stop, open noon-6pm and 7pm-midnight. Tel. 47 81 66. Restaurant with a Russian-style interior and Russian dishes. The banquet-hall is for hire. Floor show (except Mon. Tue.) and dancing to an orchestra; seats 120. Evenings could be dangerous.
KEVAD, 2 Gonsiori, open noon-6pm; 7.30pm-midnight, Sun. noon-5pm; 6pm-10.30pm. Tel. 42 55 49. A cosy restaurant in the department store building; seats 130, plus bar with 30 seats.
KOLDE, 2 Ehte, open noon-11pm. Tel. 49 21 60. A restaurant with 100 seats and 2 banquet-halls (30 seats each), dance band (except Mon.).
KULLER, 1 Kallaku. Beer and snacks.
NÕMME, 3 Jaama - in the suburb Nõmme, open noon-6pm; 7pm-11pm, Tel. 51 00 83. A dance band; seats 120, plus bar with 20 seats.
SZOLNOK, 101 Vilde tee, in the Mustamäe district, take trolly 1, 2 or 5, open noon-5pm; 7pm-10pm. Tel. 53 22 53. A nice small restaurant named after Tallinn's twin town in Hungary, seats 60, a banquet-hall for 30, plus a bar.

CAFÉS

RECOMMENDED CAFES
MAIASMOKK, 16 Pikk (or 1 Pühavaimu), open 11am-10pm, Tel. 60 13 96. Originally the oldest marzipan and chocolate producer (founded in 1864) in Estonia, today serves delicious pastries in spacious rooms. Seats 58.
NEITSITORN, 9A Lühike Jalg, open 11am-10pm, Tel. 44 08 96, 44 05 14. Situated on four floors of a city wall tower. Offers Old Tallinn charm. A balcony with a unique view over the city. Bar in the basement serves mulled wine. It seats 80.
BOGAPOTT, 9 Pikk Jalg, open every day 10am-6pm, Tel. 44 32 20, Estonian-Finnish joint venture, friendly atmosphere, Finnish coffee and tasty snacks.

OTHER CAFES
AMEREST; 1 Pääsukese, open 10am-12, 1pm-7pm. Tel. 42 58 23.
HARJU, 4 Suur-Karja, Old Town, open 9am-9pm, Sun. 10am-8pm. Tel. 44 99 60, 44 66 66. A pleasant café that seats 60 and serves tasty pastries.

Nowadays there's a history museum in Orlov's castle at Maarjamäe.

FLORIIN, 37 Pikk, Old Town, Tel. 44 37 42.
LUCKY LUKE, 20 Mere pst., Tel. 44 93 60. Saloon.
KADRIORG, 90 Narva maantee, open noon-5pm, 6pm-midnight, Tel. 43 12 00. Practically the only place in Kadriorg Park where you can enjoy a meal. Seats 150; Bar seats 40. Dance band.
NARVA, 10 Narva Rd., open 9am-8pm, Tel. 42 44 59. A small cosy café, near to the Viru Hotel, seats 64.
OLYMPIA, 33 Liivalaia, at Olympia hotel, 1st floor, Tel 60 24 89.
PEGASUS, 1 Harju, Old Town, open 11am-10pm, Tel 44 08 07. Club for the Estonian writers, accessible also to the others.
PÄRL, 2 Pikk, Old Town. Tel. 44 33 55. An almost post-modernist interior lifts this from being a run-of-the-mill cafe.
RESTKO, 29 Lai, Old Town, open 10am-8pm, Tel 60 97 28, small snacks, drinks, lunch, also rents its premises for parties.
SAIALILL, 3/5 Saiakang, Old Town, Tel 44 30 55, coffee and pastries, ice cream.
VIRU, 4 Viru väljak, at Viru hotel, 1st floor, Tel 65 07 96.
VÕIROOS, 4 Kaarli pst., Tel 66 66 00, suitable for quick lunch.
SAMAARIA, 3 Vaimu, open Mon.-Fri. 11am-6pm, Sat. 11am-4pm. Christian cafe for vegetarians.
SCHWERIN, 124 Vilde tee, in Mustamäe, open 11am-11pm, Tel. 53 28 47. Trolleybuses 1, 2 or 5. It bears the name of Tallinn's twin city in Ger-

many, seats 76. Bar seats 46.

VESIVESKI, 17/19 Suur-Karja, Located at a busy junction in the Old Town with large windows to take advantage of it.

VIGRI, 19 Narva maantee, open 11am-8pm, Tel. 42 25 13. A café for children with special decor and food. Not far from the centre, seats 65.

BARS

RECOMMENDED BARS

CARLSBERG BEER BAR, Hotel Olümpia, 33 Liivalaia, open 1pm-2am, tel. 60 24 81.

KARIKABAAR, 3 Kuninga, open 11am-midnight, fri.-sun. 11am-5pm; 7pm-1am. tel. 44 17 80. In the basement of a medieval house in the old city. Dancing. Disco on weekends.

MÜNDIBAAR, 3 Mündi, open noon-2am, tel. 44 67 41. The first bar opened in Tallinn. Very popular, seats 24. cocktail specialities.

REGATIBAAR, 1 Merivälja tee, open 7.30pm-2am, tel. 23 83 59. Seats 70. Patronized by young people. Live music, dancing. Disco on weekends.

SKY BAR AND CASINO, At Palace hotel, 3 Vabaduse Väljak, invite you to enjoy night life entertainment on the top floor of the hotel. Open 9pm-3am, tel. 44 34 61.

WESTEND, 19 Pärnu maantee, tel. 44 65 50. Pub. Open 11am-3am. "The place where gentlemen relax."

OTHER BARS

ARABELLA, 3 DUnkri, open 9am-8pm. Mainly for children and teenagers. Ice-cream, soft drinks, seats 44.

ERGO, 4 Viru. A bar in the old city.

HERAKLES, 6 Väike-Karja, open mon.-fri. noon-6pm, tel. 44 18 58.

KANNIKE, 108 Vabaduse puiestee. A bar to have a quick snack and a beer. a pleasant place to spend an evening with friends. Sauna can be booked.

KASTAN, 7 Toompuiestee, open 11am-4pm, 5-11 pm, tel. 45 06 58. An unpretentious place to have a quick snack and a drink, seats 40.

KUNINGAAIABAAR, is situated between Neitsitorn and Lühike Jalg.

MEFISTO, 23A Sakala, open noon-4pm; 9pm-3am. tue.-wed. Sex-show. tel. 66 62 86.

PELGULINN, 3 Rohu, open 10am-3pm; 4pm-8pm, tel. 47 17 88. An unpretentious snackbar, seats 35.

ROSALIE, Vene st., old town. Open midday to 11pm. A locals bar favoured for the mulled wine.

SININE BAAR, 28 Pirita tee, open 10am-9pm. 23 86 42. Bar with video and music.

TARTU, 6 Tartu maantee, open 11am-11pm, tEL. 42 33 09. Central position, seats 50. Grilled chicken, piped music, dancing.

TAURUS, 40 Narva maantee, open 2.30pm-12pm. Piped music, dancing, 30 seats.

TONDI, 26 Tondi, in the southern suburb of tondi, open 2pm-midnight, tel. 55 53 78. Seats 30. Grilled chicken, piped music, dancing.

VALGUSE BAAR, 10/12 Väike-Karja (in the courtyard), open 9am-6pm; 9pm-6am, (mon.-tue. -11pm). Tel. 44 59 66. Popular place in the old town. Disco.

VALLIBAAR, 16 Müürivahe, open noon-3pm; 4pm-10pm (sun.-7pm). Tel. 44 06 27. Live music.

VIRMALINE, 16 Viru, open 9am-8pm, Tel. 44 66 60. Ice cream, soft drinks, coffee. seats 28.

MUSEUMS

AJALOOMUUSEUM (Historical Museum), 17 Pikk, open Thur-Tues, 11am-6pm, tel 44 34 46 and 60 21 63.

A permanent exhibition of Estonia's early history. The building dates from 1410. Originally the home of the Great Guild (a merchants' guild) this is one of the finest examples of lay architecture in Tallinn.

MAARJAMÄE LOSS (Maarjamägi Palace), 56 Pirita tee, open Wed-Sun, 11am-5pm, tel 23 70 71. Bus nos. 1, 5, 8, 34, 38.

A permanent exhibition of the history of Estonia from the 19th century to the present. The neo-gothic limestone building was erected on the bluff by the sea in 1874 as a summer palace for Adjutant General Orlov-Davydov.

KADRIORG PALACE, 37 Weizenbergi, Trams Nos 1 and 3. Buses Nos 1, 5, 8, 44, 56.

Once the German theatre, now the Eesti Draamateater (Estonian Drama Theatre).

The lovely miniature baroque palace in Kadriorg Park, designed by the Italian architect Niccolo Michetti, together with the park around it were founded by Czar Peter the Great as a summer residence for his wife Catherine. In the thirties, it served as the residence of the President of the Republic of Estonia. Behind the palace lies the Garden of Sculptures.

LINNAMUUSEUM (City Museum), 17 Vene, open Wed.-Mon. 10.30am-5.30pm, Tel. 44 58 56 and 44 18 29. Several evocative items from the 14th-18th centuries. A permanent exhibition of Tallinn in the 18th-19th centuries, plus several evocative items from the 14th-18th centuries. Faience and porcelain wares and handicrafts are among the treasures. The building is a medieval merchant's abode in the heart of the Old Town.

KUNSTIMUUSEUM (Art Museum), 1 Kiriku plats, open Wed.-Mon. 11am-6pm. Tel. 44 93 40.

NIGULISTE MUUSEUM (St. Nicholas Church-Museum), 13 Niguliste, open Wed. 2-6pm, Thu.-Sun. 11am-6pm. It is the most proportioned 14th-15th century Gothic basilica church in Tallinn. The Late-Baroque steeple was added in the 18th century. During an air-raid in 1944 the church burned down. It was thoroughly restored and from 1984 it has been museum-concert hall. It contains a permanent exhibition of rare 15th-16th century works of art such as the main altar of the Niguliste Church (end of the 15th century) by H.Rode, a fragment of "Danse macabre" by B.Notke and others.

LOODUSMUUSEUM (Museum of Natural History), 29 Lai, Wed.-Sun. 10am-5.30pm, Tel. 44 42 23. A permanent exhibition of Estonian wildlife and countryside.

MEREMUUSEUM (Maritime Museum), 70 Pikk, Wed.-Sun. 10am-6pm, Tel. 60 18 03. A permanent exhibition of history of shipping and fishing in Estonia. The museum is housed in a powerful cannon tower, Paks Margareeta ("Stout Margaret") which was built in 1510-31.

TEATRI- JA MUUSIKAMUUSEUM (Museum of Theatrical and Musical History), 12 Müürivahe, Wed.-Mon. 10am-6pm, Tel. 44 28 84

A permanent exhibition of musical instruments, and an archive containing documents of historical interest, books and manuscripts. The entrance is in the old town wall.

TARBEKUNSTIMUUSEUM (Museum of Decorative and Applied Art), 17 Lai, Wed.-Sun 11am-6pm, Tel. 44 59 89. A permanent exhibition of Estonian decorative and applied art of the 20th century. The museum is housed in a 17th-century warehouse.

TERVISHOIUMUUSEUM (Estonian Health Museum), 28/30 Lai, Tues.-Sat. 11am-5pm. Tel. 60 16 02; 60 17 08. Exhibition "Man, health, family". Introduction to human anatomy and physiology by electronical models and videos. Sexual biology. Special exhibition for children at the age from 5 to 12. One room is reserved for temporary art exhibitions.

TULETÕRJEMUUSEUM (Fire Station museum), 14 Vana-Viru, Tues.-Sat. 12am-6pm, Tel. 44 42 51. This old limestone fire station has a permanent exhibition of fire-fighting equipment from the past.

A H TAMMSAARE MEMORIAALMUUSEUM (A. H. Tammsaare Museum), 12A Koidula, Wed.-Mon.11am-6pm, Tel. 427 208 and 426 300.

Trams Nos 1 and 3. Tammsaare's last home, a 19th-century wooden house, holds an exhibition of his books, letters, manuscripts etc.
KRISTJAN RAUA MUUSEUM (Kristjan Raud Museum), 8 Raua, Wed.-Sun. 11am-6pm. Estonian mythology in the works of Kristjan Raud.
KIEK IN DE KÖK 1 Komandandi tee, Tues., Wed., Fri. 10.30am-5.30pm, Sat., Sun. 11am-4pm, Tel. 44 66 86. A good exhibition of Tallinn's fortifications in the tallest cannon tower in Tallinn, built in 1475-83. The name is in Low German and means "peep into the kitchen".
RAEVANGLA (Town Hall Prison), Wed.-Mon. 10.30am-5.30pm. Museum of Photography.
ROCCA-AL-MARE VABAÕHUMUUSEUM (Open-air-museum), 12 Vabaõhumuuseumi tee, Tel. 55 91 76. Buses 21, 45. A large assembly of original Estonian peasant architecture from the 18th till the early 20th

Tallinn's shopping centre begins ...

century in extensive parkland with original domestic and farming implements.

EMBASSIES AND DIPLOMATIC MISSIONS

Canada: 13 Toomkooli, Toompea, Tel. 44 90 56, fax (358 9) 29 81 04.
Great Britain: 20 Kentmanni, Tel. 45 53 28, fax 45 53 54. Open 9.30am-12.00, 1.30pm-4.00pm.
United States of America: 20 Kentmanni, Mon., Wed., Fri. 9am-noon. Tel. 45 53 13, 45 50 05, telefax (358)-(49)-30 68 17.

CAR RENTAL

"MERCEDES-BENZ-AG" Tel. 60 62 05
"HERZRENT" Tel. 42 10 03
"REFIT" Tel. 68 26 07
"IDEAL" Tel. 21 27 35
"FINEST AUTO" Tel. 44 47 61
"ROADRUNNER ESTRING" Tel. 77 15 24 A/S ASC
Tel. 51 09 08

PHARMACIES

RAEAPTEEK, (at Town Hall square,due to renovations situated at 47 Pikk). One of the oldest pharmacies in Europe (approx. 1440). Prescriptions made up. Mon. 11am-6pm, Tues.-Fri. 9am-8pm, Sat.& Sun. 9am-3pm.

APTEEK, 5 Tõnismägi. Prescriptions made up. Night service. Information concerning medicines. Mon.-Fri. 8am-9pm, Sat. & Sun. closed.

APTEEK, 10 Pärnu maantee. Prescriptions made up. No night service. Mon.-Fri. 8am-8pm, Sat. 9am-5pm, Sun. closed.

VANATURU APTEEK, 1 Vene. Prescriptions not made up. No night service. Mon.-Fri. 9am-7pm, 9am-4pm, Sun. closed.

APTEEK, 7 Rävala puiestee. Prescriptions made up. No night service. Mon.-Fri 8 am-8pm, Sat. 9am-4pm, Sun. closed.

INFORMATION, Tõnismägi 5, phone 44 18 13, 44 36 50

TO TALLINN BY CAR

Every year more and more tourists prefer to come to Tallinn by car. Motoring tourists can travel by way of Helsinki-Vyborg-St. Petersburg-Narva-Tallinn or they can avail themselves of the Stockholm-Tallinn or Helsinki-Tallinn ferries.

PETROL. Finding petrol on your own can be a real headache. Sometimes there are queues or there is none available.

Petrol is available at **Pirita** (1 Regati puiestee, Tel. 23 84 04, open 10am-10pm, available A-99, A-95, A-76, Diesel), at **Järve** (141 Pärnu maantee, Tel. 52 92 00, open round the clock, available A-99, A-95, A-93, A-76, Diesel and also unleaded petrol 95E, service and car washing, café and shop), close to the airport and port (Statoil stations and shops). A-93 petrol is carried by filling stations 552 Pärnu maantee (Tel. 51 90 67), at **96 Paldiski maantee** (Tel. 55 91 91), at **66 B Kadaka tee, 2 Rummu tee** and **58 St.Peterburi maantee**, too. Filling stations are open round the clock.

TRAFFIC RULES. On the whole traffic regulations are international nowadays, but there are some local regulations that you should take into consideration. In built-up areas the speed limit is 50 km/25 miles per hour. The driver and the passenger sitting in the front seat must wear their seat belts. In order to drive in the Old City you have to pay entrance fee. Many streets in the city centre are closed or one-way making driving difficult and full of surprises. Keep your cool and consider driving as a challenge or an adventure.

Here are some helpful hints:

- never drive if you are under the influence of alcohol or medicine; breathalizer tests are frequent; no level of alcohol is tolerated by the police;
- there are no parking meters in Tallinn, take note of no-stopping and parking signs;
- when leaving your car, don't forget to lock the doors;
- don't leave valuables in your car even if it is locked;

TRAFFIC PROBLEMS If you have any problems consult the police) - Tel. 02, placing the call from a public phone is free or **Tallinna Liikluspolitsei** (Traffic Police of Tallinn), 31 Lastekodu (Tel. 44 54 50; trams 2 and 4, get off at **Autobussijaam** stop). Car insurance is not compulsory in Estonia. Your insurance problems can be taken care by the insurance agency "Inges", 17 Pärnu mnt. (close to the Vabaduse square), tel 44 09 18, fax 44 84 87, Mon-Fri 9am-noon, 2pm-5pm.

CITY TRANSPORT

There are trams, trolleybuses, buses, route taxis and taxis in Tallinn. Traffic begins about 5am-6am and continues until midnight. Route taxis start working at 3pm from Viru väljak and go until 1.30am. They go by fixed routes and stop where the passenger asks. Electric railway goes from Balti jaam (Baltic Railway Station) to Tallinn's suburbs - Nômme and Pääsküla. Bus number 22 connects Balti jaam, bus station and airport. Trams number 1 and 2 take you to the port (Linnahall stop), number 1 and 3 to Kadriorg. You can buy tickets for trams, trolleybuses and buses from the ticket stalls near the stops. You can also buy monthly tickets which are valid in trams, trolleybuses and buses. You must validate your ticket in a tram, trolleybus or bus. The route taxi tickets are sold by the driver and tickets for the electric train in the ticket office at the station. Warning: there are not many trolleybuses and buses on the route and you need to wait quite long. Buses, trolleybuses and trams are also often crowded. Every taxi should possess the taximeter. Some taxi drivers take more money than allowed. It is better to avoid cars without distinctive marks because of your security. The taxi stations in the City center are at Viru väljak and near the Vabaduse väljak.

HARJUMAA

Area: 4147 km^2 **Population: 128 250**

Harjumaa is Estonia's most heavily populated county, and umbilically tied to Tallinn. Tallinners' summer cottages, gardening cooperatives and children's camps are here, and its land supplies the capital's vegetables, flowers, fowl and a sizable slab of its labour force. Harjumaa is, in a sense, the diligent farmhand to Tallinn's greedy master.

The landscape is diverse. The Baltic defile, a limestone cliff at times towering 30 m, winds along the coast. Meadowland near the coast turns into primeval forests and swamps further in. History runs deep here too. Villages chronicled by the Danes show that Harjumaa was already reasonably populous and heavily fortified in the 13th century. Long before the rise of Tallinn, ancient Harjumaa was an independent land of some importance.

TOWARDS NARVA

Places of great historical and natural importance lie along Harjumaa's north coast: they're especially concentrated around Jõelähtme, Kuusalu, Muuksi and Nõmmeveski. Lahemaa was the Soviet Union's first national park and remains a favourite holiday place among Estonians.

What a piece of work

The Narva highway isn't beautiful – smokestacks pump soot into the air, storage yards look like rubbish dumps, and Tallinn's suburb of **Lasnamäe** is a splendour not. Lasnamäe is a monument to Soviet planning and a warning to future generations.

Just outside Tallinn city limits, you can gaze at **Maardu's "lunar landscape"** of chemical plants and open cast mines. If you see a pile of dirt smouldering, don't worry – it's only radioactive underground burning. Meanwhile, the passionate fishermen of Lake Maardu fish on undisturbed. A drive around the area north of the highway reveals some wonderful industrial vistas and shows you the full range of Soviet high-density living. Maardu's baroque **manor** with its singular ceiling-pieces is south of the highway. A remarkable building 1 km west of it is **Saha chapel***, 50 years older than Tallinn. The population of the graveyard has been increasing continually since 1241.

2800-year-old cemetery. Ancient stone barrows at Jõelähtme.

Rebala and the phosphorite rebellion

The plain west of here is a sort of landscape found only in Sweden and Estonia and known as "alvars". The limestone bedrock is covered with barely 10 cm of soil, which can support only sporadic clumps of grass, pines and junipers. **Around Jõelähtme village***** are a "karst" gully landscape, Estonia's Niagara, and numerous archaeological sites. These last formed the first battleground for Estonia's fledgling national movement in the 1980s.

The **"karst" area**** is south of the highway. The river has carved its way above and below ground through different consistencies of rock and created a freaky mini-gorge-land. This is a common feature of the Estonian landscape. The pastureland is full of caves, cracks and hollows, and many a river takes an underground detour. One mushroom-shaped relic is perfect for those essential group photographs, though one wonders what the ancient Estonians who considered it sacred would think. Two ways to find the place: turn south off the Narva highway at the busstop opposite Jõelähtme church, then first left, through the farmstead, then right and follow the road; or on foot follow the riverbed south from the old bridge in Jõelähtme village.

About 100 m past the Jõelähtme River, to the right of the highway, you can find over 30 excavated **ancient barrows*****. These survived for 2800 years as mounds, and one has been conserved that way. The others are presented in the gamut of barrow styles, and you can see the small stone "coffin" within a limestone ring.

Jõelähtme itself is north of the highway. **Jõelähtme church** was built at the beginning of the 14th century as a fortress-church, with walls over 1.5 m thick and embrasures instead of windows. When it was converted into a church, windows were put in, the arches were widened, and a tower was erected. You'll see a lot of churches in Estonia with a similar history.

If you follow the road west from the church you pass numerous burial mounds sporting the regulation Estonian white sign. This is the historic village of **Rebala****, which gave its name to the district, Rävala, and even to Tallinn – Tallinn's German name for centuries was *Reval*. Not far from here, archaeologists found 2000-year-old primeval fields, the oldest so far discovered in the North European forest zone. Unfortunately the Soviets wanted to mine the area for phosphorite. But this was 1985, the first days of perestroika, and historians, scientists and ordinary people banded together to fight the miners. Demonstrations were held, "We are the world"-type songs were recorded, and for the first time the ordinary people managed to defeat the powers-that-be. Rebala was saved.

Heading back to Jõelähtme along the old road, you cross en route the 19th-century stone bridge. The river reappears after its underground journey on the north side of the bridge, from where it tumbles rapidly into the Jägala river. You're on the *old* highway to Narva and St Petersburg. Keep a look-out for the **post-station** from 1824, where tired horses were changed for fresh ones and travellers could rest up on their journeys.

The witch's well in Tuhala can't hold its water in springtime.

The church of Jõelähtme was originally a fortress.

The river goes underground and carves things like this.

The Estonian Niagara

The old highway leads on to the bank of the Jägala River (103 km long, a considerable length for an Estonian river). The 8 m high **Jägala waterfall**** is often called the Estonian Niagara. There are many waterfalls in the north of the country, usually quite small. Most are formed when rivers fall into the sea from the limestone plateau. In the course of time they erode gorges in the rock. Jägala waterfall withdraws 3 m every 100 years. In the summer you can cross at the top of the falls, where the water is knee-high. **Careful** of slipping over the side. The intrepid can also cross below through the hollow cavern behind the falls.

If you're interested in old industrial architecture you can hike a few km north to a hydro-electric power station. Not far from there is the site of an ancient fortified stronghold dating back to 1500-3000 BC. It's the

Estonia's Niagara is the Jägala waterfall.

second-largest hill-fort site in the country, after Toompea in Tallinn.

Continuing along the road, a sign points to **Kalevi-Liiva*.** This sandhill was made by the great Kalevipoeg, hero of Estonia's national epic. Once, he saw an enormous ox trying to drink all the water from a lake. Kalevipoeg had a heap of sand in the flap of his coat, which he'd collected in Finland. He dropped the heap to frighten off the ox and it formed the hill of Kalevi-Liiva. Don't be surprised if you find buttons or bones in the sand. In 1942-43 the Nazis executed 6000 people here, as a monument attests.

The coast at nearby **Kaberneeme** and **Salmistu** boasts some lovely beaches. Off the coast you can see a string of islands whose inhabitants were forced out by Soviet frontier troops. Several coastal villages suffered the same fate. After crossing the river in **Valkla village** you pass the furthest point reached by the Red Army when it invaded Estonia in 1919 – barely 20 km from Tallinn. Here the Estonian counter-attack began, leading to victory in the War of Independence and an unoccupied Republic of Estonia for two decades.

The old highway rejoins the new one at Kiiu. A four-storey tower in the village is the **smallest fortress*** in Estonia. Nowadays, it's a darling bar.

The fire fairy

One of the numerous fairies Estonians believed in was a "fire fairy". When the Christians arrived, they erected **Kuusalu church**** in 1220 and cleverly dedicated it to St Lawrence, who'd been cooked alive on a grill in Rome in 285 AD and become patron saint of fire. The ploy worked, and for centuries on his feast day, 10 August, local villagers were forbidden even to light a pipe. The church has a noteworthy altar and pulpit.

The village itself is one of more than 100 parish centres mentioned in the Danish Assessment Book, composed by Danish pilgrims in 1240. Many important local figures are buried in its two adjacent, spacious **cemeteries*.** And the road behind the church leads to the place where Sweden's King Karl XII camped with his troops at the beginning of the Northern War in 1700. It's marked by 45 curly old pines, each about 25 m tall.

An underpass crosses the Narva highway on the north side of town. Between this junction and the old Tallinn-Narva highway just to the north you can find sacrificial stones and other ancient survivors. Nearby, beside the bog, is **Silmaallikas** ("eye spring"), whose waters are said to cure eye diseases. A sacrificial stone with four hollows in it lies beside the spring. Heading north from the underpass towards Alliku, half a km before the old highway, there's a **stone with a grill** drawn on it to the right. The image commemorates St Lawrence's painful martyrdom, while the pair of scissors on the stone's verso recalls that his tongue was cut off before he was fried. The same sign appears in the seal of the local congregation.

A couple of hundred metres east of the underpass, a footpath leads north through the bog to the poorly preserved remains of **Pajulinnus** ("willow stronghold", though in fact it was used more as a treasure house than a fort). It was clever of the Estonians to build a stronghold on log

Church of Kuusalu, dedicated to St Lawrence, griddled to death.

rafts in marshland, accessible only by a secret log path. Since the bog was full of springs, it didn't freeze in winter and protected the place well. If you're interested in the history of ancient Kuusalu parish, the former vicarage, now an excellent **local museum***, has information about the whole fascinating region.

Cottage in seaside Kaberneeme.

Lahemaa National Park

Continuing along the new Narva highway you enter the first national park established in the former Soviet Union – **Lahemaa National Park*****. A prolonged bureaucratic battle had to be fought in order to set up such a "dubious Estonian enterprise", and officials in Moscow refused permission until 1971. The name Lahemaa ("the land of gulfs") comes from the numerous gulfs and peninsulas that break up the coast here. Three-quarters of the park has preserved its natural appearance. It boasts a rich collection of natural treasures, including waterfalls, swamps, primeval forests and limestone plateaus. Lahemaa is also a reservation for rural architecture: an ensemble of manor buildings has been reconstructed, and barrows and sacrifice stones are preserved.

Some of the most important sites have **study trails** through them: the pocket guide is available from the

Estonia has stones aplenty – Viinistu shingle beach in Lahemaa.

hiking center in Viitna, Western Virumaa (currently only in Estonian, but it's worth picking up for its maps anyway). It's prohibited to damage wildlife or to camp out, and fires may only be lit in officially sanctioned sites. The park warden lives in splendid Palmse, Western Virumaa.

The bog-pools of Viru

Some 50 km from Tallinn take the turn towards Loksa. In about 1 km you reach a parking lot: across the road a 4 km study trail to the **Viru bog-pools*** begins. Don't worry, you won't drown as long as you keep to the plank path. Bog-pools are a rare natural phenomenon. A bog consists of 90% of water, filled with moss about 7 m thick. The water, searching for an outlet, collects into small streams and pools on the surface. Water in bog pools is among the purest in the world. You can bathe in the pools but remember, the water is icy cold near the bottom. A tower halfway along the trail gives a broader view. (To get to the other end of the trail by road, take the first right heading north.)

To the left from the Loksa road, in **Kolga,** there's a 17th-century manor house. The coat-of-arms above the entrance shows that the estate was owned by the Stenbocks, a Swedish noble family, though *Kloostrimõisa* ("cloister estate") was in fact built by monks from Gotland in the 13th century. From here, back roads lead you to another historic place, **Muuksi**.** The same monks owned the whole area around Kolga – in 1290 Muuksi village was known as Munkenkulle. Old limestone buildings, stone fences, cattle enclosures, junipers on the limestone plateau, all combine to create the feeling that time has stopped for centuries here.

There's another study trail around Muuksi's most interesting places. Just north-east of the village stands **Muuksi bluff,** 47 m high. An ancient Estonian fort stood on the bluff until the beginning of the century. On midsummer nights a bonfire is lit here and people gather to swing, sing and dance.

Gusset and a graveyard

A walkable distance west of the village there lies another hill, **Turjemägi;** down its steep northern bank a waterfall sometimes flows. In ancient times not water but pure vodka streamed down this **Turjekeldri waterfall.** Bewitching warlock girls used to sell it to passers-by. Kalevipoeg, carrying a load of planks, stopped by on his way back from Finland. Estonia's epic hero

Feel creepy in the Nõmmeveski canyon ...

was soon drunk and staggering on his way, shoulders still laden with planks ... when warlocks set upon him. Kalevipoeg smashed half the pile to pieces but couldn't manage to repel them. Suddenly a soft voice from a bush told him to turn the

... or feel much younger standing by a limestone fence in Muuksi.

planks edgewise. Our hero heeded the advice and soon the warlocks were on the run. The advisor turned out to be a small, cold hedgehog. In gratitude, Kalevipoeg tore the gusset from his fur coat and gave it to the animal – and that's how the hedgehog acquired its thorny coat. Further west there's a lovely seashore in Andineeme.

At Hundikangru, just south of Muuksi beside the road, there are more than 30 stone graves from the Bronze Age, 1st millennium BC. Each corpse was laid on the ground inside a ring of limestone blocks, then covered with more blocks. Then rounder stones were heaped on the grave.

Blight at river-mouth

The coastal highway, punctuated with small villages on both sides, makes an interesting drive. The church at **Leesi** has a beautiful altar and pulpit. But be prepared – at **Loksa** you'll see something quite different. A monster has come to this small summer resort at the mouth of the river Valgejõgi. The Loksa Marine Repair Plant, a terrible blot on the national park, has recently closed, an early victim of the new economy. The ugliness remains.

North of Loksa, at the tip of Pärispea peninsula, is **Cape Purekkari,** the northernmost point of the Estonian mainland (59° latitude north).

One way back to the Narva highway follows the west side of the river **Valgejõgi**.** The Vasaristi brook performs a vanishing act along the way: it actually flows under the road. A bit further on, take a left to Nõmmeveski mill to see some attractive rapids – a good location for kayaking, and only 55 km from Tallinn. You can follow another study trail here through one of Lahemaa's most contrast-laden areas: mini-canyons, two cascades, and a power station.

SOUTH-EASTERN HARJUMAA

If you like forests and solitude head for south-eastern Harjumaa. One good route loops: Narva highway – Jägala – Aegviidu – Vetla – Alavere – Aruküla.

Gift of the president

When you turn off the highway towards Aegviidu, the **broad, smooth road** comes as something of a shock. Such a superb road seems a bit luxurious but in fact it was a reserve airstrip for the Soviet army. A military college has only just closed in Jägala. Estonians have long traditions in gymnastics and sports of strength. In **Pillapalu** the hindmost farmstead was presented to a man named Kristjan Palusalu by the President of the Republic of Estonia, Konstantin Päts. In the Soviet period, home ownership was illegal, and the state confiscated Palusalu's house. Nowadays it's a gymnasium, which would probably have pleased its former owner. Kristjan Palusalu was a double Olympic wrestling champion, and is still the only man in the world to simultaneously hold both free and Greco-Roman wrestling crowns.

A pure land

Near Aegviidu the road passes through pine forest. The land to the left is quite scenic: eskers, dozens of small lakes, cranberry bogs. It's the northern part of an enormous forest zone extending down to Latvia. This part is particularly virgin, and for good reason: until recently about 360 km^2 of it was a Soviet army firing range. Experienced bushwalkers armed with maps can invade this pure land without risking an encounter with heavy ballistics.

The railway station in **Aegviidu** has a Russian feel. When the Tallinn-Petersburg line opened, all stations had to be built according to the Russian standard. Aegviidu's is an exact replica of the station in Grazi Tsaritson.

The Estonian Switzerland?

When you catch sight of lake Nikerjärv a couple of km along on the right it means you've reached **Nelijärve**** ("four lakes"). In fact there are seven lakes but the hilly countryside prevents you from seeing more than four at any one time. Nelijärve's constantly varied landscape, its hills and lovely valleys, make it a favourite place for skiing and orienteering. Thousands participate in the annual Aegviidu Ski Marathon. This is one of several areas people call the "Estonian Switzerland": perhaps they mean Switzerland without the mountains.

You go briefly through the next county now, turn at Jäneda to Vetla and pass the viewing tower of Valgehobusemägi (see Järvamaa chapter). The return trip to Tallinn crosses woody Vetla and the fields of Alavere. **Kiviloo bishop castle*** has fallen into ruin gradually over the past 200 years. Last century this "ghost castle" was a popular haunt of German artists.

TOWARDS TARTU

The Tartu highway leads past some ancient villages and a group of affecting monuments to the "forest brothers".

Iron and flying fish

Heading out of Tallinn on the Tartu highway, don't forget to stop at the airport. From the steps of this modernist thing you have a good view of **Lake Ülemiste** and **Lindakivi** ("Linda's stone", see chapter on Tallinn).

Jüri village is to the left near the turn-off for the Narva highway. You pass a very special **oak grove** just inside Jüri. The two oaks on either side of the road are called "the bride" and "the bridegroom". The story goes that the trees are wedding guests put under a witch's spell when two wedding processions clashed on the narrow road. If the trunks are cut by an axe, blood flows from the "wounds" (honest).

You can't see the fish from here. Lake Kiruvere.

"**Iron was smelted** from a bog here in Jüri village at the beginning of the Christian era," claims a sign on an odd monument in the park opposite Jüri church. This was one of the first places iron was smelted in Estonia. Bog ore was heated with charcoal in a clay hearth and iron flowed from the ore.
A sign on the left of the highway about 30 km from Tallinn indicates **Saula siniallikad** ("blue springs of Saula"). Curative powers have been attributed to the waters of these springs. Silver, coins, crops and animals were sacrificed to them. The right turn towards Kohila leads to a **"witch's well"*** which sometimes shoots up live fish in its springtime geyser. A sign indicating *Tuhala nõiakaev* just the other side of sweet little Kata church points the way. There are arcane sculptures not far from the well.

Lakeland

Kose*. Turn at the old tavern. You can walk through parkland downstream from the old mill, below the church, and along and across the banks of the winding river. The churchyard is attractive, with its chapel in stone of several colours. The **manor at Ravila** is now a home for the disabled, complete with inappropriate annexe.
Back on the highway, there are several small lakes, invisible from the road, on the right. To the left, closer to **Ardu,** the Paunküla reservoir and Lake Kiruvere are rich in fish.

The "forest brothers"

The "forest brothers" were Baltic partisans who fought a terrorist war against the Soviets, hiding deep in the forests from 1941 to 1953. They were particularly strong in the forests around **Kautla.** The NKVD (Soviet security service) raided and destroyed dozens of suspect households in an attempt to eliminate the brothers. A battalion of Estonians, "Erna", parachuted here after flying from Finland, and the decisive battle took place on 30 July 1941. After taking heavy losses, about 2000 "forest brothers", women and children among them, managed to make it through the enemy encirclement.
A **memorial**** to the 30 victims of the NKVD revenge was unveiled in 1942 in Kautla. It was destroyed during the Soviet era. In 1989 the memorial tablet was reconstructed, but unknown vandals smashed it

Is there enough money to restore Padise monastery?

again. In 1990 it was restored for the third time, and in December, by secret order of the Soviet Security Minister, shattered again late one night. The destroyed monuments stand next to the new one. Across the road a ruined farmhouse serves as a memorial to the thousands of farms destroyed by the Red Army.
To see all this, turn left at Ardu in the direction of the campsite, take the first good right turn after the Paunküla reservoir appears, and go about another 6 km from there.

WESTERN HARJUMAA

The west includes the ruin of Padise monastery and a few Soviet naval bases ready to be "liberated" when we went to press.

Twisting cane, encircling river

You can reach western Harjumaa along the Pärnu highway. About 40 km out, just before **Kernu**, a right at the auto service centre leads to a neoclassical manor on the shore of the Kernu reservoir. At the south end of town beside the highway there grows a thick juniper known as the "Swedish king's cane" because of its seven windings. West of Kernu lies **Nissi** village in which you can find a church in the eclectic style. The same road takes you to **Riisipere.** A manor stands 2 km west of the watertower. The handsome neoclassical facade is now shuttered and rather decrepit.
Head towards Vasalemma, and go left through **Rummu***, a mining town and military base complete with watchtowers and barb wire.
Padise monastery**, now a substantial ruin, is the oldest building in Harjumaa. It was the work of Cistercian monks, who erected the chapel in the 13th century. There are fragments of stone here remarkably similar to those in Riga's Dome. The main building of the monastery, a cloister encircled by the river, was

begun in the 14th century, but after the uprising of St George's Night in 1343 building was interrupted for some centuries. It was finally finished in the 16th century. The cloister was badly damaged during the Livonian War and finished off in a conflagration in 1766. It is currently being restored.

Non-existent Paldiski

The road to the north leads to **Paldiski****. At time of going to press there were reports of the Soviet soldiers smashing, burning, removing copper wires and chairs and light fittings, basically wrecking the place. This was heartening news since it meant that the Red Army was moving out; generally when withdrawing from their Baltic bases they took everything that wasn't nailed down, as if an order had come down from on high to leave only broken shells. The town was established as a naval port (the Baltic port or "Paldiski") by Czar Peter I. Paldiski has been closed to both Estonians and foreigners for 50 years. The peninsula of Pakri, where the town is situated, is a beautiful place, so hopefully we'll have more to say about this secret town in our next edition.

Everybody went to Klooga beach.

Kloogan contrasts

About 50 000 people spend their summer holidays in **Klooga***. The town is split in two. In the resort area are several kilometres of white sandy beach, one of the cleanest in Estonia, and a little stream called Treppoja ("staircase stream") which cascades 15 m down a "staircase" into the sea. In midsummer, the staircase and riverbed are bone dry. The "upper town" is a Soviet **military town***. This is the place to go if you want to see the poverty and

The cliff at Türisalu. Did you bring your mountaineering gear?

hardship of Soviet soldiers: appalling roads and highrises, walls, empty shops. For all that, there are a few Stalinist buildings among the blockhouses and a beautiful manor (occupied). Aptly, 2000 people were killed in Klooga's concentration camp in 1943-44.

The souls of slaves

In 1220-30 the Danes erected a wooden church on the bank of the **Keila** River. It's been rebuilt several times over the centuries and is now a spacious **two-nave stone church*** in a churchyard with collapsing headstones and a couple of crypts. Nearby, an ancient fortress once stood, and not far from its ruins is **Orjakivi** ("slave stone"). Slaves were executed on this rock and their souls are believed to inhabit the lime trees that grow around it. A 17 000 strong satellite town of Tallinn has sprung up around the church.

If you head towards Tallinn, turn off to Vääna and from that small village head back to the highway, the Vääna River appears momentarily to your left: you'll find a cascade and restored watermill here. Further on, on the right, stone **bunkers and cellars*** are all that remain of a fortified battery. In case of an invasion by land, the Russians started building a ring of such facilities south and east of Tallinn from 1910. War came sooner than expected and the fortification was never finished, leaving only a few dangerous catacombs for curious children to fall into. Other batteries on the coast and islands and at Helsinki-Porkkala were meant to cover the Gulf of Finland and prevent a naval assault on St Petersburg. The best preserved are on the island of Aegna.

Just before Tallinn, you pass **Harku.** In 1710 in Harku manor, Tallinn's Swedish garrison signed a capitulation treaty, ending both the Northern War and the Swedish era of Estonian history, and signalling the beginning of the Russian period.

NORTH-WEST COAST

The Rannamõisa road from Tallinn offers views and beaches and waterfalls.

From Rannamõisa to Laulasmaa

The Rannamõisa road out of Tallinn is the right turn from the Paldiski highway at the roundabout. From

Will Lohusalu beach throng with tourists? Not yet.

Rannamõisa cliff* you have a view of the sea and of distant Tallinn's towers and cranes. A footpath saunters near the precipice, starting at the Merepiiga cafe and campground.

Soon you approach Vääna-Jõesuu with its neat beach and the 30 m high **Türisalu cliff,** where there's a park-

Winter waterfall at Keila.

ing place. About 200 m further along, the Türisalu River has gouged out a mini-gorge before tumbling into the sea – in the wet season. There's another waterfall in the substantial park in **Keila-Joa****. The Estonian government keeps its summer cottages here; before World War II, the manor in the park was a government summer-house too. Until very recently the Soviet army occupied it, painting all the neo-gothic buildings a mute orange. The manor house itself was a clubhouse.
Lohusalu is a slim, pine-covered peninsula of summer cottages and a few sandy beaches. Last century, **Laulasmaa beach** was known as "Europe's African beach". The name comes from the singing sands (*laul* is Estonian for "song"), a low hum produced by the wind or footsteps.

TO THE ISLANDS

Aegna and Prangli are inhabited; Naissaar, Tallinn's natural island resort, is only now shaking off the Soviets.

Among the islands off Harjumaa, only Aegna (2.9 km^2) and Prangli (6.4 km^2) have local inhabitants, while Naissaar (18 km^2) was still occupied when we went to press. Aegna's silhouette can be seen from the harbour. It takes about an hour to get there by regular ferry from Tallinn. There's a good beach, as well as many workers' holiday resorts and boulders. "Jerusalem town" is a sacred maze formed from walls of heaped stones.
There are about 200 people on **Prangli** (6.4 km^2, served by a ferry once a week). The island has a school, a church and a club. The shore is stony and the coastal waters are shallow. There are dozens of small islets in the waters off Harjumaa.

PRACTICAL DETAILS

ACCOMODATION

"Peoleo" hotel & camping, 555 Pärnu mnt., Tallinn, tel 77 16 01
Kernu camping, Tallinn, Pärnu mnt. 37.km, tel 77 16 30
"Trap" hotel, Saku, tel 72 19 58
Nelijärve tourist centre, Aegviidu, tel 76 73 82
Assaku tourist house, Rae, tel 72 52 53
Kostivere camping, Jõelähtme, tel 44 12 00
Kaberneeme camping, Jõelähtme, tel 59 71 41
Kodasoo camping
Laagri camping
Kurkse camping, tel 55 70 59
Kloogaranna camping
Vääna-Jõesuu camping
Lohusalu holiday centre, Lohusalu, tel 71 82 40
Marite camping, Kõue, tel 75 32 42
Klooga hostel, Klooga, tel 74 32 42
Trawell hotel, Kuusalu, Andineeme, tel 77 25 91

RESTAURANTS

"Keila", 4. Paldiski mnt. Keila, tel 74 53 41
"Põhjarannik", 46. Tallinna mnt. Loksa, tel 77 51 75
"Rävala", Saku, tel 72 11 58
"Kibuvitsa", Laulasmaa, tel 77 22 69
"Nelijärve", Aegviidu, tel 72 83 11
"Kuld Kukk", Jõelähtme, Lagedi, tel 42 07 73

CAFES & BARS

Kuusalu, tel 77 24 46
Viimsi, tel 23 20 77
Kehra, tel 6 53 10

Kiiu torn, tel 77 44 34
Rannamõisa, tel 71 66 44
Kose-Risti, tel 75 55 46
Loo, tel 42 07 51
Haabneeme, tel 77 06 70
Loksa, tel 77 51 63
Laulasmaa, tel 71 56 22
"Musta kassi Kõrts", Kodasoo, Tallinna - Peterburi 29. km., tel 72 38 81

MUSEUMS

Harjumaa museum, 9. Linnuse Keila, tel 74 61 36
Viimsi museum, Haabneeme, tel 77 06 80

FILLING STATIONS

Kuusalu, Narva Road
Lehmja, Tartu Road
Keila
Tammneeme Viimsi, tel 77 03 11

CAR SERVICE

Keila, tel 74 43 30
Jüri, tel 72 93 70
Karla, tel 75 51 69
Jõgisoo, tel 72 08 68
Kiili, tel 72 02 05
Haabneeme, tel 77 01 28

JÄRVAMAA

Area: 2620 km^2 Population: 43 800	Capital: Paide population: 11 200

If you travel from Tallinn to Tartu, or from Narva to Pärnu, you cross the small county of Järvamaa. Järvamaa's landscape is varied and beautiful – crystal-clear springs, underground rivulets, verdant fir and broadleaf forests, untouched swamps and bogs. Its two green towns, Paide and Türi, preside over some of Estonia's best farming land. Famous manors and farmsteads are sprinkled through the north and south of the county.

PAIDE AND TÜRI

The capital and its sibling town are both pleasant, hedge-lined places. Paide also boasts a fine citadel and town square.

White stone

The capital of Järvamaa celebrated its 700th anniversary in 1991. The

Teutonic Order built a citadel here in the 1260s. The town that rose around it was originally made from Estonia's primeval building material, limestone, from which it earned its name – Paelinn ("limestone town") and thence **Paide****.

The soul of Paide in the heart of town.

The Germans called the town Weissenstein ("white stone"). Today ruins of the ancient citadel surround the recently restored watchtower, **Pikk Hermann****. The tower was first restored in the 1890s, but the Red Army blew it up in 1941. The earthen outer ramparts, in classic citadel shape, also remain. On one corner perches the latest ruin, a wooden Orthodox church; on another you can find the **bastion cellar,** a gathering place of conservators of antiquities, that hardworking brotherhood which became the vanguard of Estonia's national movement in 1986. An odd exhibition in the bastion displays bottles, locks, sewing machines, cannonballs, pool tables and archival photos of the citadel.

It's a pity the Soviets didn't blow up the town's principal blemish, the shopping centre in the **town square*.** (Of course it hadn't been built then ...) Otherwise the square features the county seat, town hall, Holy Cross church and several offices and shops. New buildings a few hundred metres away contrast with the old. The most impressive is the **community centre*,** on the Pärnu/Türi road, a sign that the folk of Paide are returning to their ancient building material. The park opposite is dominated by the town's main landmark, a **block of flats** that looks as if it was designed by a first-year student at KGB University. The local **museum,** also in the park, is quite good.

The hedge town

Barely 10 km from Paide is the county's other large town, **Türi*,** a green gem of a place. Thirty thousand green-fingered people from throughout the Baltics attend the flower fair each spring, hunting out rare seeds or valuable tree seedlings, visiting flower stalls and wandering through splendid gardens.

The local speciality seems to be **hedges.** Curved and squared, tall and short, varying in colour, weight and bouquet, the effect becomes humorous after a while. The last 3 km of the drive from Paide are hedge-lined, and even the stone wall in front of Türi's smartly-steepled, 14th-century **church** sports a hedge like a well-made toupee. Cars are not allowed to park along the prettier avenues. So take a hint – promenade, and do include the overgrown **cemetery.** One street bears the interesting name Raadiojaama ("radio station"), commemorating independence days, when Türi's radio station was the most popular in Estonia.

Little Käravete's houses glow beside the reservoir.

THE NORTHERN COUNTY

The most interesting part of Järvamaa is the north, where you'll find baronial salons, thick woods, and the home of a great writer, now a museum surrounded by historic paths through the swamp.

Two collective farms

Roosna-Alliku is north of Paide on the Rakvere road. Abundant springs flow from the soil to the left of the road just before the village. The springs are used for trout farming and are the source of the Pärnu River, the longest river in Estonia. You can canoe down the whole way: contact the Pärnu Rowing Club for details. Roosna-Alliku manor house is 200 years old. Inside are two **halls**** in rose and light-blue marble featuring tiled stoves and ornate plaster mouldings. For an acute contrast, look over the offices and homes of the state farm behind the park.

Aravete is the heart of a very different collective farm. The solid **main office***, with its fountains and granite sculpture of Linda, suggests an unexpected taste and order. The **museum** at the south end of the village is in a 200-year-old manor house. Old TVs, Lenins and relics of the last baron's days can be found alongside the usual honey vats, scales, desks and linen tools.

You can loop round to Jäneda via Rava and Ambla. Across the river from the shop at **Rava village** there's an oak grove 300-400 years old. In springtime, you can find three shades of blue anemone sheltering under the oaks. Here too is found an unprecedented mushroom species, the *Rava narmasnutt*.

The road to the north goes to Ambla via Jõgisoo. A "karst" region extends from the roadside. The waters of the

Also on sale at the Türi flower fair ...

drainage canal suddenly swirl and disappear; they plunge into underground funnels to flow out a few hundred metres away just before **Vanaveskijärv** lake, source of the Ambla River.

Ambla's main landmark is a church dedicated to Mary (*Ampla Maria* in Latin) built in 1280; in the churchyard you can see fine headstones and an impressive freedom monument. The manor in **Käravete** features a pair of colonnaded stables, no doubt to impress guests' horses during balls. The local collective farm hands out permits for fishing and crayfishing.

Landscape that inspires

Jäneda's manor and park* is a brick mansion surrounded by grey-stone buildings ... plus an original annexe designed by the Estonian architect Valve Pormeister. The interior was stripped in the 1920s to house the Jäneda agricultural school. Well-known figures have studied here (among others, Arnold Rüütel, former chairman of the Supreme Council) and were no doubt

From White Horse Hill, Estonia doesn't seem small.

charmed and possibly influenced by Kõrvemaa's mysterious landscape and crystal waters.

Behind the house, across the lake, grows a **wood****. Plunge into the forest, climb, then walk along the ridge about 500 m through magical woods with a slim rivulet to the left and lovely **Lake Kali** to the right, to the site of an ancient Estonian hill-fort. A couple of the paths from this grassy clearing lead to bumps, defensive mounds protecting the various paths up to the stronghold.

Jäneda agricultural school is a castle.

Forests and bogs in Kõrvemaa

Whenever national superhero Kalevipoeg worked for several days without pause, he had to sleep for several days afterwards. Furrows ploughed by Kalevipoeg – varyingly shaped knolls – can be found in several places in Estonia. Once, when Kalevipoeg was sound asleep, wolves attacked and killed his horse. That's why the highest peak near Mägede village is called **Valgehobusemägi**** ("white horse hill"). It's 106 m above sea level. A

The mysterious aroma of bog ...

wonderful view across Kõrvemaa's forest opens before you from the top of the observation tower. On a clear day you can see the towers of Tallinn. To get to it, you travel west from Jäneda towards Perila. Turn right where there's a left to Kihme, and follow the signs to the hill.

If you want to visit a real bog lake and bog-pools, you have to go to **Lake Kakerdaja.** Only there can you experience the heady smell of "marsh tea" and cranberry bushes. You can step on swaying islets and taste the water, among the purest in the world, though brownish and lightly flavoured with peat. If you're lucky you'll see wild ducks or noisy seagulls on the lake. Sadly, black-throated diver ducks, which once waddled in the underbrush and gave the lake its name, haven't been round this way for many years.

Truth, justice and bog paths

Heading south in the direction of Kihme you reach the land of *Truth and justice.* It's the birthplace, childhood home and inspiration of one of the country's most important writers, Anton Hansen Tammsaare (1878-1940), the man on the 25-kroon note. His novels are an incomparable depiction of the life of Estonia's peasantry at the end of the 19th century. They're translated into many languages. Local places are as well-known by the names Tammsaare gave them in his enormous, Dickensian novel *Truth and justice* as they are by their real names. Vetepere village (Vargamäe in the novel) and the farming centre of **Järva-Madise** are rich in farmhouses, landforms, gardens, even trees that are recognisable from this long work.

The **Tammsaare farm**** has been restored and includes a small theatre in the barn and an exhibition in the main house. There are several walks you can do around here. A short "writer's walk" leads past the cottages below the farm past the well and mossy rock walls, round the edge of the swamp and back to the museum. A longer path crosses the bog, complete with pools, a lake and changing flora, to Järva-Madise. Many of the prototypes for the characters in *Truth and justice* are buried in the Järva-Madise cemetery.

A lost world –

granary and traditional costume.

EAST OF PAIDE

There's another wetland on the border of Järvamaa and Jõgevamaa.

In **Koeru***, east of Paide, you should first look over Magdaleena church and churchyard. Opposite the church, **Koeru Tavern** exudes a flavour of last century. Built between 1825 and 1833, the tavern was visited several times in its heyday by Elias Lönnrot, the man responsible for Finland's epic *Kalevala*, and today is often open for lunch.

Further east is the **Endla nature reserve,** another realm of springs and drenched land. You may visit parts of the reserve and hike along pathways to springs and rivulets. One spring, Sopa, is almost 5 m deep, and the bottom is invisible despite the limpidity of the water. In parts of the reserve beavers have felled trees half a metre thick. Permits and guides for the reserve are available from the local forestry administration centre *(metskond)*.

SOUTH OF PAIDE

Amid farmland and bogs to the south you'll find a farm on unstable earth and a thick, symbolic oak.

Estonian literature bloomed in Tammsaare's childhood home.

Hollow earth and hollow oak

The Tartu highway leads from Paide to southern Järvamaa. From 1758 to 1919 the manor house, park and former creamery at **Koigi*** belonged to the Grünewalts, who had important links to the czarist court. One was even appointed Estonia's civil governor by the czar. If you turn onto the Viljandi road near Imavere you can visit the **Estonian Dairy Museum*** and its rare old milking machines. It's the large building opposite the Imavere shop.

From **Müüru farmhouse**** in Kurla village, the Estonian epic hero Kalevipoeg is said to have descended into hell ...

He came closer and found
a cave in the side of a mound,
from which fire flickered and glowed.
So that was the source of the smoke!

The ground here is riddled with "karst" funnels, underground hollows that at times boom ominously below your feet. The old housewife Anna Masa tells of the dreadful rumble when the spring flood flees underground. Here and there the earth can suddenly cave in and folk sometimes have to help a few head of cattle out of "hell". Müüru's present farmers want to turn this fairyland into a modern "fairy-farm". The farm is on the right hand side of the Viljandi road, near the turn to Kabala.For tree-lovers, in **Villevere**** there's a dendrarium with 400 species of trees and bushes, including the rare bird-cherry tree. There's also a collection of several thousand natural sculptures. Visitors are continually adding to the collection of stones and trees.

Saaresiimu oak*, the thickest tree in Järvamaa, grows near the village of

The Oostungu River begins in this lakespring in the Endla reserve.

Keeper of Villevere park.

Rassi, which is 20 km south of Türi through Põikva or 10 km west of Villevere. The tree is 6.05 m round and reputed to be 500 years old. Though its trunk is hollow and could shelter five people against the rain, it's still leafy and green every spring. Many other Estonian oaks do the same, and some would say that this is true of Estonia itself: when it seems that all is lost something happens, the oppression eases a little, and the people find enough strength to begin again.

PRACTICAL DETAILS

MOTELS

Paide, guest-house, 8. Telliskivi, Paide, phone 2 12 27
Türi guest-house, 7. Jaama, Türi, phone 7 82 62

GUEST-HOUSES

Sinisalu, Albu, phone 3 77 08
Saunametsa, Türi, phone 7 83 13
Jäneda camping

RESTAURANTS & BARS

"Paide" restaurant, 15. Keskväljak, Paide, phone 4 13 30
"Kaval-Ants" (beer-restaurant), 20. Väike-Aia, Paide, phone 2 11 68
"Presto" bar, Mäo, phone 9 41 48

MUSEUMS

Paide regional museum, 5. Lembitu, Paide, phone 4 13 30
A. H. Tammsaare museum, Vargamäe, Albu, phone 3 77 56
Dairying museum, Imavere, phone 9 75 53

FILLING STATIONS

Paide, 59. Tallinna mnt., phone 2 11 05
Paide, 12. Prääma tee., phone 4 13 72
Türi, 64. Tallinna., phone 7 84 26

CAR SERVICE

Paide, 17. Telliskivi, phone 4 18 69
Paide, 36. Tööstuse, phone 4 17 30
Türi, phone 7 85 07
Aravete, phone 3 26 03

TELEPHONE AREA CODE: 238

Would you try the ski tracks here?

Marshland.

WESTERN VIRUMAA
LÄÄNE-VIRUMAA

Area: 3464 km^2	**Capital: Rakvere**
Population: 79 800	**population: 19900**

In Western Virumaa the history is metres thick, visible as fortresses, manors, churches, national parks and factories in the north, and hilly agricultural land in the south. Virumaa used to be a single county, the largest and most populous in Estonia. The name "Virumaa" has been used for the whole country. Even today the Finns call Estonia *Viro* and Estonians *Virolaised* ("Vironians").

Vironian history dates back at least 9000 years to when hunters and fishermen lived in Lammasmäe, near Kunda. Farmers still complain of the number of awkward sacrificial stones near Viru-Nigula! In the 13th century, Danish and Swedish troops made frequent raids, although they never turned the county into a major battleground. During the following centuries about 30 fortifications and sacred buildings appeared in Virumaa, while the strongholds of the Estonians perished. The district suffered greatly during the Livonian War (1558-83), and there are a couple of battlegrounds from the Northern War (1700-21) as well. Despite its poverty, numerous manors were built, including some of the best preserved and best restored in the land. When the Tallinn--St Petersburg railway opened in 1870 the whole north coast of Estonia turned into an industrial and mining base.

Today, Western Virumaa's greatest problems are industrial. Factories pour out their gunk, the most famous being the cement works at Kunda; and army bases have added their contribution, especially the airforce base at Tapa. The Soviets introduced intensive agricultural mass-production, which continues to harm the environment.

The Pandivere Highlands in the heart of Western Virumaa feed numerous springs, the sources of many Estonian rivers. They're also rich in phosphorite. In the mid 1980s the Soviets planned to set up a huge mine near Ebavere hill. Threatened by ecological havoc, Estonians waged a "Phosphorite War" against the authorities. Their success in Virumaa spurred the Estonian independence movement.

RAKVERE

Rakvere town has two distinct parts: a medieval fortress with a dusty old upper town, and a modern centre on the plain.

Three landmarks can be seen from afar as you approach **Rakvere****, the church spire, a grain-processing factory, and the ruins of a **fortress*****. The fortress stands on the site of ancient Tarvanpää hill-fort. The bulk of

the current fortress was built by the Livonian Order in the 14th and 15th centuries. Under later owners – Russia and Sweden – it was expanded and fortified, only to be destroyed at the end of the 16th century. From the bastions you have a great **view***: grassy earthen ramparts, a windmill and a typical provincial capital.
Old Rakvere is to be found on the hillside. Just below the fortress in Tallinna St, opposite a bust of author FR Kreutzwald, is the old manor house, and nearby is the theatre. Rakvere is the smallest Estonian town with its own professional theatre. The manor is but a shadow of its former self, but its **park*** is still lovely. Further down Tallinna St, the pink **museum*** has a good collection of independence memorabilia. The building faces down Pikk ("long") St, where you can find older Estonian town architecture in wood and stone. The 14th-century **church*** has a three-tier gallery, a broad organ, a fine chandelier and a distinguished 16th-century pulpit.
Parallel to Pikk St, Lai St leads into the modern centre. Today life in Rakvere revolves around the market square, where you can see modern buildings, worthy and otherwise. The two-towered church-like thing was built in 1928. Then, as now, it was a shop.

ACROSS THE NORTH

The north coast is fascinating: here are Estonia's first national park, its finest manor ensemble, its largest boulder and its ugliest industrial monstrosity.

Viitna nature trail

The St Petersburg highway from Tallinn crosses **Lahemaa National Park*****, the other half of which is in Harjumaa. Near **Viitna** there's a Visitors Centre with accommodation, the Lahemaa Külastuskeskus, buried in pine forest by the highway. You can arrange 1-3 day guided tours in the national park, including tours of Palmse estate (see below). The centre is next to the Väikejärv lake. A 6 km nature trail begins here, and leads through some gorgeous places from the Väikejärv to Suurjärv, which has a beach, and from there to Lake Nabudi.
A wooden chapel once stood between the Suurjärv and Väikejärv. The builders vowed that if ever seven brothers entered at the same time the chapel would sink into the earth. People took great pains to avoid this common problem, until one day the innkeeper's white hen strayed and led its seven male chicks right into the chapel, which the earth promptly swallowed. On Sunday mornings, voices and singing can be heard on the site. Or so they say.
The famous Viitna inn burnt down in the late 1980s. A new one is due to open in 1993.

The beauty of Palmse Estate

The road turns north from Viitna and after about 8 km reaches **Palmse*****. Lahemaa National Park is administered here in restored buildings on the old estate. Palkemas village was mentioned back in 1286, but the estate was the work of Cistercian monks, who bred fish in Palmse brook and cattle in the fields, brewed beer and distilled their own spirits. Nobles later took over, culminating in a long period when the von Pahlens were barons. They sold to the Estonian Republic in 1923, but when Lahemaa National Park was founded in 1971 only 4 buildings were standing. Now there are 25 restored or being restored.
The estate ensemble, from the stately drive to the well-articulated park, is sumptuous though perhaps not the best restored manor in the country. The baroque **manor house** was built in the 18th century (guided tours in English can be arranged through the Visitors Centre at Viitna). The furniture is not original to the house, but was collected from throughout Estonia. Highlights include: the music box, which a staff member might play for you; the dining room's 1920s furniture and fittings, all made in Tallinn; the rococo-style stove and 1850 Meissen porcelain chandelier in the "saloon"; the original Turkish couches, the last ones remaining in the country, in the smoking room; and the baron's own chair from Ilumäe chapel in the study. Concerts are sometimes held in the ballroom.
A stable and coachhouse, distillery and conservatory are among the estate's other buildings.

You can follow paths through the **manor park,** home to the Viru Säru folklore festival every summer. On the weir at the northern tip of the pond, by the three-level cascade, the Sepa ("smith") bridge crosses the stream. The broad path takes you a few hundred metres to Presti pavilion perching daintily on a belvedere above Oruveski pond. You get an even lovelier view of the pavilion from the Palmse-Võsu road.

The path turns east and goes through the forest to the **Kloostrikivid** ("convent stones"). It is said that demons came to harass the nuns at a convent here, and when the nuns moved out the demons gathered at the edge of the forest and from great boredom turned into boulders. Here they are, leaning giantly on one another. From here you return to the main building, passing the foreman's house on the way.

Ilumäe chapel

Small yeomen's coats-of-arms were painted on the windows of **Ilumäe chapel*** in the 18th century – the originals are now in Tallinn. The von Pahlens, longtime owners of Palmse manor, are buried in their own segregated graveyard within the chapel yard. The chapel is a few kilometres from Palmse towards Loksa – watch for the round-ended "arrow" on the main road. (Interior can only be visited when the chapel is open on religious feast days.)

Two kilometres further along the Loksa road, a left takes you to the **Joaveski rapids** on the Loobu River. The river, crossing a limestone shoal, falls down several terraces. In spring and autumn the water really roars down the cascade.

Summertown

Võsu* village grows tenfold in summer into a small town of holidaymakers, becoming one long main street with cafes and wooden buildings on either side. The friendly ambience, sandy beach and clean sea give the town a peaceful, carefree feel.

If the Gulf of Finland is too cold, you might take a dip in nearby Lake Käsmu. At the top of **Käsmu peninsula*** you can walk across boulders to Devil's Island, or make a wish and add your rock to the pyramid assembled over the years by other wishfuls, or see a great boulder signed by the man himself, MK (for Mister Kalevipoeg).

An old fishing village

Eastwards from Võsu along the coast you reach the 400-year-old **fishing village of Altja*.** Last cen-

Autumn colours in Rakvere park.

Off to see Viitna's wildlife.

tury, three inns accommodated the many merchants, tradesmen and other visitors. Now Lahemaa's midsummer night bonfire is held here each year. With its traditional north-coast farmhouses, net sheds on the promontory, village swing and one remaining local inn, Altja recalls life 100 years ago.
There are restored manors at Sagadi and Vihula. The Estonian Forestry Museum is now in **Sagadi estate****, a long, low manor with a lovely lake. Besides the rah-rah forestry exhibition you can see period furniture, a pair of cloak chimneys and a small stuffed menagerie. The road going east from **Vihula**** leads back to the coast, to **Vainupea.** Off the rocky beaches there are stone piers in the water. Fishing boats were once drawn onto the shore between the rows, giving protection from storms. Church services and concerts are sometimes held in Vainupea church. The sea is occasionally visible through fir and pine forest during the drive towards Kunda. You cross the Selja River just before **Karepa,** where there's a witch's house. The painter Valli Lember-Bogatkina, whose summer house this is, has reworked natural objects. Look for the gate with twisted branches. On a small cape you can visit the attractive ruins of **Toolse castle***, founded in 1471 to protect the area from piracy.

See hell while it lasts

In order to let light into their homes, the people of **Kunda***** have to wash their windows at least once a week. The town is the victim of a cement plant, whose dust covers every little thing within a radius of 10 km around the town, and sends first-time visitors into open-mouthed stupefaction. If the hunters and fishermen who settled here 9000 years ago had seen the same picture, they would have moved on instead of founding a village. But Kunda, built on a striking coastal terrace, was for a long time one of Estonia's prettiest places. The site of their settlement can be seen on **Lammasmäe** hill beside the road to Rakvere.

Palmse estate, baronial grandeur restored.

Terminus for the boulders

A village of huge boulders stands on the coast to the north-east, near Letipea. At the edge of the village is Tagaküla Suurkivi, a 4 m high rock with a 30 m circumference. The biggest Estonian boulder of them all, **Ehalkivi****, is in shallow water near the shore. This granite thumper is 7 m high, and its circumference is 48 m. Glaciers snapped the rocks from Scandinavian mountains and carried them here, where they were stopped by the limestone bank.

Sanctuary

At **Viru-Nigula****, the Maarja chapel was built on the battlefield where German crusaders defeated the Russians in 1268. The destination of many a pilgrimage in the Middle Ages, now only a single imposing free-standing wall remains for photographers. The local 14th-century gothic **church** is still in good nick, spacious, cool and architecturally interesting. There's a **"secret" hiding-place,** used by those seeking sanctuary, on the vault above the southern entrance. The secret entrance is clearly visible 4 m up – and you can see an arrow-slit from the outside. The "Celtic crosses" around the church date from the 17th century.

Beyond Viru-Nigula, quite close to the highway, is an 11th-century fortress mound at Pada, just inside the turn-off to Sonda.

"Signe" loves flowers: a statue in the Käsmu cemetery.

TOWARDS THE SOUTH

The road to Tartu crosses the highest part of the Pandivere Highlands. There's little in the way of wild landscape to be seen, but plenty of historical and cultural monuments, and farming land galore.

Heroic horse hills

The Tartu road goes south. **Around Assamalla** Kalevipoeg, Estonia's epic hero, performed heroic deeds. His horse was killed in the Battle of Assamalla. The steed was worthy of

Altja's inn dates from the 1970s.

its puissant master, and its harness and corpse form the hills round the village: Maksamägi ("liver hill"), Salumägi ("saddle hill"), etc. Turning west at Kullenga crossroads, you come to **Porkuni***, where an old manor house, a Stalinist building and a vassal tower built in 1479 form a set piece overlooking a beautiful lake. The manor house is now a school for the deaf.

Onward to the ancient parish centre of **Väike-Maarja,** which played an important cultural role in the national awakening last century. In 1873 a parish school was established here,

Altja celebrates midsummer's eve the traditional way.

Rather a nice building for a forestry museum: Sagadi.

in 1875 a mixed choir was founded, in 1880 the local library and in 1896 a brass band were set up. Educated people from the surrounding countryside gathered here at the school and formed a group that was later called the Parnassus of Väike-Maarja. This area's most famous son is Georg Lurich, a famed strongman early this century. You can find out more about him in the chapter on Raplamaa.

A 14th-century **fortress-church** towers over the centre of Väike-Maarja, its spire a lofty 62 m high. The Krusensterns, indefatigable seafarers for the Russian Empire, are buried in the churchyard.

The phosphorite war

The trees of **Ebavere hill,** south of Väike-Maarja, were the homes of ancient Estonians gods. In 1220 the Germans took axes to them and the locals were amazed when blood didn't spurt out. From the road you can see Ebavere hill's observation tower poking up over the woods. A magnificent **panorama**** of the Pandivere Highlands opens from the tower. It's not *too* hard to find. Park at the busstop and climb up through the forest. Follow the forest road, turning left once onto a steeply rising track, then right onto a footpath at the top. **Careful:** the ladder is not protected and the flooring at the top is rotting away.

Here, you're in the heart of Western Virumaa, at the nub of a little political problem a few years ago. The Pandivere Highlands are so porous that surface water instantly disappears, and although there are no springs or ditches in 2000 km^2, the sinking waters feed an abundance of springs that issue at the edges of the plateau. Many Estonian rivers, flowing in all directions, begin their journey here. Ah, but Western Virumaa has large deposits of phosphorite. The Soviet Fertiliser Industry Ministry planned to establish an enormous mine here, which would have required a new town to be built and thousands of workers to be brought in from outside Estonia. The phos-

Innocent picture of dusty Kunda.

phorite industry would have taken nearly a third of the highland area. Pollution on the usual Soviet scale would have sunk with Pandivere's water and fed into Estonia's rivers, creating ecological catastrophe through much of the country. Luckily this was the time of perestroika and glasnost. When the people learned of the threat in 1987, the so-called "phosphorite war" broke out against the Soviet authorities. This successful national protest movement was one of the seeds of the Estonian independence movement.

The Äntu lakes

The **Äntu lakes*** are 4 km from Ebavere in the direction of Tartu. A nature track starting at the parking place to the left of the road wends its way between the seven marshy lakes. A hill-fort once stood on Äntu Punamägi ("red hill"). Watch out for horseflies – take a comb just in case. The track crosses the road twice and the river a few times. If you're short of time you might head straight to **Äntu Sinijärv**** ("blue lake"). A spring pours forth from a funnel-shaped dip on the lake bottom, clearly visible 8 m down.

Some estates and views

A westward turn at Ebavere gives you a detour through Kiltsi, Vao and Liigvalla. A turn towards **Vao** collective farm takes you to a square castle dating from 1375. There's an early neoclassical, circular estate en-

Undercut trees on the Selja River.

The Toolse fortress, a defence against pirates, had no defence against time.

semble in **Kiltsi,** south at the same crossroads. There are also manor houses in **Varangu** and **Liigvalla.** The lake at Liigvalla is ice-free in winter and wild ducks come here to hibernate.

Back on the main road you come to dusty Rakke village, and a little further south, enjoying the surrounding landscape from the drumlin at Edru, to the border of Jõgeva county. In the **land around Salla village*** there are several high points on roads from which you can see the rural landscape rolling away splendidly. One is **Emumäe*,** the highest point in northern Estonia. It was pawed up by Kalevipoeg's horse. To the south-west, in **Piibe estate,** grow oaks planted by the founder of embryology, Karl von Baer, the man on the 2-kroon note. A monument in the park commemorates his birth here.

WESTWARDS

Tapa is a Soviet relic; in Kadrina the chimneystack competes for prominence with the church spire.

Epic birthplace

West of Rakvere is the rail-junction town of **Tapa*.** The army base is known for its pollution: sometimes the river catches fire. There are also some of Estonia's most hideous concrete housing blocks here. **Kadrina** is a small, though rather lovely industrial centre. The **freedom monument*** in the churchyard is rather large.

A few kilometres south of Kadrina you can find furrows ploughed by Kalevipoeg. They're called the **Neeruti hills** after their former baron, Nieroth. In the local community centre in Kuresüüdi you can visit an exhibition on the Neeruti hills and get information about hiking tracks. In these hills in 1803, in **Jõepere village,** the maker of Estonia's national epic was born. Friedrich Reinhold Kreutzwald composed *Kalevipoeg* based on folklore he collected across Estonia, though with a sizable Virumaa bias.

SOUTH-EAST OF RAKVERE

Manor houses amid fertile farmland lie to the south-east, and beyond them swamps and forestry lands.

The fate of Rägavere

Rägavere manor*** lies near the Tudu road quite close to Rakvere. It suffered the classic fate of Estonian manors: the landlords left in 1920, the estate was turned into a local schoolhouse, then the small schools were closed, people left, and the empty buildings became dilapidated, and were at one stage used to store vegetables. But thanks to the local collective farm, Rägavere is one of perhaps twenty manors in

Another proud tradition: a perfect garden on a Karepa farm.

Estonia that have been restored, while hundreds are ruins or gouged out shells. The neoclassical mansion, dating from the 1780s, had the same architect as Toompea Palace in Tallinn.

The collective farm collected the furnishings too: they include Japanese dishware and armour, clocks, chests and a painting by one of the first German painters of peasant life, Hoffmann. The large dark rooms upstairs were the baron's office and the dining room. A door in one corner used to contain a lift for servants and food. You can attend classical music concerts here now, and in summer there's an international accordion festival. (Ring ahead if you want to see the manor house at other times.)

From a wounded warrior

Heading west from Rägavere, take the turn to Vinni. On the way you pass the mansion, park and Valgehobusemägi ("white horse hill") of **Mõdriku***. The second "mansion" used to be a distillery. Lord of the manor, General Kaulbers, erected a monument on the hill 250 m behind the house to celebrate the Russian defeat of Napoleon. But locals like to explain that it was really built in memory of the general's white horse, which carried its wounded master home from the battlefield. Trees in the oak wood in **Vinni*** can reach 20 m upwards and 4 m around.

Viru-Jaagupi, a typical Estonian small town, has a 15th-century gothic church. The Russian seafarer F P Wrangel is buried in the churchyard, where you can also find an unusual **memorial*** to those deported and killed by the Soviets.

The form and size of the Earth

Roela manor* is now the administrative centre of a collective farm that has retained the quality of an estate, though today it's the lord of blocks of flats and tractor-farmed land. There's a fortified tower in a backyard near **Muuga** manor, and a windmill that doubles as a bar. The town square in **Laekvere** already has several stone buildings; its new postmodern council house deserves to be painted a better colour.

Simuna is one for geographers. Just before the village, a **stone column** on the edge of a field recalls the spot where F. G. Struve determined the form and size of the Earth. In 1816-55 the world-famous astronomer measured the meridian curve here. Also in Simuna are a pastorate and the Avanduse manor.

Alutaguse, the region to the south-east, is a sparsely populated land of vast forests and marshes inhabited by, among other creatures, bears.

PRACTICAL DETAILS

HOTELS

"Rakvere", 25, Tallinn mnt., Rakvere, phone 4 34 20
Viitna motel, Viitna, phone 4 56 59, 9 36 51
Kadaka motel, Viitna, phone 4 94 19
Sõstra motel, Viitna, phone 3 41 37
Võsu hostel, Võsu, phone 9 91 89
Lahe hostel, Võsu, phone 51 00 38
Porkuni hunters-house, Porkuni, phone 4 30 66
Mõedaku ski-base, Kaarli, phone 4 05 01
Võsu guest-house, Võsu, phone 4 41 14
Võsu puhkekodu 21, Mere, Võsu, phone 9 92 70
Vinni Spordikompleksi hotell, Vinni, phone 4 71 64

RESTAURANTS

"Kolhida", 68. Tallinna, Rakvere, phone 4 44 64
"Rakvere", 1/3. Koidula, Rakvere, phone 4 27 43
"Viru", 8. 1. mai, Kunda, phone 5 16 20
"Videvik", 2. Lillaka, Tapa, phone 7 41 59
"Muuga tuulik"(wind-mill), Muuga, phone 9 30 12
"Neptun", 12. Laine, Võsu, phone 9 92 33

CAFES & BARS

Kadaka bar, phone 4 35 76
Võsu Grillbaar, phone 9 93 00
Võsu Jokker

TRAVEL BUREAU

AS VIRU TUUR Ltd., 21 Tallinna Rakvere, phone 4 10 00
1. Liimi, Tallinn, phone 58 60 06

MUSEUMS

RAKVERE regional museum, 3. Tallinna, Rakvere, phone 4 43 69
Kunda cement museum, 9. Jaama, Kunda, phone 5 15 94
Rägavere estate-concert hall, Rägavere, phone 4 73 12
Spirit's museum, Tapa, Moe, phone 76 541
Sagadi Forestry museum, Vihula, Sagadi, phone 9 86 42
Viru-Nigula regional museum, Viru-Nigula, phone 93 586

FILLING STATIONS

46. Rägavere tee, Rakvere, phone 4 31 21
Viitna, phone 9 36 58

CAR SERVICE

Rakvere, phone 3 85 07
Rakvere, phone 4 17 75

TELEPHONE AREA CODE: 232

EASTERN VIRUMAA
IDA-VIRUMAA

Area: 3198 km²
Population: 222 030
Capital: Kohtla-Järve, population: 78 000
Largest town: Narva, population 82 000

Historic Virumaa, once the largest and most populous county in Estonia, has been sliced into Western and Eastern provinces. Eastern Virumaa is a special place in several ways. Estonia's most important mineral resources are here. Great deposits of oil-shale, peat and sand have created urban industrial centres. Russian immigrants who've settled here since World War II make up most of the population. Estonians form only 4% of the population in Narva and 23% in Kohtla-Järve. The Estonians who still form the majority in rural areas may have to face the fact that many in the north-eastern region want to secede from Estonia and become a Russian-speaking republic. So Ida-Virumaa is a symbol for Estonia – of what is and what might be.

A steep limestone defile marks the north coast, the Narva River the eastern boundary, and enormous Lake Peipsi the south. Though mines and open-cast pits have transformed some parts into lifeless landscapes, you can still find untouched spots. In the southern part of the county there's a land of forests and bogs, Alutaguse, with the 40 lakes of Kurtna lake country at its heart. The virgin forest is a home for lynxes, bears, flying squirrels and other wild animals. Cosy beaches can be found on the top side of Lake Peipsi, and waterfalls and rapids dot the northern coast. Ecological catastrophe threatens all this natural beauty. Many tourists visit the region for powerful photo-opportunities.

As in industrial areas the world over, Eastern Virumaa can be dangerous for foreigners, especially at night. Crime will worsen as the factories are privatised or closed and unemployment grows. While the country areas are relatively safe, you should be careful in the big towns.

Those unnatural hills

The whole economy of Eastern Virumaa is based on **oil-shale.** Rich layers of "brown gold" were deposited several hundred million years ago. They've been mined for the last 75 years, a process which involves breaking through and digging up the limestone layer just

A cracked cross, symbol of Eastern Virumaa.

above the oil-shale. Though it's a waste to use oil-shale in furnaces, in Estonia the stuff is mined chiefly to heat thermal power-plants: two massive ones near Narva put Estonia among the top ten per capita producers of electricity in the world. The plants produce enormous amounts of oil-shale ash. There's al-

ready over 100 km^2 of spoiled land, extending for several kilometres around the plants, both ash hills and limestone hills. You can find tar pools at the bases of the limestone hills, and sometimes the pressure causes them to overheat and catch fire. They can burn for ten years. Gas seeps underground into people's cellars and there are mass evacuations. Old mine-passages fall in and land is left useless by the mining. During mining the local wells are empty, and afterwards the groundwater is unusable.
Besides the "brown gold", for years Sillamäe has had to cope with radioactive waste. Health and life expectancy in Eastern Virumaa are the worst in Estonia. Finland and Sweden have also protested at the situation.

KOHTLA-JÄRVE AND NARVA

The two biggest towns are industrial centres with mostly Russian-speaking populations. Narva's Old Town was razed in World War II, but its fortress has been restored and overlooks the economic border with Russia.

Industrial sleeping quarters

The county centre, **Kohtla-Järve***, Estonia's third-largest town, came into existence during the oil-shale boom years. Kohtla-Järve actually consists of five different sections, mainly dormtowns with Soviet-modernist buildings that have mushroomed around the new mines. The most interesting is **Kohtla**. For more information about Kohtla-Järve, a town of contrasts and political strains, visit Kohtla's Oil-Shale Museum *(Põlevkivimuuseum)*.
The old parish centre was nearby **Jõhvi,** which celebrated its 750th anniversary in 1991. The **fortress-church*** of Jõhvi dates from the 16th century, though there's not much else to see here. Between Jõhvi and Kohtla, at the settlement of **Kukruse,** the first mine was founded in 1916. The spot is now marked by an artificial hill; it takes a wee bout of exercise to get to the top but there's a good **view****. Remember, any hills you see are artificial, either limestone or ash. Neoclassical Kukruse manor house beside the highway is to be restored if any money ever arrives. Before Jõhvi you pass the park of Edise estate. The old manor stable has been turned into a pub, the **Valgehobu** ("white horse"), an attractive place to eat.

Rearrangements on the Narva River

Narva** is on the left bank of the Narva River on the Estonian-Russian border. Road and railway bridges lead across the river to the Russian town Ivangorod; thousands commute across every day. In July 1992 Estonia instituted border controls between the two towns' spectacular fortresses. Once upon a time the river flowed here in a deep valley from Lake Peipsi. After the war a canal was built for a hydro-electric power station and the riverbed fell dry. Later came the Narva reservoir, at 200 km^2 the country's third-largest lake. The Narva waterfall is also now dry. It's divided in two parts by Kreenholmi island, and you can see interesting geological layering in the waterfall valley. Several villages were submerged when the reservoir was built. Nowadays, ironically, only Ivangorod uses the energy produced by the hydro-electric station.
Narva's most outstanding historical monument is on the riverbank near the bridge. The **fortress*****, mentioned as far back as 1256, was built as a Danish frontier fort. The Danes sold their share of Estonia to the Teutonic Order, who sold it on to the Livonian Order. Under the knights of the Orders, the main citadel and the imposing **Pikk Hermann** tower were built. Later the Swedes constructed a fortified wall around the large courtyard and erected low bastion towers, thus creating a first-class fortification. The ramparts have often been drenched in blood. The fortress was half-destroyed by Soviet bombardments in the last war and has since been quite well restored.

The inside of the citadel powerfully evokes medieval times. You can climb the tower and view the city from the walkway round Pikk Hermann's neck. The various floors on the way are filled with art galleries and a good **museum***. As well as the history of the citadel and old photographs showing the beautiful Narva that used to be, there are some fine historical artefacts, craftworks, military equipment and costumes on display.

Pimeaed ("blind garden"), founded in 1853, is a park on the upper bank of the Narva River north of the border post. A memorial with an anchor chain was set up to Russian soldiers killed in 1704. In the spring of 1944 Narva's beautiful baroque Old Town was virtually razed by interminable barrages of the Red Army. One of the few buildings to survive is the **town hall***. Others include two churches, which you can find between the town centre and the railway station, and the buildings of **Kreenholm's factory*** on an island in the middle of the river. Kreenholm's factory, with 12 000 workers, is the biggest enterprise in Estonia, though its future is uncertain now.

The six smokestacks at the edge of town are part of the thermal-electric power station. The **winged statue**** in front of the plant is a monument to Soviet industry, much as can be found throughout the former USSR. The new Narva rebuilt since the war has a radically different culture and people to the old. Estonians were not allowed to move there, even if they were born in Narva. Only a few thousand Estonians remain and they've formed an Estonian Society.

ALONG THE NORTH COAST

The northern part of the county is home to oil-shale and uranium towns, as well as good beaches and holiday places.

Ancient castle?

North of the Tallinn-Narva highway at the western edge, **Kalvi estate*** has a small castle. Corner-towers, staircases and crenellations seem to come from the Middle Ages, but the mansion actually dates back to the year 1913. The interior, with its lovely ceiling mouldings, was remarkably well preserved until 1975 when, at the height of the Brezhnev era, it was converted into a Soviet-style holiday home. Former barons the Stackelbergs want it back.

Estonia doesn't accept the Narva River as border. Narva on the left, Ivangorod administered by Russia across the river.

An unsinkable fortress

Seaside Aseri is a new industrial town. Continuing past it, the highway reaches the sea at Kõrkküla. The **view*** along the way is splendid. The valley of the river Purtse and the fishing villages at its mouth are straight ahead. Behind the villages rises Hiiemägi ("sacred hill"), a sacrificial lime tree at its summit. Further off, the Saka-Ontika-Toila cliffs climb from the sea.

In the middle of Purtse stands a 16th-century **vassal fort****. It was destroyed in the Northern War and rebuilt, and then gutted by fire in 1950 (fortunately the castle ghost had already departed). The local collective farm tried to destroy the ruin to build a youth club but their bulldozer wasn't powerful enough for the walls. The limestone building has recently been restored, a good example of slightly too neat a restoration job. Concerts are sometimes held here, and when they are the bar's open too.

Oil rock town

In the distance to the south you can see the tower of the **church at Lüganuse***. The unusual round upper section is unique in Estonian medieval architecture. A large cross reminiscent of Finnish medieval churches decorates the gable, and you can find an 18th-century altarpiece inside. On the road south of Lüganuse, hidden behind a 1.5 m stone wall, is an estate ensemble, the **Maidla manor.** Though right now it's just a pretty face (plus some former buildings such as workers' quarters and a cow shed), it's due for restoration as a town hall. The mortar on the wall was mixed with glass and ash, thus giving it that strident grey colour.

Kiviõli** means "oil rock"; this is a good place to see the shale hills in action. Otherwise south of the railway line are the usual wooden houses and well-maintained vegetable gardens, over which the hills loom ominously.

Purtse fortress ready to do cultural battle.

The cliff of Ontika

The coast road is more interesting than the highway. **Aa** is the closest beach to Kohtla-Järve. The **Saka-Ontika-Toila cliffs*** extend more than 20 km along the coast, reaching a height of 56 m at Ontika, where you can stand on the edge (careful!). Thick deciduous forest hides most of the cliff face. There's no way down for several kilometres; fishing folk used complicated rope-systems to lift their catch up the precipice.

After Ontika you cross a ditch at **Valaste,** where a waterfall plummets more than 20 m to the sea. A strong sea breeze will whirl the water back up to the road.

The surfaced road from Valaste to Toila follows the very edge of the cliff before descending to the valley of the Pühajõgi ("holy river"). An expansive **park*** has been laid out on the lower reaches of the valley on a natural terrace. The Aluoja waterfall on the left-hand tributary of the Pühajõgi is also rather picturesque.

The village at the mouth of the Pühajõgi is **Toila.** A Russian merchant named Yeliseyev laid the foundation of Toila when he built **Oru manor** here of white stone. During the previous republican period it was the summer residence of the Estonian president, Konstantin Päts. The castle was destroyed in the war – only some terraces, annexes and avenues have been preserved. Toila was already a

Little Valaste brook drops 20 m.

famous summer resort before World War I. Summer cottages were built on the high bank among shady pines. The next village along, still on the same road, is **Voka.** In the English-style manor you can find two stone bastions, on which stood the cannons that used to salute the arrival of VIPs.

Good beach? Aa yes.

Enriched by uranium

The road rejoins the highway before **Sillamäe**.** The town was behind a barbed wire fence for many years – not even Estonians were allowed in. What was being produced here? Only after the town had stopped enriching uranium and burying radioactive waste was the truth revealed. For their pains the people of Sillamäe earned more and could buy more than most people in the Soviet Union – but people whisper of deformed animals and a cemetery that contains an uncommonly high number of young men. The centre of town boasts some excellent **Stalinist buildings and monuments*.** When last we checked, you could still see **Lenin** clenching his fist across the river at the west end of town, defiant to the end. There's still plenty of radioactive waste, but it's perfectly safe as long as it doesn't leak.

Autumn chill hits avenue in Toila.

Resistance hills

The **Sinimäed** ("blue hills") are real hills next to the road. In 1944 the front line stayed here from spring to autumn, and tens of thousands lost their lives. The tenacious resistance, which may have owed some of its vim to the number of Estonians fighting in the German army, gave the rest of Estonia the opportunity to hide its treasures and flee. Once they'd broken through the Sinimäed, it took the Soviets only a month to conquer the rest of the country, perhaps because of the number of Estonians fighting in the Red Army.

Turning left onto the seaside road you reach **Narva-Jõesuu*** ("Narva river mouth") via Meriküla and Udria. The erratic boulders on Udria beach are Kalevipoeg's discarded shoe stones. Narva-Jõesuu has been a health resort since the last days of the czars. Its sandy beach and shady pinewood extend for 7 km. The town **park*** is pretty. Pleasure-trips are organised up the river to Narva.

DOWN TO LAKE PEIPSI

Much of the south is swampy, but on Lake Peipsi itself there are many beaches. And Kuremäe has a classic Orthodox convent.

From a vision of Mary ...

You *could* go south along the main road, which hits Lake Peipsi at Kauksi. On the way you pass villages and old manors and the settlement of **Iisaku.** Iisaku is on an esker, a ridge gouged out by glaciers in the last ice age; highest point is the hill Tärivere (94 m).

A more interesting road leads southeastwards from Jõhvi. En route, in the heath east of **Kurtna***, you can

"Tchaikovsky pavilion" at Narva-Jôesuu.

find over 30 clean, beautiful lakes lost among the hills and ridges. The ancient hill-fort of Edivere is now an overgrown though attractive mound by the roadside just before the Konsu busstop. Just beyond, a left

turn leads into the lakeland itself.
A few kilometres further is **Kuremäe****, on a hill in the heart of the Alutaguse area. This was a sacred place even in ancient times: there's a "2000-year-old" oak in the cemetery and a holy spring. Nowadays thousands gather here on Russian Orthodox feast days. The story runs that in the 16th century Mary, dressed in a divine blue, appeared to shepherds at the sacred oak, where they later found a sacred icon. The sacred spring is down the hill along the road behind the cemetery. Here you can drink or bathe in the miraculous springwater.
In 1892, at the high time of russification, the **Pühtitsa convent**** was built here. The finest structure and oldest building is the bold **gate,** in which there are seven bells, the largest weighing 2.5 tonnes. Murals on the inside of the gate commemorate Mary's dramatic appearance to the shepherds. In the **main church*** you can see the **sacred icon** itself on the far right column, while in front of the far left column is another icon containing bits of the bodies of 32 saints. You may be surprised at the nuns' comfortable houses. The sisters themselves cultivate the land, growing all they need. Life in the nunnery is quiet,

Some fall, some stand. Kauksi River near Lake Peipsi.

Traditions with an air of dignity.

though many outsiders attend the services, and the nuns are quite agreeable to you looking around – they may even give you a guided tour!
The road reaches **Lake Peipsi** near **Vasknarva***, an old bastion-town and port. Ruins of a German Order fortress rest in peace with a view of the Narva River.

Beachland and beyond

The northern coast of Peipsi is a bather's mecca, with warm water and sandy beaches at Smolnitsa, Jõeküla, Uusküla, Kauksi, Rannapungerja and Lohusuu. Peipsi offers beautiful views, both in Kauksi and in nearby Rannapungerja. Russian fishermen have lived along these shores since the Middle Ages, making a living from the plentiful bream and smelt that thrive in the lakewater.
Lohusuu village actually consists of Russian Lohusuu on the lake and Estonian Lohusuu on the river. While relations in the "industrial north" are somewhat complicated, here these two peoples and cultures have been living side-by-side in harmony for centuries.
On the border of Jõgeva county, at the mouth of the Preverniku stream between Ninasi and Kalma, a **boulder-strewn area** extends several kilometres into Lake Peipsi. About 4 km out, in the middle of 8 m waters, there's a strange shallow where the stones almost reach the surface. The

The splendor of Kuremäe convent had humble miraculous beginnings.

boulder-strewn area is a bridge made by Estonia's epic hero Kalevipoeg so he could step across the lake and make that strange platform ... though why he wanted to do it, no one remembers.

The biggest centres of the south-western part of the county are Avinurme and Tudulinna. A large area of bogs and swamps separates them from Kohtla-Järve. The **Muraka bog,** the **Sirtsi swamp** and a few other places have retained their original Alutaguse qualities. Over a thousand bears live here, and several rare species of eagles, flying squirrels and other creatures build their nests in the area.

PRACTICAL DETAILS

ACCOMODATION

NARVA
"Vanalinn" hotel, 6, Koidula, phone 2 24 86
"Narva" hotel, 6, Puskini, phone 2 27 00
NARVA-JÕESUU
"Mereranna" guest-house, 17 Aia, phone 7 39 81
"Narva-Jôesuu" guest-house, 3 Aia, phone 3 15 35
"Noorus" guest-house, 19 Koidula, phone 7 33 11
"Kajakas" guest-house, 12 Vabaduse, phone 7 41 91
"Pôhjarannik" guest-house, 75 Vabaduse, phone 7 11 81
"Liivrand" guest-house, 21 Koidula, phone 7 43 91
"Ookean" guest-house, 10 Raja, phone 7 01 31
"Energia" guest-house, 14 Pargi, phone 7 21 01
Sillamäe hotel, Kirovi 23, phone 71 964
JÕHVI
"Jôhvi" hotel, 11 Tsiolkovski, phone 2 26 01
"Kitzbergi" hotel, 10 Kitzbergi, phone 2 22 88
KOHTLA-JÄRVE
"Kohtla-Järve" guest-house, 42 Narva mnt., phone 4 44 34
"Reet" hotel, 27 Môisa tee, phone 4 37 33
KIVIÕLI guest-house, 2 Vahtra, phone 5 89 21
Kauksi tourist-house, Kauksi, phone 9 38 19
Uusküla camping, phone 9 37 08
Uusküla camp, phone 9 31 63
Kauksi camp, phone 9 38 40
Niinsaare tourist-house, Illaku, phone 9 21 74
Narva-Jôesuu camping, 6 Koidu, phone 2 24 86
Loogna motel, phone 2 26 55
Karjamaa motel, Alajôe, phone 9 31 78
Sillamäe hotel, 23 Kirovi

RESTAURANTS

"Baltika", Narva, 10 Puškini, phone 3 15 31
"Joala", Narva, 6 Kreenholmi, phone 3 35 63
"Regatt", Narva, 26 Anveldi, phone 4 01 55
"Fööniks", Jôhvi, 12 Rakvere, phone 2 27 70
"Valge hobu trahter", Jôhvi, Edise, phone 2 27 42
"Jôhvi", Ahtme, 19 L. Tolstoi, phone 3 41 37

"Turist", Kohtla-Järve, 23 Kesk-Allee, phone 4 41 53
"Triboliit", Kohtla-Järve, 10 St. Peterburi phone 4 41 01
"Ported", Kiviôli, 1 Kesk-Puiestee, phone 5 80 98
"Kevade", Kiviôli, 33 Kesk-Puiestee, phone 5 73 39

CAFES & BARS

"Narva", Narva, 6 Puškini, phone 3 30 56
"Vikerkaar", Narva, 1 Vôidu, phone 2 40 20
"Bistro", Narva, 10 Puškini
"Kevade", Narva, 6 Kesk-Allee
"Oksana", Narva, 19 Tallinna
"Randel", Narva, 12 St. Peterburi
"Meretare", Toila, phone 9 56 96
"Kajakas", Jôhvi, phone 2 18 40
"Maiasmokk", Jôhvi, phone 2 27 72
Kiikla bar, phone 9 95 72
Kalma bar, phone 9 36 52
"Mikro", Jôhvi, phone 2 12 01
"Tuuleke", Kohtla-Järve, phone 4 57 33
"Vigri", Kiviôli, phone 5 70 67
Alajôe, phone 9 32 11
Aseri, phone 5 12 65
Kauksi, phone 9 38 33
Sillamäe, phone 7 43 80

TRAVEL BUREAUS

Virumaa Turismikeskus, 15 Pargi, Jôhvi, phone 2 29 05
Toila Reisibüroo, 13A Pikk, Toila, phone 9 55 39
A/S "Suvi", 15 Kesk-Allee, Kohtla-Järve, phone 4 71 56
Narva Reisibüroo, 5 Peetri väljak Narva, phone 3 35 10

MUSEUMS

Oil-shale museum, 9 Narva, Kohtla-Järve, phone 4 57 54
Narva town museum, 2 Peterburi, phone 3 32 01
Museum of the Kreenholmi Manufaktuur, Narva, phone 2 41 18
Iisaku regional museum, Iisaku, phone 9 34 61
Jôhvi museum of art, 40 Pargi, phone 2 23 00
Purtse castel, exhibition-hall, Purtse, phone 5 93 88

FILLING STATIONS

Narva, 64 Tallinna, phone 4 98 53
Narva, 55A Tallinna, phone 4 24 00
Kohtla-Järve, 5 Narva mnt., phone 4 54 91
49 Ahtme, phone 3 33 66
64 Tallinna, phone 4 98 53
Kiviôli, 86 Lepa tee, phone 5 74 17
Sillamäe, 40 Tallinna, phone 7 55 14
Ahtme, phone 3 33 71

CAR SERVICE

Narva, 1A Kirovi, phone 4 92 49
Kohtla-Järve, 34A Narva mnt., phone 4 57 88
Kohtla-Järve, 1 Kaevuri, phone 4 01 44
Sillamäe, 19 Tallinna mnt., phone 7 33 77
Avinurme, 6 Tööstuse, phone 9 75 16

TELEPHONE AREA CODE: SILLAMÄE 249, NARVA 235, KOHTLA-JÄRVE 233

JÕGEVAMAA

Area: 2604 km²	**Capital: Jõgeva,**
Population: 42 650	**population 7100**

Jõgevamaa is the Land of Drumlins. Lines of the narrow hills run diagonally, north-west to south-east, through much of the county. The East European plain has many such "basket of eggs" landscapes, but it's here that they are at their most majestic. According to legend the drumlins are furrows made by Kalevipoeg, the hero of Estonia's epic poem. According to geology they were left by receding glaciers.

In ancient times these lands belonged to two small Estonian "parishes", Vaiga and Mõhu. In 1220 a Finnish priest, Pietari Kaikkivalta, baptised the people with the help of Latvian Hendryk. The land was divided, a feudal order of knights seizing one part while the southern part remained under the control of the Bishop of Tartu. The district of Palataguse was founded in the western part, and Põltsamaa castle, around which a town later arose, became the bailiff's residence. Another order castle, Laiuse, became the eastern centre. In the 16th century, the population on the shores of Lake Peipsi was increased by Estonian and later Russian fishing folk.

The county has suffered its share of wars. During the Livonian War (1558-83) the castles of Laiuse and Põltsamaa surrendered to Russian troops. After the Battle of Narva in the Northern War in 1700, Sweden's King Karl XII and his army established their winter quarters in Laiuse. A longer period of peace under the Russian thumb began in 1709, lasting two centuries, until the Estonian Independence War (1918-20). Then, at Laiuse castle the Bolshevik troops attacking the southern part of the country were stopped. The partisan troops of Julius Kuperjanov were based in Puurmani.

Perhaps the Soviets craved revenge: Jõgevamaa suffered severely during World War II. The Soviets deported great numbers to Siberia and ruined churches, estates, clubs and the beautiful palace of Põltsamaa.

The monument to the War of Independence in Põltsamaa.

JÕGEVA

The capital is a small town making good.

Admin centre

Jõgeva was a tiny village for centuries, until 1876 when the railway line to Tartu was completed. Soon an inn, shops, a post office and a horse post-station were built. In 1903 the landowner, Count Mannteuffel, began to redistribute land along 2 km of road connecting the railway station (which he didn't own) to his estate. This became Station St, the main street. Even in 1919 there were only 95 houses and 817 people in Jõgeva. Later it was given the status of town and became capital of its own new county, Jõgevamaa.

Today the town's most prominent institution is the **plant research centre.** There are also some lovely gardens in Jõgeva. The flower gardens of Rudolph Tamme are decorated with statues by the Estonian sculptor Anton Starkopf. Otherwise this is a dusty administrative centre.

AROUND PÕLTSAMAA

Põltsamaa is a delightful park town with a castle ruin. The farming centres around it are splashed with history.

The residence of the "king"

The verdant town of **Põltsamaa**** has led a famous life. In 1558 Russian troops conquered the town and Põltsamaa briefly became the residence of Duke Magnus, King of Livonia. But the town's real king ruled in the second half of the 18th century: Major Woldemar Lauw established a glass factory, a copper foundry, a mirror factory and a china factory. In 1770 he built a superb three-storey palace, now a **ruin in a park****, on the remnants of the old castle. The interior featured rococo decor and the walls were covered in yellow, pink and pale-blue imitation marble. The palace of Põltsamaa and

Põltsamaa – a pretty river is a great addition to any town square.

its park were created in the style of western European and St Petersburg models. Pathways, arbours, niches in hedges and Chinese bridges were all part of the design. Even Empress Catherine II came to see this sumptuous dwelling. (At the moment it's under reconstruction. A restaurant and bar are completed, and there are plans for a hotel.)

The enterprising major also established a hospital and a pharmacy. He invited a man named Peter Wilde to be its doctor and manager. This staff selection proved successful and Wilde founded the medical school annexed to the hospital. Wilde also had time to establish a printing office in Põltsamaa, the sixth largest in the Russian Empire. Between 1766 and 1780, 16 works in Estonian, Latvian and German were printed, and 41 issues of Wilde's magazine, *A Brief Instruction Containing Some Medicines and Some Knowledge,* were published. Wilde's German article "Eine arztiche Anweisung für den Landmann" was translated into Estonian by August Hupel, the pastor of Põltsamaa, marking the beginning of Estonian periodical publication. By the way, the first Latvian periodical *Latviesu Arste* was published in the same way in Põltsamaa. Jakob Lange was not only its translator, but also general superintendant of Riga.

Today the highlight of town is the **river**** -- and the parks and bridges that criss-cross its leisurely course. There's a stirring white War of Independence monument and a general atmosphere of languorousness such as one finds in Estonia's greener towns.

The central point of Estonia

A rock in **Adavere,** north of Põltsamaa on the Tallinn highway, marks the geographic centre of the Estonian mainland. The village's French-style park is full of different plant species. And Adavere windmill, north towards Tallinn, has been restored with some verve as a restaurant.

Near Põltsamaa in **Võisiku** lived Timotheus von Bock, who in 1816 drafted a proposal for a Russian constitution. His proposal criticised the czar and serfdom, and von Bock suffered 20 years in prison after he sent the work to Alexander I. On release he was deemed insane. Jaan Kross, the most famous living Estonian writer, a recent nominee for the Nobel Prize and a member of the Estonian parliament, has written a novel *The czar's madman* based on von Bock's life; it's now available in English.

Brother Vahindra or Barefoot Tõnisson

The only Estonian saint, Brother Vahindra, came from **Umbusi village** near Põltsamaa. He was born Karl Tõnisson in 1883. In his youth he raced against horses and taught about reincarnation. In 1915 he started to preach Buddhism and became known as Barefoot Tõnisson since he went about barefoot. He called himself Brother Vahindra after hiking to Tibet and returning to the Baltics as a Buddhist priest. During World War II Tõnisson emigrated to Burma where he governed a large Buddhist monastery. After his death, his thin body did not suffer normal deterioration, and after three weeks he was buried with great ceremony. In 1962 Brother Vahindra was canonised a saint.

Puurmani* is south-east of Põltsamaa, 39 km from Tartu. A superb estate was built here 110 years ago. Originally, it had 42 rooms, a billiard hall, wine cellar and central heating throughout. This grand home belonged to the Count Manteuffel. The countess built one additional room, planned as the count's bedroom -- she called it the snoring room. The estate is surrounded by a park wealthy in different plants.

EAST TO LAKE PEIPSI

A monster drumlin, a ruin and a pleasant lakeside town ...

Laiuse

The **drumlin of Laiuse** is a real giant -- 10 km long and 2 km wide. The road that used to cross the Laiuse mountain was so steep that carriage wheels had to be tied. The **sweeping view*** from the mountain of domesticated land and one or two forests was breathtaking. It still causes a gasp today; there's a viewing platform on three large tanks.

The **church in Laiuse** stands out in what is otherwise a dusty collective-farm town. In the north-eastern part of the churchyard, beyond the teachers' house, grows a lime tree planted by King Karl of Sweden on 29 May 1701 when he abandoned Laiuse. He planted four oaks slightly later when he returned: they're in the SW corner. Reinerus Brocmann, son of the Laiuse pastor, moved to Sweden to escape the Northern War, which Sweden lost, and later published *The entire Swedish household book*. He'd learnt a lot in his life in Laiuse to recommend for the development of Swedish agriculture.

Long, thin villages merge into one another along the coast of Lake Peipsi.

The ruins of the 15th-century **Order castle*** are a little further along the Mustvee-Jõgeva road. This was the first Estonian castle built to cope with firearms. Goodly portions remain, including a corner tower that gives some idea of the original look and shape of the castle.

Torma lies between Laiuse and Mustvee. In the 18th century, the Riga-St Petersburg post-road ran through the town, and Czars Paul I, Catherine II, Alexander I and Nikolai I all passed through. After the Riga-Pskov stone road was built in 1859, Torma was cut out of international travel. But Torma replaced its golden age and crowned heads with a writer: the local pastor, Johann Eisen von Schwarzenberg gained international fame with a book about preserving fruit and vegetables.

Bits of Laiuse's Order citadel stand firm.

From the Laiuse drumlin you can see almost as far as summer.

Black water

On the shore of Lake Peipsi at the mouth of the Mustvee River, the town of **Mustvee*** ("black water") lies near the Tartu-Narva road. Since ancient times, most of the inhabitants of Mustvee have grown cucumbers, onions and carrots. Looking south you can see a continuous line of settlements stretching along the coast of Peipsi to the mouth of the river Omedu: Russian fishing villages. Mustvee is a popular lakeside holiday town among Estonians, and relatively undiscovered by foreign visitors.

NORTH OF JÕGEVA

A place to explore marshes, visit rose gardens and see Peace Parks from peaces made long ago.

The roses of Kurista

Only 5 km from Jõgeva you reach **Kurista** where within the forest east of the road you can visit a **rose garden.** There are almost 500 varieties of roses in the sunny glade surrounded by fir trees.

There's a farm museum not far to the north in **Paduvere,** while Estonia's popular comic writer Hugo Raudsepp (1883-1952) came from **Vaimastvere.**

Legends of Kärde

Around **Kärde hill** lie boulders with stories attached to them. On Peter's Stone, in the forest on the western side of the road, Czar Peter I once had his dinner. The Lady's Stone east of the road recalls the unhappy love story of a lady of Kärde manor, Miss Stackelberg. She fell in love with a peasant and, because of the disapproval of her parents, felt she had no choice but to drown herself. In the **Peace Park** in Kärde, the Peace House is a unique memorial of architecture and history. On 21 June

1661, the peace treaty ending the Russian-Swedish War in 1656-58 was signed here. The Peace Ditch reaches the road a little beyond Peter's Stone. It was dug during negotiations to keep the soldiers occupied.

The **Tooma Research Station,** where swamps have been studied for almost a century, is also in Kärde. Several kilometres of narrow boardwalk cross the pool-filled bog. This is a centre for the Endla Nature Reserve.

The last village in Jõgeva county in the direction of Tallinn is **Vägeva.** One branch of the crossroads leads towards Rakvere, and in the beautiful forest between the branches of the road you used to be able to meet an old man with a white beard sitting at a fire telling stories about Kalevipoeg. The epic hero once rested right on this spot.

Nowadays the old mills work as taverns.

SOUTH TOWARDS TARTU

The impressive drumlin landscape hides lakes and manors.

Ducks, trout, quail eggs

Just west of Jõgeva, **Siimusti** is the place for crockery and ceramic vases. And just south of the county capital, across the Pedja river at Painküla, is the Kaarepere experimental forestry centre. Southern Jõgevamaa is domestic game country. People in Kaarepere village raise musk ducks and mallards, they breed trout and perch in the pond of Härjanurme, and quail in Kaiavere. To keep their fowl free from neural lymphomatosis, many countries buy Kaiavere's germ-free quail eggs.

Approaching **Kassinurme** you meet more places connected with Kalevipoeg. Certainly the hero's bed is here – on a hill where an ancient

View over Lake Prossa from Nava's drumlin – your everyday Jõgevamaa landscape ...

... but Gooti ("gothic") avenue in Luua park is unique.

hill-fort once stood. It was a convenient sleeping place because there's a deep round hole at the foot, Kalevipoeg's washbasin. Close by, a deep oval pit was the hero's bath. Further off are Kalevipoeg's footprints and the lake he once drank dry (it stayed like that). Local people like to walk in **hills round Kassinurme***, where there's a song stage, benches and swings.

Five kilometres separate Kaarepere from **Palamuse.** The history of the village dates back to the year 1234, when a three-aisle granite church was built according to an edict of Pope Gregory IX. Around the pulpit you can see the figures of six apostles, above it the figure of an angel and a ladder to heaven. The landscape of Palamuse is magnificent, though the place is best known for its writer. A young chemist's apprentice, Oskar Luts, wrote a novel based on his school reminiscences, the eternal schooldays' novel, *The spring*. He gained great and instant success and is still one of Estonia's best loved writers. A musical version for children is part of the repertoire of Tallinn's Estonia Theatre. In the museum of Palamuse you can see Luts's other works.

Aidu Laisaar has carved out a niche for himself.

Schooldays at Palamuse inspired Oskar Luts to write his classic novel, The Spring.

Kuremaa** was near the head of the queue when they were handing out the landscapes. A glittering lake with a sandy beach, a park with terraces, a neoclassical ensemble of buildings are all in gentle harmony here.

They just keep rolling

South of Kaarepere, the drumlin landscape keeps on rolling. A lake called Pikkjärv hides in a deep valley east of the highway. In the village of Pikkjärve is **Kaarepere mansion** in an ancient park. To the north-east

A cottage made famous by Oskar Luts.

you can find Lake Luua. The buildings of **Luua manor**** form one of the most beautiful estate ensembles in Estonia, and the park is rich in flora.

The 100 km^2 **Vooremaa area**** begins here, where Jõgeva and Tartumaa meet. In the ice ages, glaciers left hundred of drumlins behind as they retreated. The spaces between have filled with lakes, and in modern times bungalows have been built on their sandy shores. Near **Elistvere** you can climb a tower for a **view**** of the drumlins, the deep narrow lakes, the cattle and the fields.

Tabivere is almost on the border of Tartu and Jõgeva counties. The local church once had a famous vicar, Otto Wilhelm Masing (1763-1829). Masing founded the first weekly newspaper in Estonian and wrote some ABC-books and schoolbooks. He introduced the "õ" into written Estonian. The **War of Independence monument** opposite the church recalls the sacrifices this county has made with a certain special 1930s poignancy.

PRACTICAL DETAILS

ACCOMODATION

"Virtus" hotel, 40 Aia, Jõgeva, tel 2 13 19
Jõgeva guest-house, 4 Jaama, tel 2 14 54
Põltsamaa hotel, 1 Jõe, tel 5 14 60
Avi motel, 9 Tähe Mustvee, tel 2 65 32
Tabivere camping

RESTAURANTS, BARS, CAFES

Adavere Windmill-restaurants, Adavere, tel 5 73 11
"Ranna" restaurant, 1 Veski, Põltsamaa, tel 5 14 92
Jõgeva restaurant, 33 Gagarini, tel 2 29 82
"Ankur" resturant, 5 Tartu Mustvee, tel 2 44 40
Tabivere windmill-cafe, tel 3 63 02
Adavere BISTRO, tel 5 72 17
Põltsamaa grill-bar, tel 5 13 66
Põltsamaa Kurvebaar, tel 5 12 55 (Põltsamaa crossroads)

MUSEUMS

The writer Oskar Luts school-museum, Palamuse, tel 3 30 32
Kaarepere Forest museum, Luua
Vaimastvere farm-museum, Paduvere

FILLING STATIONS

Jõgeva, tel 2 17 65
Mustvee, tel 2 44 26
Põltsamaa 1, tel 5 16 02
Põltsamaa 2, tel 5 23 95

CAR SERVICE

Jõgeva, tel 2 12 78
Pajusi, tel 9 57 16
Neanurme, tel 5 14 70

TELEPHONE AREA CODE: 237

TARTUMAA

Area: 3051 km^2	Capital: Tartu,
Population: 41 400	population: 114 240

Tartu county is bordered by two giant lakes to the east and west, and split by a majestic river, the Emajõgi. The fertile valley formed by the river and its tributaries over millions of years and has created some magnificent countryside – such as the rolling landscape around Elva and the valley of the Kavilda River. Old Russian communities inhabit a string of one-street fishing villages on Lake Peipsi while the rest of the county is the breadbasket for Tartu town. (Tartu itself has its own chapter.)

In the past Tartumaa was more than twice its present size. Many times the county has acted as shield for Estonia against eastern assaults ... fields that now host collective farms have oft been soaked in blood.

Birth of the Emajõgi river

God was angry, for the animals took no pleasure in life but spent all their time quarrelling and devouring one another. So God decided to give the animals a king to rule over them, and ordered them to dig a deep river where the king would live. The rabbit and the fox found the site for the river, the mole dug the first furrow, the badger dredged, the wolf scraped, and the bear dragged the soil away. Finally God poured in water from a golden dish. And that's how the river Emajõgi was born.

The **Emajõgi** ("mother river") begins from the Võrtsjärv, Estonia's second-largest lake, in the west. It slowly makes its way across the county, fed by twelve tributaries including the lovely Elva, Kavilda, Amme and Ahja rivers, through Tartu itself before emptying into Estonia's largest lake, Lake Peipsi. The last few kilometres of its course it crosses the inaccessible Great Emajõgi Marsh. For centuries the Emajõgi has been the principal trade route and

A river called "Mother".

food source of the local people. In the distant past it flowed the other way, from Lake Peipsi through the Võrtsjärv all the way to Pärnu. Nowadays the best way to see the river is on a cruise from Tartu downriver and onto Lake Peipsi itself.

TOWARDS JÕGEVA

A watermill with a monastic legend attached and a landscape of lakes and drumlins lie north of Tartu.

Hard life

Travelling along the Jõgeva road, **Vasula manor,** home of the 17th-century poet and philosopher Stiernhielm, who was Sweden's first Copernican, lies to the east of the highway just before the river Amme. A left from the Jõgeva road just north of the river Amme, another left at the Nõela tee busstop, and a right turn a few hundred metres along the dirt road takes you to the site of **Kärkna monastery.** All you can see is a 19th-century watermill being used as a barn, standing where the monastery's mill used to. Which is sad because there's a classic Estonian tale about the place.

It seems Cistercians monks founded the monastery on the bank of the Amme river in 1233. The numbers grew quickly and they decided to squeeze funds out of the Pope to build an extension. Two brothers were sent to Rome with a letter complaining about the "hard life" and "severe rules". The letter claimed they were allowed to eat nothing but bread and fish (probably Peipsi lavaret, with its tender, white flesh). Especially horrid, they said, was the "mortification", in which the naked monks beat themselves with switches and poured cold water over themselves. Unbearable! The Pope chose an Italian brother to take these bizarre practices in hand. After being treated to dry fish and bitter beer, the guest was taken to a sauna where the monks began to birch themselves with whisks, as one does in a sauna. "No, for heaven's sake!" cried the envoy as he dashed out. "No one should live as harshly as this!" The monks didn't have to wait long for the Pope's beneficence.

Lakes and drumlins

The 100 km^2 **area of Vooremaa**** is further north along the Jõgeva road, where Jõgevamaa and Tartumaa meet. In the ice ages, glaciers formed hundred of drumlins here. The largest and deepest of the many beautiful lakes between the drumlins is **Saadjärv***, 25 m deep. A right turn at the Tabivere church takes you there. Once, Kalevipoeg and his brothers had to choose a ruler among them and finally agreed that whoever could throw a stone the furthest would rule in the place of old Kalev. The oldest brother's stone (1.3 m high) fell in the middle of the lake. The second brother's stone (4.5 x 2.8 x 2.1 m) landed on the beach in **Äksi village.** Kalevipoeg hurled his stone all the way over the village. Millstones and gate-posts have been made from the upper part of that stone. The other half is in the ground in a field 5 m to one side of the road, marked by a rowan tree.

The Saadjärv has been known as a lovely place to spend the summer since czarist times. Local **Kukulinna estate** was used as a summer cottage by the Pallas art group in the 1920s, and was until recently a Young Pioneer's camp. Nowadays it's a run-down hotel.

EAST TO KALLASTE

Russian towns and fishing villages lie along the shore of Lake Peipsi to the north-west. Alatskivi's manor is a fake castle.

Pharmacist

The Kohtla-Järve highway zooms through flat farmland. If you take the turn towards Kallaste you soon come to **Väägvere,** cradle of Estonian music culture. Väägvere brass band, established by a local teacher, Taavet Wirkhaus, with the help of his son, gained renown throughout the country after the first song festival in 1869.

Now the road begins to ride up and down the drumlins of central Estonia. Just before Alatskivi you pass the **home of writer Juhan Liiv,** now a museum. From the outside Liiv's life and work seem straightforward, but the man suffered deep bouts of depression. A little boy from one of his novels knows that the great Lake Peipsi is nearby but cannot find it, and summarises his situation with a sigh: "If only that forest wasn't in my way!" Liiv lived his whole life in the area, working as a pharmacist.

Alatskivi** is a classic Estonian farming centre. You'll find in this dusty place the usual shop and blocks of flats and wooden private houses and palatial manor with splendid tree-lined avenues. The local landlords were wealthy Stackelbergs and Nolckens. They left behind a **manor house** in the fake-English-castle style so popular among Balto-Germans last century. It needs a lick of paint and a complete internal restoration. They also bequeathed to the village its fine **park, avenues and ponds,** though the lake view was already there.

The cemetery of Old Believers at Kallaste.

One long village

The road to Kolkja mosies past Lake Lahepera to Lake Peipsi. From here south is a great example of an old **Russian fishing community****. The houses, some semi-detached, some with trademark blue doorways, some of stone and brick, line a single street through three long villages, Kolkja, Kasepää and Varnja. People will tell you that Russians paint their houses or doorways blue to keep the flies away. Occasionally you can glimpse the lake along boat-paths

It's a castle! No, it's Alatskivi manor.

Moment on the Saadjärv.

through the rushes. The road ends at the Great Emajõgi Marsh.

Just out of Alatskivi in the direction of Pala, you can clearly pick **Kalevipoeg's bed***, once an ancient Estonian hill-fort. Now there's a swing on it. The knolls across the road were carried here by the hero in his coat flap. Some of the sand slipped out on the way and formed a 2 km long morainal ridge, and the pits from which Kalevipoeg took the sand formed several lovely lakes. They lie on either side of the road through **Savastvere,** hidden by roadside brush.

Shore town

In the 18th-19th centuries Russian families from the opposite side of the lake came to live on this side. Many were Old Believers – those who hadn't accepted the Orthodox religion and were suffering persecution. They got along with the local Estonians quite well, and traded onions, cucumbers, mushrooms, and fresh fish. There were good potters, masons and brickburners among them, and in the course of time many of the Russians adopted Estonian culture. From one such settlement grew **Kallaste** (from the Estonian *kallas,* "shore"). This small town on the shore of **Lake Peipsi** has

The lakes in Vooremaa formed between ice-age drumlins.

seen some good times, judging by the imposing buildings on the main square in Nõukogu ("Soviet" or "community") Street. Russians call Kallaste *Krasnaya Gora* ("red mountain") because of the area's red sandstone: in the southern part of town there's a spectacular escarpment by the **beach.** The cemetery has a good view, too.

SOUTH-EAST TO MEHIKOORMA

Võnnu was the home of several important personages, while Mehikoorma is a port on Lake Peipsi.

Survival

As you leave Tartu by the Räpina road, you pass new tower blocks in the suburb of Anne and the Institute of Forestry before coming to the old village of **Lohkva.** Garden villages like this one show how dependent Estonians are on the soil. One tradition the Soviets didn't oppose was that of keeping a small plot of land where one could "grow one's own" fruit and vegetables. Even high-rise dwellers keep gardens somewhere; without them many probably wouldn't survive the winter and tough economic times. There's a **horse stud** where you can ride horses at **Ihaste** south of Lohkva.

The collective farm that's moved into **Luunja** has managed to maintain some of the stateliness of the old manor on the bank of the Emajõgi. The manor house now has a bar and the park a couple of unusual statues, including one dedicated to famous Luunja horses.

Conqueror of Estonia – a Soviet tank from 1944.

Memorials in Võnnu

Your way turns off to the east through **Võnnu.** Some famous Estonians and Baltic Germans have lived here. Parson Eduard Körber (1770-1850) established a park and planted an oak to commemorate the liberation of the peasants. There's the childhood home of the Estonian poet Gustav Suits. In the church is buried Baron Nolcken's son, killed in the bloody Battle of Borodino. The **"porridge school"** opposite the church was one of the first schools of housekeeping (1876) in the Baltic countries and the Russian Empire. Here, girls who'd finished at the village school could learn the secrets of managing a household.

An iron wolf guards **Järvselja nature reserve.** No visitors are allowed, but you may admire silver spruce and the metre-high witch-hazelnut that blossoms in winter in the local dendrological park.

The road gets to **Lake Peipsi** at **Mehikoorma*.** Besides several coastal villages, you may also sail to **Piirissaar island*.** Before the Treaty of Tartu in 1920, the island was divided between Russia and Estonia. Young men hid there from czarist military service, which in those days lasted 25 rather longish years. During the War of Independence naval battles were fought in the lake. A cruise around Lake Peipsi (there are several from Tartu in the summer) is a cruise through history to some beautiful places. There's also a regular ferry.

SOUTH TOWARDS VÕRU

A museum for tractor buffs and a gorgeous lake.

Agriculture

The Võru highway leads south from

All aboard for Piirissaar in Lake Peipsi.

Tartu past **Ülenurme,** a collective farm centre and home of the **Estonian Museum of Agriculture*.** Bridal couples often come here and are received according to the old wedding customs, though not all of the museum is housed in the old stable, smithy, barn and carriage shed. Out in the weather are tractors and other farming equipment dating from 1909-50 and clearly outlining the effect of Soviet agriculture on Estonia. There's a windmill and a group of old beehives too. The exhibition was developed under Brezhnev but has coped rather well with the changing times. Old peasant equipment, now the flavour of the year, is beautifully displayed in the main building.

Across the highway, planes fly to all sorts of odd destinations from Tartu's airport.

In Kambja's newly restored **church*** there's a memorial to Estonia's first schoolteacher, Ignatsi Jaak, and two more in the grounds. The cock has been a symbol of education in Estonia ever since Jakobson put one on the cover of his Estonian ABC book a century ago. An oak growing here was planted by the Swedish crown prince Gustav for Tartu University's 300th anniversary in 1932. The church is attractively located beside a lake, and the cemetery's up the hill on the way to Vana-Kuuste.

You can turn towards Otepää before you reach Kambja. One of the loveliest lakes in the Otepää Highlands is **Lake Pangodi*** to the southwest. Elva is west of here, and there's a view of hills blurring into treeline from the road.

DIRECTION RIGA

South-east are a war atrocity memorial and a woody holiday town, Elva.

Lake Artsi lies next to Elva, sprouting waterlilies.

Elva ...

Warcrime

Heading from Tartu on the road to Riga, you first pass **Maarjamõisa,** where a hospital and a suburb of private houses were founded at the beginning of the century on what was once the Tamme manor. Near Lemmatsi village 12 000 men were slaughtered in an anti-tank ditch. From December 1943 to April 1944 the Nazis had the bodies dug up and burned in order to conceal the crime. The unfortunate diggers, Polish, Czech and Slovak prisoners-of-war, were burned alive. The **memorial to the atrocity*** is a wall of dolomite with Soviet-style figures in relief, which you can see by the parking place not far outside Tartu city limits.

The domes of the **Wilhelm Struve Astrophysical Observatory** swell from the hilltop in Tõravere. The centre is internationally known for its research into noctilucent clouds.

The resort that thundered

The landlord of Meeri, von Seidliz, who had a Swedish accent, built eleven villages, and the last was named **Elva**** after the Swedish word for "11". No it wasn't. What happened was, the Georgian who built the Elva railway was terrified of thunder and lightning, and often cried to the sky: "Elva, elva!", which means "thunderstorm" in Georgian. This lovely summer resort really did arise beside the Tartu-Valga railway. It began to flourish when Estonians first involved themselves in larger-scale business enterprises and an Estonian middle class formed. Wooden holiday homes are built across the hills by Lake Verevi amid a virtual forest of pines.

Continuing south, the "Uderna park" sign points to an old schoolhouse where several important Estonians studied, including short-

... and its heraldic tree, Artsi pine.

story writer Friedebert Tuglas and sculptor Konrad Mägi. They're commemorated in a small **sculpture park** around the school.

The church in **Rõngu*** is the only single-nave church in south Estonia. It has 16 valuable altarpieces, a bell, an organ and stained-glass windows. The current "civic" facade dates from 1901. The building across the road used to be Rõngu tavern ... and is again today. The town's song festival ground is on the north side of town. It was once a sacred grove and burial place. You can see the ruins of a vassal town 2 km away along the road to Sangla, now forming part of someone's farm.

TOWARDS VILJANDI

The westward road from Tartu to Viljandi 80 km away crosses pretty Kavilda valley and passes two historic churches.

Tragedy

A hundred years ago folk had to make a great detour to reach Viljandi during the spring high waters. You can see plentiful peatland on both sides of the road as you leave Tartu, a remnant of those damp times. But the landscape holds a fascination not only for peat producers.

The road dips and rises at the **valley of the Kavilda River***. A thousand years ago an ancient Estonian **stronghold** stood on the western bank (it's to the right at the top of the valley). The present wall remnants are from the medieval castle founded in 1361. Now the place is called Kiigemägi after its swing *(kiik)*, and festivals and midsummer night bonfires are held here. In caves in the side of the valley lived devils, knights and even barons. South of the road on the same side of the valley stands an **Orthodox church.** Many Estonian peasants converted to Orthodoxy in the hope of being rewarded with land; they built this church, dedicated to Alexander Nevsky. The waters of a sacrificial well near the church are said to make people young.

Kavilda manor near Kiigemägi belonged to the mightiest clan of early feudal times – the Tisenhusens. Barbara von Tisenhusen, barely 20, fell in love with the secretary of the manor, Franz Bonnius, who was from a merchant family. Custom and law forbade marriage between social classes. The lovers escaped to

Lake Pangodi dwells amid the pastureland.

Riga to marry, intending to go abroad. Alas, Barbara was caught and the family decided to drown the young woman in the Võrtsjärv. Two Estonian peasants refused to perform the vile deed, so her own brother, Jürgen von Tisenhusen, carried out the sentence. In revenge, Bonnius became a highwayman and waylaid and killed dozens of nobles. The tragic tale spread through the courts of Europe, and Eduard Tubin wrote an opera based on a ballad by the Finnish-Estonian writer Aino Kallas, *Barbara von Tisenhusen*. Only uninteresting foundations remain, but it's a great story, eh!

To the Võrtsjärv

In the churchyard of **Puhja's gothic church** you'll find ancient stone crosses and the stone of an Estonian peasant's grave. During the Northern War Käsu Hans, the first Estonian man of letters, worked in this church as precantor and schoolmaster. His poem "Oh, our poor Tartu", completed in 1708, was a lament for Czar Peter I's demolition of Tartu. The church's key is kept at the pastorate next door.

You reach the Võrtsjärv, Estonia's second-largest lake, at Sangla. Heading south, **Rannu church**** is a distant landmark rising above a farming plain. Inside this 15th-century church there's a finely wrought chandelier from 1699 and a 16th-century chancel (key available from the house behind the church). Nearby Vehendi is a resort on the Võrtsjärv.

Heading back north, once past Sangla you're travelling a couple of hundred metres from the **Võrtsjärv:** typically for Estonia you only get to glimpse the lake once through the trees. From Jõesuu bridge you can see it again – here the Emajõgi begins its languorous journey to Lake Peipsi – but you're already in Viljandimaa.

PRACTICAL DETAILS

ACCOMODATION

Elva guest-house, tel 5 61 71
Elva guest-house, tel 5 63 33
Vehendi motel, Rannu, tel 5 45 56
"Tare" guest-house, Tähtvere, tel 9 53 75
"Poldri" guest-house, Tõrvandi, tel 1 23 89

RESTAURANTS, BARS, CAFES

Elva restaurant, 1 Pikk, tel 5 61 30
Nõo bar, Voika 23, tel, 5 53 64
Tõrvandi bar, Tõrvandi, tel 1 53 45
Kuldkirve, Tõrvandi

MUSEUMS

Tartumaa Regional Museum, 2 Pikk, Elva, tel 5 61 41
L. Hansen home-museum, 2A Vilde, Elva, tel 5 62 89
Estonian museum of agriculture, Ülenurme, tel 1 23 96
Uderna local museum, Kalme, tel 5 71 00
Juhan Liivi Museum, Alatskivi

CAR SERVICE

Külitse, tel 9 73 44
Elva, tel 5 63 07

TELEPHONE AREA CODE: 234

TARTU

Population: 114 240

If Tallinn is the centre of Estonian political power, then Tartu is the intellectual centre. Tartu was the headquarters of the Estonian national awakening in the second half of the 19th century. The first song festival was held here, and the first Estonian theatre established. Most importantly, a great university was founded back in the 17th century, and Tartu's intellectual spirit has long been a focal point for national culture. An uncompromising academic idealism has forged links of iron between Tartu and those "outsiders", be they Finns, Russians, Baltic Germans or others, involved with the university.

Athens on the Emajõgi

Tartu is on the Emajõgi ("mother river"). From the banks of that ancient river-road you have a view of a pale neoclassical city with its own Mount Olympus, Toome Hill, in the centre, and one of the oldest universities in Scandinavia (1632) – all giving the town a special aura and a slightly boastful nickname, "Athens on the Emajõgi".

The town was first chronicled back in 1030, making it historically the oldest town in Estonia, and second after Tallinn in population. Fate has not always been kind to Tartu. Not a single house survives from its days as a flourishing Hanseatic centre – Czar Peter I razed the old city, which then had to build itself from scratch in the 18th-19th centuries. Modern Tartu includes the Ropka industrial district, turn-of-the-century wooden houses in Karlova and Supilinn, villas in Tähtvere and Tamme and new concrete housing blocks in Ülejõe. The town offers the chance of peace and contemplation, rather than glitzy entertainment and greedy commercialism. Many celebrities prefer to live here. It allows them to stay in opposition to the mentality of government in the capital. Thus you will find a town whose cultural basis was created by German scholars, whose exterior was shaped by Romanov (czarist) tastes, and which has been the seat of Estonia's lofty nonconformist spirit.

HISTORY OF TARTU

From ancient fort ...

In the times when gods lived in trees and stones, when gnomes and fairies bustled beside humans, the local Estonians built a mighty wooden fortification on Toome Hill in the Emajõgi river basin. The river was a busy waterway crossed by trade routes from the northern coast to Latvia and from Russia to the Baltic Sea. For 500 years the **Tarbatu fort** offered shelter to traders from near and far and a sanctuary for locals from the frequent invaders. In the year 1030 Kiev's sovereign, King Yaroslav the Wise, reached Tarbatu. The old Russian chronicle *Tales of ancient times* tells us that Yaroslav (first name Yuri) established a fortification here, which was called Yuryev after him. Thus Tartu gained a birthdate and a new name. Russians would call the town Yuryev until the

19th century. The sensible Germans called it **Dorpat.**

Meelis and Vyatshko in defence of Tartu

Under the Soviets, Estonian children had to choose whether to believe the stories their textbooks told them or the home-taught versions of their parents. In the age of the Crusades, the small castle of Tarbatu was the only fortress still held by Estonians. In 1224 the Germans, Livonians and Latgals were threatening the town, so the local Estonian ruler, Meelis, called on a Russian, Prince Vyatshko from Novgorod, for help. He came, though with only 200 Russian warriors. Vyatshko, his soldiers and the townspeople who'd taken refuge inside, all were slaughtered. And so 750 years later children learnt that even in medieval times the Russians had been altruistically helping Estonians.

But too many details ring false here, and the current revised version suggests that Vyatshko, with whom the Estonians had no quarrel, was a guest at the castle. Unbeknownst to the locals, he was preparing to annex the whole country, but his plans went awry when an army turned up on the doorstep. Till the last moment the prince was waiting for Russian reinforcements. As an old adage says: "No one has ever seen a fish eat a cat."

A Hanseatic flourish

Tartu became the seat of the powerful **Bishop of Tartu,** who controlled a vast swathe of south-eastern Estonia. But it was also a **merchant town** and grew very handsome. Simon, a monk from the Russian town Suzdal, enthused about the great stone mansions of medieval Tartu. Like Tallinn there was a castle on the hill walled off from the merchant's town in the valley. The lower town was surrounded by a stone wall with gates and towers. There were 12 churches and four abbeys. Of the few survivors from those times, the Peter & Paul cathedral on Toome Hill and St John's church are ruins. But the medieval street network has been preserved, and the old street names have recently returned. The main streets were Lai and Suurturg, running from Toome Hill to the river. They were crossed by Jakobi, Jaani and Rüütli Sts.

Birth of a university

After bloody wars between Germans and Russians, Russians and Poles, Poles and Swedes in the 16th-18th centuries, a period of relative peace and prosperity came to Tartu. The Swedes, somewhat democratic compared to their predecessors, gave the peasants greater rights and allowed an education system to develop in the countryside. It was in 1632 that they made their most decisive contribution.

The opening of Sweden's second university, in Tartu (the first was in Uppsala in 1477), was the work of one man, Johann Skytte. Talented son of a merchant from Nyköping, Skytte wandered through European universities and became tutor to Gustav II Adolf, the future king of Sweden. Thanks to Skytte, young Gustav enjoyed an excellent education, and for the rest of his life had a great belief in its importance. The grateful king knighted his former tutor and made him governor-general over Livonia, Inger and Karelia. Johann Skytte settled in Tartu. As one of his first deeds he established a high school in 1630, then in 1632 asked the king for permission to transform the high school into a university. On 15 October 1632, at 8.00 am, all the churchbells chimed, a procession descended from the governor's residence on Toome Hill to the university building where a ceremony was held, the first rector was sworn in in the Maarja church, and the day ended with a festive supper in the town hall. The University of Tartu was founded under the name **Academia Gustaviana.**

Pity me

The university existed for only 76 years, until the Northern War brought ruin on the town. Czar Peter I himself led his army at Tartu. In 1708 he commanded that the whole town including the wall, towers and gates, bastions, houses and the fortress on the hill be **razed.** One of the oldest surviving works of Estonian literature is "Käsu Hans's lament", a long narrative poem written in 1708 and modelled on the story of the last days of Jerusalem. The poem begins: "Pity me, I'm poor Tartu town". The people fell into dire poverty; until 1730, when a wooden town hall was built, the council had to hold its meetings in a rented room in a private house.

Stone buildings were prohibited in all Russian cities except St Petersburg, so it's no surprise that in 1775 a fire destroyed everything again. (The town's third apocalypse, World War II, still lay ahead.)

After the fire they switched the situation and banned inflammable houses. But how could enough stone be collected to rebuild the city of stone? By order of the czar every peasant coming to town by wagon had to bring along a pood (about 16 kg) of stones. More help came in the form of loans and grants. Empress Catherine II presented 15 000 roubles for a stone bridge, which became a symbol of Tartu until World War II, when it was destroyed. By the end of the 18th century Tartu was beginning to look like the present town.

The churches of Tartu remember the Swedes, Germans and Russians.

University born again (and again)

The University of Tartu reopened only in 1802, basically because Czar Paul I, terrified of the contagion of revolution, had ordered all Russian scholars home from abroad in 1788 and commanded that new universities be established in the empire. Tartu won over Pärnu, Tallinn and other towns because it had had a university before. Academia Gustaviana was now **Yuryev University;** students and teachers were still mostly German, so they called it, melodiously, **Dorpat University.**

The few Estonian students had extra difficulties. In order for one "serf" student named Jürgenson to receive his diploma in the faculty of philosophy, he had to become a freeman. He applied to the rector to be liberated from serfdom by the government, but he was in a legal bind, because the university couldn't accept peasants without their landlord's permission. Jürgenson's documents were sent up and down. Historic changes came to his rescue when serfdom was abolished in 1819.

In the middle of the 19th century, **russification** policies became more active. The university was steadily isolated from other European universities. Soon the language that classes were taught in was changed from German to Russian, and many gifted German scholars left. In World War I studies stopped completely. A plan to evacuate the university to Voronez in central Russia was only half-effected - property went, and little else. Bureaucratic cunning has dragged the issue on till

today, despite the fact that the return of all property was agreed in the 1920 peace treaty between the Estonian Republic and the Soviet Union.
The day the great clock of the university's main building began to work again on 1 December 1919, **higher education in Estonian** commenced at last, in a school that could call itself the **University of Tartu.** The qualities of the old renowned German university within the Russian empire remained; but now Estonians taught and researched their own history and language, created their own art movements. Tartu became the intellectual seat of pre-war independence.
As one Estonian in exile described 1930s academic life: "Academic Tartu did not live only within the walls of the university and its organisations, nor even merely walk along the streets wearing distinctive marks. It spread to other places as well – cafes, homes, societies. While in Tallinn money was the measure of a person, in Tartu academic titles and academic credibility determined status. Academic merits were the first things mentioned when talking about someone; they were essential information on a calling card. One was esteemed according to the position and status of one's organisation."

Soviet times

In the **Treaty of Tartu,** signed in 1920 at 35 Aia St (now Vanemuise St), the Russia gave up all claims to Estonia forever. The treaty between Soviet Russia and the Republic of Finland was also signed in Tartu, at 1 Tõnissoni St, the Estonian Students Society building.
The Treaty of Tartu was honoured only in the breach. During World War II the university operated under difficult conditions. After the war those who could escape did so and those who remained and were not killed fighting had to toe the party line or else. Tartu University was left with only 5% of its pre-war faculty. In areas where the Soviets didn't feel threatened, research and achievement continued. Tartu was one of the best **Soviet universities** and even in the worst times some links remained with the west. But the theology department was disbanded at once, the brains were surgically removed from the philosophy department, and any studies around Estonian culture were feared for their "nationalist" taint.
The old student fraternities and sororities were banned. One day a week the men had officer training while the women studied nursing and civil defence. About 20% of every student's course-load was "red": subjects such as Marxism-Leninism, History of the Communist Party, Civil Defence and Scientific Communism were compulsory. Students were expected to join Comsomol or the Students' Construction Group; ironically these summer holiday work groups were the training ground for today's leaders. In the early 1960s any humanities student who'd come straight from school had to work in a factory or building site during the day and study at night, though only for the first year. Even into the late 1980s, the first few weeks of the everyone's university year were spent digging potatoes, building apartments, doing the spade-work on archaeological digs, and so on.
Nowadays 5500 students study in the university's nine departments, and extracurricular life is flourishing again. Theology and social science are being taught. The old student societies have been re-established, and new ones are starting. Student life today is more and more reminiscent of 50 years ago.

ON TOOME HILL

The hill where the old fortress and cathedral stood is today the spiritual centre of the university town, a fascinating historical place and a beautiful park to boot.

The symbol and fortress of Estonian intellectual life, the University of Tartu.

Realm of fairies

In ancient times every living soul came to the sacred Taara oak grove on **Toome Hill***** to listen to the god of song, Vanemuine, sing and play psalms. His music was so enchanting that the river Emajõgi stopped flowing, the wind forgot to blow, animals and birds stood stock still to listen, and the cross-eyed ghost looked out from behind a tree. To this day the trees on the hill recall the rustle of the god's clothing, the birds the sound of his singing, and the wind the highest notes. Only the fish in the river failed to lift their ears out of the water and doomed themselves to dumbness.

The 1920 Treaty of Tartu was signed here.

Later Toome Hill was treated less piously. In the 18th century, after Tartu was razed, it was used as a rubbish dump, cattle-breeding ground and gravel pit. When Czar Paul I presented the hill to the re-established university, the first rector, Professor Parrot, decided to make the place a park and thus cultivate noble feelings in the minds of students and citizens. Opposition between rector and citizens was so great that an armed guard had to be mounted to keep cattle away and arrest agitators. Today Toome Hill is virtually an open-air museum, with monuments and memorials at every

The way from dormitory to university passes through the land of fairies, Toome Hill.

corner. It's split by **Lossi ("castle") St** running from behind the town hall up and over the middle of the hill.

Cathedral-library-museum

It was quite a task to build the **Dome Church**** (originally Sts Peter & Paul church) in a pagan land. The devil destroyed the day's work every night, and he was appeased only when a virgin was sacrificed, or so they say. Anyway the church suffered from dithering too. Its design was changed several times during building. The western facade with twin towers dates from the 15th century and in its day was magnificent. But the walls soon began to crumble and in the 17th century the building was used as a granary and hayshed. In 1806 one end was rebuilt into the university library, which quickly became one of the best libraries in the Russian Empire. In 1980 the library moved into a new building and the Dome Church became what it is today, a museum and concert hall.

The Museum of the History of the University* shows the university's activities from 1632 until the present. Part of the elegant library has been restored. The splendid collection includes scientific equipment and a diagram of the human body showing the sites of some of the 200 diseases named after Tartu profs and grads: Vogel's investigation and Pirogov's triangle are both here.

There's also some memorabilia from the old student "corporations" or fraternities. When the university reopened, German students started Caronia and Livonia corporations in 1805-10. Tartu was the only university in the Russian Empire that allowed student organisations. In 1870, in the time of national awakening, Estonian students formed their own company, later called the Estonian Students Society. The Estonian Republic would adopt the society's flag as its own.

Alongside the fraternities, culture clubs were active. The Estonian Society of Learned Men, established in 1838, started to explore the nation's history, language and culture. Literature published by this society fired the country people with nationalist ideas.

The walker near kissing hill

A long-haired, inspirational figure stands near the Dome Church. Dressed in peasant clothes, stick in hand, **Kristjan Jaak Peterson*** (1801-22) walked from his hometown of Riga to Tartu to study at the university. The last line in his diary reads, "Farewell, Tartu, city of muses": Peterson was a gifted Estonian poet whose life was lopped by TB. Lines of one of his odes, glorifying the Estonian language, are cut into the base of his monument.

Beyond Peterson's statue there's a small mound made out of ancient stones. This was probably the foundation for a tower in which Russian merchants were imprisoned during battles between Russia and Hanseatic countries. Today it's **Musumägi***** ("kissing hill"), a favourite place for lovers since olden times. There's an artificial grotto in the hill where star-crossed lovers carried out suicide pacts. History tells other tales about the place. In

Tartu's cathedral is a splendid ruin and museum.

1880 F von Villebois's statue "Vater Rhein", depicting the Rhine river and its three sons (tributaries) was put up in the grotto. But Estonians read the work as an allegory for Germany and the three Baltic provinces, and blew it up early one morning.

Karl Ernst von Baer, Baltic-German scientist, relaxes in the peaceful parkland.

The tiny, pretty, meaningless bridge leading to Musumägi is called the **Bridge of Sighs.** Open air concerts are performed here.
The **sacrificial stone**** by the bridge comes from ancient times, when people made offerings at the sacred Taara oak grove. Each age has its own sacrificial rites: nowadays students burn their lecture notes on the stone after their exams.

Angels, devils and embryologists

Not far from the Bridge of Sighs an elderly man sits in an armchair, an open book in his lap. This is **Karl Ernst von Baer*** (1792-1876), a Baltic-German scientist at the university, founder of embryology and current incumbent on the two-kroon note. The statue was erected with money collected among the town's citizens.
A simple **limestone obelisk** bearing the words "Area Morgensterniana"

stands behind von Baer. Once a high fence stood here to hide the goings-on in the garden from passing ladies. This was a pleasure and exercise garden for students, who were then exclusively male. There were bowling-grounds, swings and gymnastic apparatus. Professor Morgenstern bequeathed the garden to the university.

Two bridges stretch over Lossi St, connecting two peaks of Toome Hill. Neoclassical **Angel Bridge** (1836-38) is closer to the Old Town. A Latin saying, *Otium reficit vires* – "rest restores strength" – greets those climbing the hill. On the other side of the bridge there's a bas-relief of Rector Parrot above the words *Primo Rectori Universitatis Dorpatensis* ("first rector of Dorpat University"). **Devil Bridge** was built in 1913 and dedicated to Alexander I, who reopened the university. There's a 100-year-old custom to hold song concerts on the bridges. Female choirs sing on Angel Bridge and male choirs on Devil Bridge: women were only admitted to the university two years after the Devil Bridge was built.

While the main building of the university was being constructed in 1806, several human skeletons were found in the former Maarja church cemetery and reburied in Toome Hill valley. Their memorial is Tartu's **oldest surviving monument,** known as the "people's monument". It's at the base of the hill below Devil Bridge.

Kristjan Jaak Peterson stands up for the Estonian language.

Museum or clinic?

Soviet power did not enrich Tartu University. Buildings that would be museums in other places still serve their original functions. The university's **internal diseases** and **women's clinics,** either side of the Devil Bridge, and the domed **old anatomical clinic*** are good examples. People are still trained there today. In front of the old anatomical clinic is the bust of **Friedrich Robert Faehlmann,** a doctor and leading light of Estonian culture,

Angel Bridge in the depths of autumn.

At one stage the world's most perfect telescope was in this observatory.

who collected folklore and was the university's first lecturer in Estonian philology. He died while still gathering material about Estonia's traditional hero Kalevipoeg, and the project of writing it up was given to another doctor, Kreutzwald.

A hundred metres further across the hilltop, an ancient settlement and later the great bishop's palace stood. Now there's a former **observatory***. In the first half of the 19th century this observatory, with its 9" Fraunhofer refractor telescope, was one of the world's great centres of astronomy. It was founded by Georg W Struve (1793-1804), whose statue you can see here (not a good likeness). The **Observatory Museum** shows historical astronomical equipment.

Gunpowder cellar, beer cellar or physics lab?

An engineering detachment built a **gunpowder cellar*** *(püssirohukelder)* into Toome hillside. The building was part of a plan of Catherine II's to transform Tartu into a fortified town. There was still gunpowder in the cellar when the plans had been dropped and Toome Hill belonged to Tartu University; it took a power of letter-writing and paper-shuffling to get rid of it. The next owner of the cellar was a brewer named Schramm, who used it for 70 years. Then a Professor Lewitsky decided the stable temperature and solid walls made it an ideal place to instal a pendulum to study earthquakes. More recently the cellar has been renovated into a roomy, atmospheric **restaurant.**

The Soviets refused to see any connection between the old Swedish Academia Gustaviana and the Russo-German university founded in 1802. In 1952, on the 150th anniversary of the *Russian* university, a monument to 19th-century Russian scientist **Nikolai Pirogov** was un-

Town Hall Square is the heart of town.

veiled in a prominent position at the base of Toome Hill, next to Lossi St and behind the town hall. Pirogov, founder of experimental surgery, was a teacher at Tartu.

THE LOWER OLD TOWN

The old merchant town is in the main a neoclassical town centred around the town hall and the university buildings. There are several fine literary monuments along the Emajõgi.

Artistic leanings on Town Hall Square

Town Hall Square***, the heart of Tartu, is on the site of the medieval market. The **town hall** was built in 1782-89. The three-storey building with its hip-roof recalls 17th-century towered Dutch palaces. Buildings on the northern side of the square are venerable and interesting. The so-called "Old University" at no. 6 was built by Baron Ungern-Sternberg in 1789 and sold to the university. The house at 16 Town Hall Square is also imposing. The Great Guild, Bank of Estonia and other important establishments have been quartered here. When the wife of Russo-Scottish general Barclay de Tolly bought the building at 18 Town Hall Square last century it was an upstanding young thing. Today it leans drunkenly like the Tower of Pisa and is known as **Barclay House****. All the old houses of the city have sunk a little because they were built on swampy terrain and stand on oak rafts and posts. One side of the house was set against the medieval town wall, which has started to lean because of car vibration and dropping groundwaters.

In the upper two floors of Barclay House resides a gallery of **Tartu paintings****, one of the best surveys of Estonian art. The gallery is run by the Tartu Art Museum which also has temporary exhibitions at its HQ in 14 Vallikraavi St. It seems amazing that Estonian fine art is essentially a 20th-century thing. The national awakening in the 19th century was powered by literature; the only recognised 19th-century Estonian artists were Johan Köler, who was based in St Petersburg, and the heroic sculptor Amandus Adamson. The first wave of Estonian artists studied at the drawing school of the German Handicraft Society: nouveau/romanticist Kristjan Raud, sculptor Jaan Koort and expressionist Konrad Mägi were educated there. Raud opened an art studio, which also worked as a school, in 1904. Even more important was the Pallas Art Society, founded in Tartu in 1919, which later developed into Estonia's first art institute. The first graduate was the brilliant Eduard Viiralt. The Pallas teachers had travelled to Germany. Later Paris was the main destination and a Pallas "style" developed, similar to the post-impressionism then popular in France. An alternative gathering, the Estonian Artists' Group founded in 1923, showed more of an avant-garde cubist influence.

Unsurprisingly, war and the victory of socialist realism sent Estonian art to the four winds or scrunched it into a Stalinist corner. The stores of Tartu Art Museum hold 20 000 artworks, including several by 19th-century Baltic-German artists, masterpieces from the Pallas times, and made-to-order works by social realists depicting harvests and first-rank lathe operators. Artists gradually gained a measure of freedom from the 1960s on, and have taken up virtually every international style. Today there are galleries and remarkable artists everywhere. The **Tartu Artists' Union** exhibits at 26 Vanemuise St.

The walls of this bar don't shudder – the Gunpowder Cellar.

The impressive university

You can find a great, six-columned, neoclassical building on the narrow street behind the town hall, Ülikooli ("University") St. The **university building***** designed by Johann Wilhelm Krause is one of Tartu's symbols. Krause also designed the observatory, old anatomical theatre and former library-in-a-ruined-church on Toome Hill. This one was a devilish toil to build. About 5000 pine beams were needed as posts and rafts to make the terrain solid under the foundation. Maarja church had previously been there and the ruins of its wall, tombs and basement demanded extra work. On 31 July 1809 the new building was consecrated.

The **ceremonial hall** is in the same style as the building's facade. A vaulted ceiling, mirrors, colonnade, elaborate grating, chandeliers and a neoclassical lectern help to create an air of high pomp at graduations in July. Portraits of all the university's chancellors line the **Hall of the Learned Council**; and in the lobby of the staffroom are portraits of the scientists thanks to whom the university reopened in 1919.

The **Museum of Classical Archaeology** in the left wing was the third largest such museum in the old Soviet Union. Its walls are covered with Pompeii-style frescoes. The museum exhibits copies of classical sculptures, Egyptian mummies, copies of gems, examples of the ancient art of miniature engraving, and so on.

Various departments are housed around the main building. Number

Vanemuine Theatre.

16 Ülikooli St briefly functioned as the main building. There's a cafe and students' dining room at **20 Ülikooli St;** the presses of the first Estonian printing house turned here in 1831. The former University Church, behind the main building, now serves as the philology library and history department. **Gustav Adolf Square*** is just beside it. A bronze statue of Gustav II Adolf stood here since Swedish times. The Soviets sent it for remelting with other "erroneous" statues such as those of Kalevipoeg. In 1989 the king reappeared – made by the students out of snow. And today he is standing there again, in bronze, looking very enlightened.
All these buildings, once houses for students and tutors, together with the row of houses opposite the main building, form a **harmonious group****. The ensemble is completed by a fine baroque building at **1 Gildi St,** home to the editorial staff of *Postimees,* a newspaper that has served national movements last century as well as this one.

Jaani and Lai Sts

Ülikooli St becomes Jaani St, taking its name from **Jaani church**** (St John's). The church was built in 1310 by a Lübeck master and is unique

The new "shopping centre" was built in 1989.

with its tiny clay moulded statues in tiny recesses. Wrecked in three wars (Livonian, Northern and World II), Jaani church is under restoration. When completed it will be one of Estonia's most significant architectural masterpieces. The ugly brick buildings next door were built in Nikita Khrushchev's time: flats were built big, cheaply, and with inadequate kitchens because everyone was supposed to eat in canteens. A quadrangular group of buildings here has been a seat of learning for over 180 years. One of them, **Princess House*** beside the church, belonged to Baroness Tsherkassova (Princess Hedvig of Kuramaa before her marriage) and was left to the Livonian Noblewomen's Institution after her death. The block now belongs to Treffner High School.

The building opposite Princess House was part of the Swedish Tartu University; it was restored in 1766 but in Soviet times served as a **prison,** where in 1941 the NKVD secret service killed 192 people. Now it's a drying-out tank for drunks. A Citizen's Museum is to be set up at 16 Jaani St. A former warehouse at the corner of Lai and Jaani Sts is the **oldest stone building** in Tartu. It dates from the 16th century, and Peter I is said to have taken shelter there during the Northern War. Across the road at 24 Lai St is Tartu's **oldest wooden building,** built in the mid 18th century and restored since, though remnants of a mantle chimney are in their old condition.

Lai St acted as border to the medieval city. Now it has a row of neoclassical buildings and the lovely **botanical gardens**.** In the grounds are the famous palm house, a small rose garden near the first greenhouse (designed by Krause), a couple of monuments and a pond. In one green glade you can find a wooden totem pole celebrating the 350th anniversary of the Swedish university in chilly 1982. In parkland across the street the last few surviving metres of Tartu's **medieval wall** are hidden.

Monuments along the Emajõgi

Along the Emajõgi river, parks have been laid out. A stroll through them is also a journey into Estonian literature. Near the end of Lai St you can see a 1978 monument to Armenian friendship. Further along, opposite the stylish Tartu Commerce Bank, is **Friedrich Reinhold Kreutzwald** (1803-82), composer of the Estonian epic *Kalevipoeg.* Originally Kalevipoeg, the mythical hero himself, had stood on the same spot, a provocative symbol of freedom and independence for Estonians until the Soviets took it away. Kreutzwald replaced him in 1952. Some would like to change the figure of the creator back to that of his creation.

Oskar Luts* (1887-1953) is the Mark Twain of Estonian literature. His novel *The spring* has been a second *Tom Sawyer* for Estonian children for several generations. A monument to him stands further along from Kreutzwald's. (And his home in Riia St is a museum.)

The **cement footbridge** at the bottom of Town Hall Square is another ring-in – here stood that famous symbol of Tartu, the stone bridge erected at the end of the 18th century, bombed in World War II. Former Baltic-Germans have raised a great deal of money to build a new bridge, but some would like to see the money used to help restore Jaani church.

Across the river to the right, a **bronze baby** is sitting on the number 100 000, commemorating the birth of the city's 100 000th citizen in 1977. They left room for a couple more 0s.

To the left there's a flash bust of Estonian literature's greatest stylist, short story writer **Friedebert Tuglas*** (1886-1971). The statue is on the site of the original Treffner High School, which offered schooling to children of the poor. One student, A. H. Tammsaare, is often labelled "Estonia's greatest writer". He set a volume of his masterwork, *Truth and* *justice,* in the school. "Every Estonian schoolchild must learn like a madman," says one character, the schoolmaster Maurus, whose prototype was Hugo Treffner himself. The park is now called Tammsaare Park.

MODERN CENTRE

Tartu people shop around the old market and along Riia St, where you'll find a theatre, museums and memorials.

Green heart of town

Tartu's modern citizens mill around Town Hall Square and Riia Street. The centre of the city has shifted a few hundred metres to the south since medieval times. **Tartu Market*** *(Tartu turg)* is the only building to retain the sense and style of the prewar times when this area was full of shops, hotels, cafes, clubs and student buildings. After the bombardment in 1944, the ruins of central Tartu were mainly replaced by greenery. Arnold Matteus, chief architect of the town, considered the preservation of the town centre, empty as it is, his main achievement. The market is the only European-style covered market in Estonia.

The **department store** on Riia St demonstrates bleach architectural styles of the sixties. A more pleasing new **"shopping centre"** *(kaubahall)* lies uphill from the Tartu Market. It's part of a planned new commercial district.

Barclay Square

A **monument to Barclay de Tolly** stands in the middle of Barclay Square just near the shopping centre. As well as the house in Town Hall Square, Madame de Tolly owned an estate in Jõgeveste, Valgamaa; she's buried there in a mausoleum with her husband. The first **parking meter** in Estonia opened in Poe St in October 1992. **Illegaard Photo Gallery** is in a cellar off Ülikooli St north of Barclay Square. In 1983 Tartu daringly opened the first nude photo exhibition in the Soviet Union here. The gallery still exhibits today.

Theatre, theatre ...

The birth of Estonian theatre is tinged with sexual irony. At the end of the 19th century Estonian audiences were too puritanical to accept actresses on stage. Yet the national theatre was founded by a woman, Lydia Koidula, a poet of the national awakening era. Lydia Jannsen, penname Koidula ("dawn"), was the daughter of a nationalist newspaper editor; she wrote and directed the first Estonian plays, though to her great regret she had to cast men in female roles. Inspired by the birth of Finnish National Theatre, the first Estonian play *Cousin from Saaremaa* was staged in 1870. Find out more about Koidula in the Pärnumaa chapter.

That stern face belongs to Oskar Luts, great comic novelist.

The 1967 version of the **Vanemuine Theatre** stands above the shopping centre where there was once the handsomest theatre in the Baltics; the current model isn't. Today, opera, ballet and drama companies live under the same roof and there are two theatres, this large monster and a little one further along Vanemuise St (see below). In Estonia several small centres such as Tartu, Viljandi and Pärnu have substantial

Treffner School educated the poor.

theatres. In the '70s and '80s the theatre was usually the only place where one could say what one really thought. Of course one had to say it in theatrical language!
Every town occupied by the Soviets had a Lenin statue. Tartu's stood up Riia St in front of the **Agriculture Academy** until 1990, when independence demonstrators put a noose around his neck, hoisted him in the air with a crane and paraded him around the city for half an hour ... without the approval of the city authorities. There was great controversy over where to put Lenin and the other anti-republican monuments. One idea was to create a Stalinland of monuments to Soviet saints, examples of characteristic architecture, a museum of the KGB, together with various entertainments – interrogations, trials, sentences in squalid prison cells, tortures – according to the client's taste, nervous system and wallet-size. The Agriculture Academy grew out of the university. The building used to belong to the Defence Union, a military organisation in the first Estonian Republic, making Lenin's placement especially symbolic.

And the cornflower wept

The people of Tartu have felt the claws of state oppression for centuries. Deportations were carried out in the Livonian War (1558-83) and Northern War (1700-21). In Soviet times the scale of oppression increased. Between the October Revolution in 1917 and the Estonian Republic on 24 February 1918, 154 Tartu people were deported to Siberia. In December 1918 the Soviet government took power for 24 days and killed 300 more. During the next brief period of Soviet occupation 200 were killed in Tartu just on 8 July 1941. Exact details about the victims of deportation and murder during the German occupation are unavailable. One place where people were tortured and murdered in Tartu is the so-called **"Grey House"**, further along on Riia St, home of the KGB until 1955. Tartu District Administration now works here. A **monument of a weeping cornflower** was put up across the street in 1990 – the cornflower (in Estonian *rukkilill*, "rye-flower") is the national flower.
The **Sports Museum*** at 27a Riia St is a rather enjoyable introduction to Estonian sports history. It's in an an-

nexe to a modernist church, St Paul's, designed by the Finnish architect Eliel Saarinen.

Along Vanemuise St

The Vanemuine Theatre's beautiful **Small Theatre*** behind St Paul's used to be the German Theatre, which burnt down but was restored and reopened in 1990. The **water-tower*** across the park dates from 1939.

Heading back down the hill you pass the **Zoological Museum***, which has a reasonably stuffed collection of animalia from across the globe, and the **FR Kreutzwald Literature Museum***, as much an exhibition as an archive and research institution. Jakob Hurt's collection of folk poetry is its most valuable treasure. The archive includes almost all publications printed in Estonia or about Estonians. The **Treaty of Tartu** was signed at 35 Vanemuise St, then 35 Aia St.

Here, in 1869, the first National Song Festival was held.

ETC ...

Around Veski St there are more museums and some fine buildings. Tartu's cemeteries are historic and beautiful.

Museums behind Toome Hill

The area around Veski, Von Baer and Kuperjanovi Sts is a historic district of stone and wooden houses.

Singing everywhere in summer.

Oru St begins just below Kissing Hill. At **Tartu City Museum*** you can see the history of Tartu from the town's birth until now. Next to the museum, **Meelis and Vyatshko*** gaze into the wide green bowl below, planning tactics. Originally made in 1952 for the anniversary of Tartu as a Russian university, this most political sculpture was kept in the museum and only moved outside in 1980. Around the corner in Veski St part of **Karl von Baer's house** has been preserved as a museum in his honour.

The current home of the **Estonian National Museum*** is round the corner in Veski St. The National Museum was founded in 1909 based on collections begun in the late 19th century. Its heyday began in 1922 when Ilmari Manninen, a Finnish ethnographer, was appointed director. The museum opened in **Raadi estate,** north of the Emajõgi but still in Tartu, and quickly became one of the most visited spots in the country. People remember the view over the pond towards the white palace where there were 30 halls full of treasures. In 1940 this came to an end. The manor was set on fire and taken by the Soviet army which only recently moved out, having allowed the manor house itself to fall into ruin.

The museum holds 850 000 ethnographic items, among them 100 000 material objects. What it doesn't have is room for a permanent exhibition. Currently a single room of the building in Veski St serves, but they hope to move across the road to the Railway Club building in the next few years. Fingers crossed.

Monuments, graves and swimming spots

Over the Emajõgi there are several cemeteries on the top of the valley slope. In **Uus Jaani cemetery** along the road to Narva you can find war graves and the bust of the school principal Treffner. **Raadi cemetery**** is one of Estonia's finest. The headstones oft show a more artistic bent than usual. Kreutzwald, von Baer, Hurt, Uku and Otto Masing, Wirkhaus, and Rector Parrot himself are all buried here.

Not far away, across from St Peter's church, a monument erected in 1959 marks the spot where the **first Estonian Song Festival** took place in the high days of the Estonian national movement. This was an event of special significance, for it began a tradition that lives till today, climaxing with the "Singing Revolution" in the late 1980s. In 1869 in Tartu, 46 choirs with 800 male singers and four brass bands performed in front of 15 000 at the first Song Festival. Although choir music is of an exceptional standard in Tartu, composers and performers tend to live in Tallinn, and the national song festival is now held there. Tartu still provides fine concert halls at which the masters from the capital can perform. The current song ground is on the south side of the Emajõgi near **Tähtvere manor** on the way to Tallinn.

Komsomol Cinema*, erected in a shock-work campaign, shows how the centre might have been, full of stalinist works, though at least these are preferable to the Soviet-modernist buildings of the 1960s. Now the cinema is aptly called Illusion. You can find it in Raatuse St, not far from the road and foot bridges across the Emajõgi.

Half a kilometre south-east of there, the high-rise suburb of Anne towers over the best swimming spot in Tartu, the **Anne Kanal.**

And the cornerstone

The era of education for Estonians began in earnest in 1684, when Bengt Gottfried Forselius founded the first Estonian Teachers Seminary. In its first four years, 160 country-school teachers graduated, and a proud Forselius took four of his pupils to the King of Sweden to demonstrate the fruits of his work. There's a **memorial stone** to him in a park on Tähe St on the south side of town.

A very educational town, Tartu.

The Museum of Zoology is a haunt for wild animals and little folk.

PRACTICAL DETAILS

HOTELS

"Taru", 9 Rebase, tel 7 37 00
"Park", 23 Vallikraavi, tel 3 36 63
"Tartu", 3 Soola, tel 3 20 91
"Pro", 13 Tuglase, tel 6 18 53
"Salima", 1 Kopli, tel 7 08 88
"Rändur", 25 Vasara, tel 7 56 91
"Sepa", 26 Sepa, tel 7 24 94
"Remark" guest-house, 94 Tähe, tel 7 77 44
"Tare" motel, Tähtvere vald, Ilmatsalu asula, tel 9 91 45

RESTAURANTS

"Tarvas", 2 Riia, tel 3 22 53
"Kaunas", 2 Narva mnt., tel 3 48 47
"Kaseke", 19 Tähe, tel 7 06 08
"Püssirohukelder" (The Gunpowder), 28 Lossi, tel 3 42 31
"Fox", 9 Rebase, tel 7 39 54
"Volga", 10 Küütri, tel 3 39 60
"Taverna", Raekoja plats
"Rüütli kelder", 1 Rüütli
"Pro Studiorum", 13 Tuglase, tel 6 13 86
"Sigma", 1 Filosoofi, tel 3 70 70

BARS & CAFES

"Avar", 12 Tiigi
"Jaani", 14 Lutsu
"Grill Bar", 2 Narva mnt.
"Kassioru", 3 Näituse
"Cavern", 5 Ilmatsalu
"Oskar", 52 Kreutzwaldi

"Otto", 116 Tähe, tel 7 06 38
"Säde", 2 Küüni
"Rukkilill", 2 Tuglase
"Kokoko", 5 Küütri
"Silva", 2 Tuglase
"Visiit", 23 Vallikraavi
"Saloon", 15 Rahu, tel 7 17 79
"Sigma", 1 Filosoofi
"Männi", 40 Anne, tel 3 62 15
"Taverna", 20 Raekoja plats

MUSEUMS

City Museum, 2. Oru, tel 3 20 33
Fr. R. Kreutzwaldi Literary Museum, 42. Vanemuise, tel 3 33 96
Art Museum, 14. Vallikraavi, tel 3 25 21
Anton Starkopf Museum, 2. Vilde, tel 6 20 64
Kivisilla Art Gallery, 18. Rajekoja plats, tel 3 30 63
Estonian National Museum, 32 Veski, tel 3 22 54
K. E. von Baer's House, 4 Veski, tel 3 35 14
Zoology museum, 46. Vanemuise, tel 3 47 44
Tartu University History Museum, Toomemägi, tel 3 26 35
Student Museum, 61. Veski, tel 3 30 03
Tartu Observatory, Toomemägi, tel 3 49 32
Oskar Luts Museum, 38. Riia, tel 3 37 05
Karl Ristikivi Museum, 18. Hermanni, tel 61 745
Tartu University Classical Art and Antiguities Museum, 18. Ülikooli, tel 3 14 14
Sports Museum, 27a. Riia, tel 3 46 02
Botanical Garden, 40. Lai, tel 3 26 43

TRAVEL BUREAUS

E-tour, 59. Kalevi, tel 3 21 23
Teele, 35. Lai, tel 3 33 70
Alexela, 4. Rüütli, tel 3 30 70
Livoni Reisibüroo, 28. Vanemuise, tel 3 09 56

FILLING STATIONS

Külitse, Valga, tel 9 73 44
Aardla, Võru, tel 3 17 13
52. Ringtee, tel 2 88 64

CAR SERVICE

21. Sepa, tel 7 48 16
56. Ringtee 56, tel 2 87 75
2a. Tulbi, tel 2 89 80

TRANSPORT

Bus Station, 2 Turu., tel 7 53 55
Railway Sation, 6 Vaksali., tel 3 09 37
Airplane tickets, 10 Võru., tel 3 24 55
River harbour, 5 Soola, tel 3 45 53
"Marser" (Ship tickets Helsinki), 45-40 Mõisavahe, tel 3 71 38

TELEPHONE AREA CODE: 234

PÕLVAMAA

Area: 2165 Km^2	**Capital: Põlva,**
Population: 36 150	**population 7270**

This small county in south-eastern Estonia is rooted in the land, with traditional farmsteads, watermills and rural churches. Winding old roads and deep riverbeds with outcrops of sandstone twist and turn among the hills and lakes. Restaurants and hotels tend to be few and far between, but there are plenty of lovely places where you can put up a tent.

Ethnically the territory is splintered. Though 90% of the population is Estonian, there are old Russian communities in Räpina and on the shore of Lake Peipsi. Traditionally the Russians have built villages within shouting distance of each other and grown onions and cucumbers, which is why Estonians call them "onion-Russians". The eastern part of the county around Värska is the land of the Setu people, who briefly had their own county in the 1920s and 1930s after centuries of Russian rule. Setumaa today is a mix of Setu, Estonian, Russian and other national traditions, some of which have died out elsewhere.

PÕLVA

Põlva is a small, often pretty rural town.

Town in the valley

The valley of the river Ora, spilling over with greenery, and a reservoir at its centre make **Põlva*** rather picturesque. A walk or drive around the lake offers some postcard views, especially when you can see the bright red **church tower**. According to an old tale, the town earned its name when the church was being built. At Satan's command, everything built during the day was destroyed at night. He was only placated when a kneeling virgin ("knee" = *põlv* in Estonian) was immured alive into the wall. The building with the wire hat that now dominates the town is the **community centre,** a sibling to Paide's in Järvamaa. It opened in 1991. It's rather large for such a small town, but Põlva's population has been increasing steadily from only 700 in the 1940s when it first became a county capital. If you walk or drive along the Võru road south of Põlva you soon pass a motocross track on the left while just

All singing, all dancing traditions.

over the hill to the right is Põlva's song festival ground. Then you reach **Rosma***, a tiny village with a mill and gardens. Behind the village is the site of an ancient **hill-fort:** most of the earthen defences have survived. A settlement once lay at the base of the hill.

NORTH & WESTWARDS

Põlvamaa's most famous attraction, Taevaskoja, is right near Põlva. Kanepi and Valgjärve to the west are laketowns set in farming land.

Sky chamber

If you drive north-west towards Tartu, a right turn after 5 km takes you to Taevaskoja railway station. Keep going 1.5 km further, where a signpost points to the right to *Väike ja Suur Taevaskoja* in the Ahja River valley. The parking station is near a weir and the small hydroelectric Saesaare power station. You're a short walk from **Taevaskoja**** ("sky chamber").

A broad forest path leads downstream to **Väike Taevaskoja** ("small Taevaskoja"), a low sandstone cliff gouged from the valley by the Ahja river. The crag, 190 m long and 13 m high, is continued upward by a wall of lordly pines. A small bridge leads over the Emaläte ("river source"), whose pure water issues from a tunnel that curves back into blackness. This way climbs above the cliff and leads to the top of Suur Taevaskoja.

To see the cliff from below, cross the larger bridge and pass the **maiden's cave** *(Neitsikoobas).* If you listen carefully you can hear a maiden's cry and the shuttling of her loom. The flaxen-haired virgin in the cave has been weaving for an age. On midsummer's eve she reveals herself, though only to those who can find a **fern flower.** Scientists say that no such flower exists, but is anything impossible on St John's eve?

Continue downstream to **Suur**

Suur-Taevaskoja's just a bend in the Ahja River.

"Cave drawings" at Väike-Taevaskoja.

Taevaskoja ("great Taevaskoja") itself, 24 m high. *Taevas* means both "sky" and "heaven" in Estonian. Standing on the natural lawn across the river, an old place for local celebrations, you have the sense of being somewhere sacred. This hasn't stopped people from signing every reachable part of wall, and even some spots that aren't so reachable. The rock is 150 m long, and its layers of pink, burnt orange, cream and gold sandstone, some swirled and candy-striped together, are up to 500 million years old. Completing the scene is a large, oddly-shaped block at the edge of the rapids called Nõiakivi ("witch's stone").

You can get back to Väike Taevaskoja along the top of the cliff, and a trail leads upstream along the right hand side back to the weir. From here, you might like to hike on along the river to **Kiidjärve***, or even further to the woody summer village of Valgemetsa, where there's a witch's house. Alternatively you can get to Kiidjärve, a pretty river-town with a millpond and a working three-storey watermill, by road.

Childhood

In the village of **Ahja,** north of here, lived one of Estonia's literary heroes, Little Illimar, from Friedebert Tuglas's children's story. Older Estonians visit this corner of the country hoping to relive a sentimental novel of village childhood. What remains of Ahja itself is a wreck of a manor house with a nice lake in an ordinary village. They'd be better off visiting Kiidjärve or Valgjärve.

There's a manor ensemble with a smart facade at **Mooste,** south-east of Ahja. South of Ahja towards Vastse-Kuuste there's a unique **wildlife reserve,** which you may not visit, because walking 1 km through it you could destroy 300 lives. The 200 ha honeydew ant reserve includes over 1200 nests, the oldest dating back to the 1830s, the highest reaching 2.3 m.

Threshers and schooldesks

The road leading west from Kiidjärve crosses the Tartu-Põlva road; keep going, and turn left onto the Tartu-Võru road. Not 1 km south you come upon old buildings, a fine windmill that you can go inside, ancient steam tractors, threshing machines and all kinds of household equipment. It's a former school, now a **farm museum*** where you can see an evocative classroom from last century. About half the museum's buildings are used by locals and therefore unvisitable, including the traditional smoke sauna. The collection is not systematic: the windmill isn't typical for the region; that bizarre collection of neat bushes is in fact a model of Põlvamaa in shrubs!

South and then west of here is **Kanepi,** reached through lake-spotted valleys. The statue at the south end of Kanepi's **cemetery** was created by one of Estonia's greatest sculptors, August Weizenberg, and is called "Hope". The figure decorates the tomb of the sculptor's family. The Estonian on the back translates: "Here is my happiness, my world, my heaven, and here dies my last memory." Kanepi's church is also lovely. You can swim in Põlvamaa's largest and deepest lake, on the northern side of town.

Driving towards Tartu from Kanepi you reach **Kalevipoeg's boat,** a 2.3 m high chunk of rock at Sirvaste near the Palava busstop. Estonia's epic hero is thought to have hidden his golden oars and golden-fingered gloves under the boat.

Village turns into lake

At Saverna your way goes to the left, to **Valgjärve*** ("white lake"). A nearby hill gives you a good view over the lake. Before Valgjärve, Valgeküla ("white village") stood here. One day, when the villagers were celebrating a marriage, they refused to let a beggar and his little son inside. That night it rained so heavily that the village and all its people drowned. Stop at the community centre and walk through the **manor park***, through a delicious deciduous wood, including some grand oaks. A drive around the lake via Puugi reveals shifting scenery of typically rural Estonia – rolling hills populated with various sorts of woods, people leading cattle or working outside sheds, wooden houses and some new collective farm buildings.

The top of **Valgjärve TV tower** is 500 m above sea level, making it the highest point in the land – the tower transmits TV to the whole of southern Estonia. Valgjärve is a hop, skip and a jump from the lakeland around Otepää in northern Valgamaa.

EAST & SOUTHWARDS

Southern Põlvamaa has some of the loveliest country scenery in Estonia. The south-east is the heartland of the Setu people.

Comsomol shock-work

Off to Lake Peipsi now, via a small, drab building of grand historical importance at Leevaku. In 1947 the first Comsomol shock-work assignment in Estonia was created here – the **Leevaku power station.** Comsomol was the Communist Party's youth organisation. Membership was not compulsory, but it was advisable if you wanted a university education, for example. While the gigantic dams, canals and roads of Stalin's five-year-plans were built by "prisoners", Comsomol members were drafted into smaller projects like Leevaku. The poet Juhan Smuul wrote a poen to the power station, which children had to study at school. In a blast of propaganda it was put into operation on 7 November, the anniversary of the Great Socialist October Revolution. A little later, certain faults turned up. It was rechristened a museum of youth and given to the "ideological education" service. It never did operate as a

Lords of the lake.

Reflections of wee Orsava village in Värska's river.

museum. At least the weir is pretty.
The main town of eastern Põlvamaa is **Räpina.** By the reservoir you can find neoclassical **Sillapea manor.** The country's biggest school of horticulture has settled in the ensemble of manor buildings, parks and gardens. Tree-lovers can practise their Estonian plant-names. The only thing worth looking at inside the main building is the view from the balcony. To get to the manor, turn right when you cross the reservoir, and follow the road round the lake.
The Võhandu river flows into Lake Peipsi near **Võõpsu.** One-street villages, fishing boats and drying nets are a sure sign of a Russian fishing settlement.

Setu singer

Setumaa** begins at Võõpsu. The poorest area of Estonia is also one of the most interesting. Setu people have their own traditions, a mingling of the Russian and Estonian. They are mostly Orthodox Christians, yet their language is similar to Estonian and they consider themselves Estonian. During the last time of independence Setumaa was a separate county, now sadly dismembered: two-thirds of their territory is currently under Russian rule, and the culture is in decay. Few speak pure Setu now; instead the tongue is a melange of Setu and Estonian. The historical market town, Petseri, is stuck behind the border.
Setus tend to live in tiny groups of 5-8 houses, which you see from the road throughout Setumaa. Groups of these form villages. The people are most renowned for their unearthly **singing.** The music is unforgettable, but tourists usually only hear it at folk festivals. You may be lucky. When larger villages have parties or weddings, people gather from all over the region to listen. Every village has its own sounds. In days gone by, songs might be im-

A late passenger on the Värska inlet.

provised for hours. The full women's costume included a silver ornament weighing several kilograms worn round the neck. If you're *very* lucky you might witness a village declaring itself a nation, setting up roadblocks and electing a monarch.

You can discover a piece of Setumaa's history on your way to Värska. At Karisilla busstop a left along rough roads leads to Võporzova and Tonja, two classic Setu villages. **Võporzova*** is a network of houses linked by gardens and gates. Near the river there's a memorial to the greatest ever Setu folksinger. Anne Vabarna knew over 100 000 verses of folk-songs – of all Balto-Finnic people she handed down the greatest number of songs to the next generation. It was a Finnish specialist in folklore, Väisänen, who found Vabarna in 1923, after which the Setu singer became an inexhaustible treasury to all folklore collectors until her death in 1964. Nearby **Tonja** is a straight one-street village, the yards of all eight farms facing the lake.

Deep Setumaa

The land is sinking and Lake Pihkva now often floods little Värska inlet, which has great reserves of curative mud. Värska mineral water makes for a healthier tipple than Tallinn's water supply. **Värska*** town is on the other side of the inlet. A little harbour, school, mud resort, Orthodox church and Setu culture centre are all here. Song festivals take place at the local song-ground.

Saatse is almost in Russia. On the way you cross an Estonian checkpoint. Don't worry about a Russian visa here. This isn't the actual border. The guards are trying to police a difficult frontier, one which Estonia doesn't recognise anyway. Saatse's Setu Museum is small and down-at-heels (key available at the yellow

Setu harmonies can seem unearthly.

building on the left with the small statues in the yard).

The beautiful south

Northwest from Värska, a turn onto the Petseri road leads into beautiful southern Põlvamaa. Petseri's splendid **monastery**** is currently locked away inside Russia; so is the picturesque **Mõla church*** by a lake in a valley. For an accessible lake, turn right at Soe towards Orava, then left after 3 km onto a soft road. Over a thousand beavers inhabit southeastern Estonia. You may well see some in **Kõvera forest lake.** *Kõver* means "crooked" – a good description of this narrow, clean, dog's-hind-leg of a lake. **Piusa*,** south of Orava and Kliima villages, is a sand-mining centre, so careful of getting stuck on sandy roads! On the left outside town, there's a tremendous open pit, a display of sandstone left by miners. A subterranean labyrinth of caves lies between the village and the railway. The most impressive cave is also the easiest to reach and safest to explore, **Sammaskoobas*** ("column cave"). Follow the *kauplus* sign: the caves are up the hill behind the shop. Chambers up to 6 m high covering about 400 m^2 are as shivery as tombs of pharaohs. From 1922 to 1966 sand for glassworks was mined here with pickaxes. Some pickaxe scars can still be seen on the columns.

Hell's grave

Back through Orava take a left towards Ilumetsa along a road dotted with sweet villages and stop at the parking place, **Põrguhaud**** ("hell's grave"). Follow the signs through Põrguväravad ("gates of hell") to an eery circular lake, 12.5 m from lip to bottom. A church once sank beneath the earth here when three brothers entered it. Since then, Põrguhaud has been a haunt for devils. It's particularly risky to call a

In defence of Petseri's monastery.

Põdramüür ("elk wall") relaxes in the sunshine on the Võhandu River.

devil by name, because the demon may well materialise at once. For centuries the locals avoided the place, apart from the bravest lads who only looked from a distance. Scientists claim this is the biggest of a group of three meteorite craters, all about a kilometre apart. The other two – "deep grave" and "devil's grave" – are harder to find. Either explanation, the legend or the scientific story of a rock puncturing three round wounds in the earth's side, gives pause for thought.
Estonia also has the famous Kaali crater on Saaremaa island, and there are many more pocked across the country. Nowhere else in the world are there so many quality meteorite craters per head of population.

Võhandu's charms

West of Ilumetsa is Veriora. The left to Lepassaare travels by the Nohipalu lakes: **Valgejärv** ("white lake") and **Mustjärv** ("black lake"). You might like to camp here, if you've got the essentials with you.
North of **Leevi**, on both sides of the **valley of the Võhandu river****, stand sandstone walls, sometimes 20 m high. An overgrown hiking trail starts across the river from the Leevi watermill. Or you can get to a parking spot by turning left at the stone

Where miners have dug for sand, a mini-canyon remains.

barn on the north-east edge of Leevi. The view of the **Viira watermill** from the top of the cliff halfway along the river is especially pretty. During the Northern War (1700-29) the local people took refuge in one of the biggest caves, **Sõjatare** ("war cottage"). The enemy, camped across the river, noticed nothing. Unfortunately, a cat strayed from the encampment, climbed the rocks and suddenly disappeared. Looking for the cat the soldiers discovered Sõjatare and some hundred frightened people. They burnt them to death inside. Rather than hike, you might like to explore the Võhandu on a canoe or boat trip.
Põlva is 20-odd km north-west of here, along more country roads with some serious bends.

PRACTICAL DETAILS

ACCOMODATION

"Pesa" hotel, 5. Uus, Põlva, tel 9 00 86
Taevaskoja hostel, Põlva, tel 44 72 74 (Tallinn)
Värska camping
Värska sanatoorium, tel 9 47 93, phone 9 46 39
Tonja camping

RESTAURANTS

"Põlva", 10. Kesk, Põlva, tel 9 50 55
"Võhandu", 29. Vööpsu, Räpina, tel 9 12 96

BARS & CAFES

Põlva, tel 9 69 90
Ahja, tel 9 71 58
Jõksi, tel 9 78 48
Saarjärve, tel 9 25 65
Tilsi, tel 9 91 82

MUSEUMS

Põlva Peasantry Museum, Karilatsi, tel 9 92 13
Setu Museum, Saatse
J. Käisi Museum, Rosma, Põlva

FILLING STATIONS

70. Jaama, Põlva, phone 9 60 06
18. Räpina mnt., Räpina, phone 2 12 23

CAR SERVICE

18. Räpina mnt., Räpina, tel 2 12 23
16. Piiri, Põlva
Kauksi
Kanepi
Vana-Koiola
Põlva, Tännassilma
Põlva KEK, tel 95 696

TELEPHONE AREA CODE: 230

VÕRUMAA

Area: 2305 Km²	Capital: Võru,
Population: 45 360	population 17 900

The highest hills, vast valleys, the deepest lakes and swiftest rivers, old watermills still turning, horses dragging heavy loads, tidy farms scattered across the countryside, country folk speaking in dialect – this is Võrumaa. Võrumaa, with Võru 265 km from Tallinn, is the furthest county from the capital. Its core is the Haanja Highlands, and its highest point is Suur Munamägi ("great egg hill"), at 318 m the highest hill in the Baltic states. Rapid rivers start in the Haanja Highlands, and over 170 lakes lie among the hills. Most are deep and tiny, and in some places, such as the lake district in Rõuge, gorgeous archipelagos of lakes have formed. Good maps for hiking along the many tracks are available from Võru's Kalev sports society.

Elsewhere Võrumaa is plain. In the south-west of the county mighty forests grow. The people live by farming, and almost all are Estonian. In the county's north-east corner the Setu folk live in their tiny villages.

VÕRU

The county capital is a small country town surrounded by marshes, factories and a lake.

Võru* was established by order of Empress Catherine II in 1784 to be the centre of a tiny part of the Russian Empire where there were no large towns. The town grew rapidly from the end of the 19th century up to the year 1944 when it was virtually levelled during World War II. Several old wooden houses and stone buildings in the centre survived the devastation.

Legend's cradle

One house in Kreutzwaldi Street has a special meaning for Estonians. The doctor who lived and worked there last century was Friedrich Reinhold Kreutzwald (1803-82). He put

Where's our place, Dad?

together Estonia's national epic *Kalevipoeg* in the garret of this very house, which is now a **memorial museum*** to him. That's his original plaque on the door. The house, sauna and cellar retain their original look. His furniture, books, medical instruments and correspondence have been conserved.

At the time of the national awakening, Estonian intellectuals felt that their people needed an epic. After all, the Finns had one, the *Kalevala*. Kalevipoeg ("Kalev's son") was a popular figure from local legends, a good-hearted though bumbling figure responsible for the shape of the land, a fairytale hero spoken of round the cottage fire. Kreutzwald put ads in newspapers asking for legends and contributions, and travelled the country in search of tales. *Kalevipoeg's* importance now tends to be historical rather than literary. The poem was one of several galvanising forces in the national awakening, and the first edition was banned. But most of the material came from Kreutzwald's own childhood home, southern Virumaa, and anthropologists dispute just how ancient the stories really are. Kreutzwald went on to produce Estonian almanacs and reference books and to have a platonic love affair with the poet Lydia Koidula. There's a statue of him by Adamson in the park on the shore of Lake Tamula, a favourite spot of the townspeople.

Baroque 18th-century **St Catherine church** in Jüri Street has a theatre-set altar and pulpit. The **Võru Museum** at the corner of Koidula and Kreutzwaldi Streets is rather good.

Just out of town on the Rõuge road is a quiet place, complete with pine forest and motel, **Kubija.** The Tourism Centre here organises canoe trips and walking tours, some lasting several days, in Põlvamaa and Võrumaa. English-speaking instructors can be hired.

NORTHWARDS

A ruin and a manor.

Below Kreutzwald, the god of song pauses to listen.

The ruins of **Kirumpää bishop's castle** lie outside Võru to the left of the road. They're on a hillock just before the Võhandu River, and date from the 14th century.

Further north, an agricultural school has been established in **Väimela's baroque manor.** There's a view from the house of lakes on three sides, including the overgrown manor lake surrounded by broad-leaved trees.

WEST SIDE

Estonia's thickest oak, a church on a valley, and relentless beauty.

A valley with an oak

West of Võru along the Antsla road, you pass Lake Vagula and reach Sõmerpalu. Here flows the **Pühajõgi** ("holy river"). A water sprite lives in its waters, which twist and turn between steep banks. The Pühajõgi has been considered a holy river since ancient times – in sacred groves along its banks, sacrifices were made to the thunder.

Further west **Lake Lõõdla** appears to the left. This is the southernmost lake of the unspoilt **Urvaste valley.** Driving on the sideroads around here, the beauty is relentless. The valley is steep and deep and long lakes such as the Uhtjärv lounge along its length. About 200 m north of Urvaste village school is the oak with the largest circumference in Estonia, 8.1 m. It's known as **Tamme-Lauri**** *(tamm* means "oak" in Estonian). Oaks were believed to be holy trees in ancient times. Food, fabric, beads and other offerings were made to them. Several of these "1000-year-old" trees still grow in open fields, untouched by local farmers, though scientists tell us that most of them are half the age that custom says they are. There's a small door in the tree, and in the hollow were found a German machine gun and a diary from about 1950: the Forest Brothers, those partisans who continued to resist the Soviets well into the 1950s, used the tree as a hideout. So it's fitting that Tamme-Lauri appears on the 10-kroon note, based on a painting by Gunther Reindorff.

Estonians at the sacred Tamme-Lauri oak in Urvaste.

To the south-west, poised on a hillside, is Võrumaa's oldest church. **Urvaste church**** has a noble front. It was built as a basilica and fortress church some time before it was first chronicled in 1413, though it's been reshaped drastically since. One of its pastors was the first to translate the bible into Estonian ... and in the south Estonian dialect. Alas plague took the man in 1657 and his version was never printed, so a later north Estonian translation became the standard and the northern dialect became standard Estonian. A century later another pastor, Johannes Quant, was the first to translate fiction into Estonian. At the Urvaste pastorate you can ask about how to find a forest where the locals have created a menagerie from trees.

To the Latvian border

South of Urvaste beyond Antsla the **Karula Highlands** begin. A favourite lake for painters is the **Ähijärv***, with its little coves and islands.

South of the Ähijärv, you reach **Mõniste's Village Museum***, actually in Kuutsi and some 45 km from Võru. A chimneyless hut and sauna, a teepee-shaped summer kitchen, a granary and a well were all built here in traditional local style. A 25 000-year-old mammoth's tooth, baskets for brooding hens and a horse-powered standing saw are some of the collection's oddities. The river Mustjõgi, which flows across the floodplain, grows to 1 km wide during the spring thaw.

Heathen's land

While driving along the road parallel to the frontier you can find the tracks of Vanapagan ("Old Heathen", an enemy of Kalevipoeg in Estonian folklore). The area round **Krabi** is called **Paganamaa**** ("heathen's land") and the Paganamaa Lakes are the old man's footprints. Several hiking tracks, which visit bogs, stone graves,

The Mustjõgi ("black river") isn't black.

springs and "the footprints of Vanapagan", start at the parking place outside Krabi. There's a 20 m high observation tower nearby and a good lake to swim in, the **Liivajärv.** Heading north in the direction of Võru you cross the **Pärlijõgi** ("pearl river"). The czar's court was ravenous for treasure found in this river: *Margaritifera,* fresh-water oysters, which make pearls. Thousands of the animals were slaughtered for every pearl found.

THE HAANJA HIGHLANDS

The south-eastern part of Võrumaa is a scrumptious rural highland. Many roads wander through the traditional farming landscape; not all are mentioned here.

Valley of the nightingale

Rõuge*** is 14 km south of Võru and 17 km north of Krabi. For many this village is in the midst of Estonia's most beautiful scenery. **Rõuge church** sits in a poetical pose up the side of the valley, while below seven spring-fed lakes rest patiently. Across the street from the church is an intrepid monument to the War of Independence, one of several in the country kept hidden on a private

A legendary spring, Paganamaa Neitsiallikas ("maiden's spring in heathen land").

farm during Soviet rule. The valley is called **Ööbikuorg** ("nightingale valley") because the birds sing constantly through the spring. The **Suurjärv** ("great lake") is the deepest lake in Estonia at 38 m; it served Kalevipoeg as a well.

If you turn off the Vastseliina road where the sign points to Ööbikuorg, then turn right into the parking space and climb, you come to the top of an ancient hill-fort site. The valley is laid out below you. Again from the parking place, follow the path eastwards along the rim of the valley past fields to a farmhouse, then descend at the green railing. This takes you down to the valley floor. Over 20 springs bubble from this side of the valley, and in springtime they can form geysers. One of them is connected to a type of artesian well known as a "water ram", built in 1939 and still pumping. Water falling 1 m from a spring is circulated 20 m uphill to the farm at the top of the valley. In the winter hills of ice freeze round it.

The same Ööbikuorg road continues to **Kure dendrarium,** the biggest private dendrarium in the country. Over 400 species of trees and bushes grow here, some rare.

From the edge of a cloud ...

The road curls around the hills to Haanja. The 19 "mountains" in the highlands have created a sodden microclimate where annual precipitation is about 800 mm and snowfall is twice as heavy as Võru's. About 40 000 people a year climb to the top of the neat, 1930s-design observation tower on **Suur Munamägi**** (tower closed in winter). At 318 m above sea level this is the highest hill in the Baltic states. On a clear day you can see the Tartu TV tower and the towers of Pihkva 80 km away. Down steps on the east side of the observation tower is **Kunder's Stone.** The poet Juhan Kunder was so struck by the view that he sat down on this stone and wrote verses now familiar to Estonians. "From here, from the edge of a cloud..." he began.

Haanja's soil is poor – its people depended on handicrafts to make ends meet. Farm people have long made wagons, sledges, spinning-wheels and baskets, and since the 19th century pipes have been made for sale. The Kriisa brothers from this area built most of Estonia's pipe organs.

Relentless beauty

The road south of Haanja passes tatty Ruusmäe manor, with its enclosed courtyard, and comes to the Riga-Pihkva highway. Towards Riga, a turn towards Sarise passes a

Rõuge Liinjärv is deep, very deep.

The Haanja Highlands seen from the highest peak in the Baltics.

small farm belonging to one Viktor Kuklane: his **dendrarium*** is younger than the Kure dendrarium, but the farm is idyllically situated and boasts some naive sculptures with nationalist themes and an island the man himself made from a bend in the river. He's happy for you to look around.

Harvest time.

Towards Pihkva (Pskov) you come to **Misso,** in the most south-easterly region of Estonia. **Lake Hino*** south of Misso has several islands. If you go north through Vana-Saaluse, the road is relentlessly beautiful. **Lake Kavadi**** is in Uue-Saaluse. There's a **view** of the lake from the south, and you can cross onto an island in the lake along the Räpo road. The manor house on the island is a ruin, and you can camp if you don't mind the mosquitoes. Võru is a few km to the north-west.

EAST TO SETUMAA

Deep valleys, sandstone crags, the ancient land of the Setus, and legends ancient and modern.

Blood lake legends

On the road to Vastseliina, the first lake below the road on the right a few km out of Võru is the **Verijärv** ("blood lake"). On stormy nights the

One shard of Vastseliina's fortress helps you to picture the whole.

noise of a vicious quarrel rises from the bottom of the lake. It's the carry-on of a landlord whose serfs loathed him. One stormy night his much-abused coachman turned the carriage down the embankment and drowned with the landlord in the lake. On moonlit nights you can see the carriage's silver harness glinting. Võru's Lenin was so badly made that a local clerk had him buried in the rubbish dump. Some wit dug him out and mounted him on top of the tip, master of all he surveyed. In a panic, the clerk had the statue reallocated to the Verijärv, and on moonlit nights his hand gleams as it makes a dramatic point. That's the more recent legend.

You cross 80 m deep **Kütiorg*** ("hunter's valley") at the Holsta busstop. In every county there's a hunting club that'll gladly issue you a licence and may organise a hunt. Kütiorg is better known for its slalom track with 2 ski lifts.

Into Setumaa

Vastseliina is a farming centre with a chilly monument to the War of Independence. Tiny **Vahtseliina*** 6 km away was the original town and for a long time there were two Vastseliinas, until the Soviets changed a letter. This was a Hanseatic trading post and the historical border between Russia and old

Möldri müür ("miller's wall") beside the Piusa River glares down.

Setu women in weighty costume.

Livonia. Roadside Piirikõrts ("border tavern") has recently reopened. Behind the tavern is a ruin's ruin, **Vastseliina fortress****. The shape of the original castle and the site of its keep are obvious; walls and circular towers still bear their decoration. The ruins lie on a thin strip of land between the Meeksi and the Piusa Rivers. Pilgrims used to visit in the Middle Ages – a crucifix in the castle chapel was believed to grant miraculous cures.

From Vahtseliina take the Petseri road. You're in **Setumaa****, an ancient land now divided between Russia and Estonia (for more on the Setu people see Põlvamaa chapter). **Meeksi*** is 4 km south of the road. Across the road from the church there's a spring that cures eye problems and a mossy rock above it that cures everything else. Inmates of the local low-security prison built the small wooden church under the cloak of night in the early 1950s. It's one of only two new churches built in Estonia under Stalin.

The other is in **Obinitsa***, north of Meeksi through Meremäe. The primitive, effective church sits beside a classic Setu cemetery, and beyond that you can find **ancient burial mounds*** running for 500 m

There's 1000 lakes in Võrumaa ...

through the pine woods.
The road back to Võru crosses the **valley of the Piusa river**** at Tamme. From here you can hike along the river to some impressive sandstone outcrops, reaching up to 19 m. The west bank has the best views; the east bank has easier trails; but there are a couple of bridges over the river. The exposures near **Härma village** are 44 m across. In the village itself you can see a sacred, many-branched pine. The beavers who live in the Piusa valley's pine forests are breathing Estonia's purest air. Breathe deep.

PRACTICAL DETAILS

ACCOMODATION

Kubija hotel, Võru-Kubija, tel 4 24 98
Igimäe ski-house, Lasva
Kurgjärve Sports Centre, Haanja-Rõuge, tel 51 24 93 (Tallinn)

RESTAURANTS

"Võru", 8. Pioneeride, Võru, tel 2 17 72
"Kubija", 43. Männiku, Võru, tel 7 14 05

BARS & CAFES

Kubija, tel 4 11 16
Antsla, tel 5 55 95
Lasva
Puiga
Vastseliina
Sõmerpalu
Võhandu trahter, 18. Koidula, Võru
Põrgu kelder, 6. Katharina, Võru

VÕRU TOURIST CENTRE, 43. Männiku, tel 4 24 98
Kütioru skiclub, tel 3 31 42

MUSEUMS

Võru Regional Museum, 16. Kreutzwaldi, tel 4 14 79
Dr. Fr. R. Kreutzwald House-Museum, 31. Kreutzwaldi, tel 2 17 98
Mõniste village-museum, Kuutsi, tel 9 36 22
Ruusmäe school-museum, Ruusmäe, tel 72 231
Suur Munamägi-Hill Tower, Haanja, tel 7 88 57 (closed mid oct. - mid apr.)

FILLING STATION

Võru, 10. Räpina mnt., tel 2 12 23
34. Antsla mnt., tel 3 15 23

CAR SERVICE

Võru, 4a. Roopa, tel 4 10 42
23. Antsla mnt., tel 2 23 54
13. Paju
41. Kreutzwaldi
Antsla
Vastseliina

TELEPHONE AREA CODE: 241

VALGAMAA

Area: 2044 km^2	**Capital: Valga**
Population: 41 380	**population 17 530**

Like Võrumaa and Hiiumaa, Valgamaa suffered from its isolation from Tallinn for half a century. Money, building materials, food, production, commerce, everything was allocated according to the principle that the further you were from the centre, be it Tallinn or Moscow, the less you got. For all that, this border province with a border-town capital includes some yummy lakeland around Otepää and Karula, an intriguing large town in Valga, battlegrounds of several wars, one of Estonia's most famous manors, and extensive skiing country. While the autocratic eyes of Soviet bureaucracy were turned elsewhere, Valgamaa managed to retain its gentle rural qualities.

VALGA

Valga and its Latvian sibling Valka have had bloody histories. What survives is a curate's egg of an industrial town.

Bloody history

Two things strike you about **Valga****, the county capital. The first is that this is one of those towns that refuses to live in one country. It forms a big sister to Valka (population 8000) in Latvia. Konnaoja ("frog creek"), which separates Valga and Valka, was accepted as border between the Order of Teutonic Knights and properties of the Bishop of Tartu in 1224 by the Bishop of Modena. The town itself was first chronicled in 1286, and grew up beside the Riga-Tartu and Riga-Pskov trade routes. It never had any defensive buildings, something unique for Estonia, but fatal for Valga.

This was a prosperous town until the Livonian War (1558-83). Over the next hundred years, plague and starvation harried Valga almost to extinction. In 1577 Ivan the Terrible besieged the town, but the area had already been so ravaged by war that his army began to starve and had to

Monument to the beginning of Estonian schooling at Karula, 1687.

leave, too weak to take its cannons with it. The small Konnaoja now divided Russia from Poland. In 1627 there remained "three citizens, a priest and a widow," according to one record. In all, Valga has been burnt down 15 times.

Gradually Valga recovered some of its prosperity, becoming a beer centre, amongst other things. When the border question arose again in about 1920, this time between Estonia and Latvia, it almost caused a war. International experts headed by an English colonel named Tallents fixed the frontier again at Konnaoja, where it still is today. Nowadays this is a large, mildly industrialised country town.

Highlights of the town

The second thing that strikes you about Valga is the **architectural mish-mash****. It's as if all the forms of architecture used in Estonia over the last century or so were shuffled in a bag and placed at random on a town plan.

The town's main landmark is **St John's church*** with its tower clock, built in late baroque style and the only oval church in the country. It was commenced in 1787 when Catherine II was trying to make a name for herself as a great builder, but the money ran out. Finally in 1816 the town raised enough money to finish the project. The organ was made by masters from Leipzig. Every spring the church's excellent acoustics can be appreciated at the Festival of Youth Choirs.

The group of wooden council buildings forms a set piece. In 1865 the **town hall** was built on the site of a smithy from Swedish times. The street is now called Sepa ("smith") St. Head along Sepa past the clothing factory towards Valka. Your Estonian visa allows you to visit Latvia, so you might like to take a Valkan tour (see below). A right off Sepa follows **Raja St.** There's an old post station on your right, a winebottler's on you left, and a border post. A **monument** commemorating the 400th anniversary of the town's foundation was unveiled in 1984, but you'll have to pop into Latvia if you want to see it up close. The mansion behind the border post is the only reminder of Raja St's heyday when the town's most important personages resided there and it was known as Härrade ("gentlemen") St.

Valga's oldest building, a **Catholic chapel** from the 18th century, is now a shop near the corner of Riia and Raja Sts. Across from it stands a warehouse that used to be a prison and before that a police station and before that the town hall and before that a radical newspaper office. Originally it was built as a courthouse in 1783.

Riia St becomes Kesktänav. An old German bank on the left has been given new life as the district council house. The **community centre** on the right is classic Soviet architecture: looks good on a drawing, but ages badly and who'd want to live in it? In the park behind the culture house you can see an effective **monument.** The image isn't a ladder to the stars, it's the railway that took prisoners to their doom in Russia in 1941. Kesktänav crosses Vabaduse ("freedom") St, which points to a great grain mill.

East of Vabaduse St

East of Vabaduse St you'll find an interesting district of wooden houses and blocks of flats. The **railway station*** in Jaama St was built by German POWs in 1949. Typically for a Stalinist building it looks more like a church. The **Catholic church** nearby has no steeples because the Russian government refused to allow any. It's being restored with German money.

The market and the **Orthodox church,** with five steeples and a belltower, are in Pargi St. And buried in the **Metsa St cemetery,** one of four in town, are more than 300 men killed in the War of Independence. Generally the bodies of fallen Estonians were returned to their home towns, but these ones died in mid summer, and no such luxury could be accorded them.

Stalag 351

The gloomiest place in town is the site of **Stalag 351,** a World War II prison camp in which 29 000 Red Army soldiers died. They're buried under firs and have earned an imposing monument. To see it, head out of town along Kuperjanovi St, take a left after the large furniture factory, then the first right. Don't mind the **Soviet tank** en route -- the cannon's not loaded.

On the Latvian side

Valka is a clean, residential town whose people work in Valga's fac-

tories. If you **cross the border** and go along Riga St you pass Valka's finer community centre, and come to the **Church of St Luke,** with a cockerel on top of its steeple. The building at the end of the street is **Cimze Seminary,** where teachers and parish priests were trained in the second half of the 19th century. These men became the leaders of the Estonian and Latvian national movements. The seminary is now a local museum. **Lenin's head** lies out the back of one of the buildings.
You can also stroll along the picturesque shores of a lake, the Veskijärv, and admire the sculpture of a **zither-player*** across the river from Valka's festival-ground.

AROUND SOUTHERN VALGAMAA

Not far north of Valga there are towns on lakes and rivers, and even more lakes in the Karula Highlands to the east. Sangaste manor is the finest surviving manor house in south Estonia.

The secret of the Valgejärv

Karula east of Valga is the centre of the lovely **Karula Highlands***, a forgotten corner near the Latvian border full of lakes and rural hillscapes.
The **Valgejärv** ("white lake") lies west of Valga. To get there, drive north from Valga and turn left at Piiri. The lake lies 3 km south of Koorküla. Through its clear waters you can see a **pile of wood** 4 m down. Once a rich lord lived with his sister in a glorious mansion. The lord wanted to marry her and a priest agreed to wed them for a large bribe. They even got permission from the Pope. All the neighbours, including the peasants, were invited to the wedding, but a grey old man asked the peasants not to go there. Before the ceremony, the lord's uncle asked him to change his mind and not marry his sister. The groom laughed and produced the Pope's letter of permission. Finally the uncle said, "If you're looking for disaster, you can have it," climbed onto his horse and rode away. When the uncle returned the next day there was no mansion on the hill but only a lake, and the castle's towers sticking out of the water.

Valga railway station's been quiet lately.

Over the centuries people have tried to discover the "true" secret. In 1640 the local landowner engaged some divers, who ran off with the treasures they found. In 1958 the Academy of Sciences discovered 74 nine-metre beams and some pottery shards dating from the 5th-10th centuries. The archaeologists have suggested that the buildings belonged to a rich man who left his village and built his own houses on piles in the middle of the lake.

Battlegrounds, other towns

Further north on the Viljandi highway is **Hummuli,** a small village first mentioned in 1226, which has had a bloody history. Vicious battles were fought here during the Northern War in 1702 and during World War II in 1944. Perhaps the Väike Emajõgi ("little mother-river") creates the illusion that you're safe on its opposite bank and can fight against your enemy forever. The **manor** is a small version of Sangaste manor, built by the baron's children, and will prepare you for the main event.
Tõrva* is a young town on the picturesque bank of the River Õhne. In spite of its lake, fresh air and pine forests Tõrva hasn't yet become a resort. The lake has a 10 m diving

board. Near the site of a hill-fort south of town, there's a **view*** of a footbridge over a bend in the river carpeted with waterlilies. North of town on the other side of the cemetery you can find **Orjakivi** ("slave's stone"). The rock turned soft when a tortured slave rested on it. The slave died but the impressions have remained.

Just 2 km from Tõrva, **Helme** has a good local museum. On the highway on the outskirts of town you can find the caves and the ruins of a **German Order castle***. The ruins extend deep into scrub along a natural ridge.

A mausoleum in Estonia!

East of Tõrva near tiny Jõgeveste is the **mausoleum**** of the husband of a local landowner, built in 1823. It's about 1 km north of the village. Barclay de Tolly was born in Scotland and after the Scottish uprising migrated to Livonia. He joined the Russian army, rising to the rank of field-marshal. He led the army at the Battle of Borodino, the bloodiest battle of the 19th century. The statue shows Pallas-Athena crowning the general; the other figure represents Russia. The relief shows de Tolly reaching Paris: he captured Napoleon's capital on 31 March 1814. (There's a monument to him in Montmartre to prove it.) The coffin on the right belongs to his wife.

Short tour of Sangaste manor

The most interesting building in Valgamaa is **Sangaste manor house****, about 3 km from Sangaste along the Tsirguliina road. To see inside, you might try to find the manager or ring 91 343. Unfortunately tours are not in English. This tudor-style building, built in 1874-81 by Friedrich von Berg, is a solidly built redbrick version of Britain's Windsor Castle. The von Berg family hopes to get the mansion back and return it to the style of the years before it was a Young Pioneer's camp. Though eclectic in style, a brief tour gives you a taste of the lives of barons in the late 19th century.

Among the mansion's 149 rooms, the finest today is the 300 m^2 **ballroom.** The orchestra balcony is obvious, but look up at the dome. The space between the bottom and second layer of glass was an aquarium. The Soviet army, as well as burning all the furniture and most of the paintings, used the ballroom as a stable. Next door is the **Spanish salon,** whose fine mouldings and arches betray a Moorish influence.

Upstairs, above the rear balcony that overlooks the pleasant lake and park, you can see the monogram of the architect, Otto Pius Hippus. He also designed Kaarli church in Tallinn. There are some original tiles on the stoves in the **reading room,** painted by the owner's obstinate Russian wife in bourgeois English style. Hooks in the library doorway were for children's swings. The library has been refloored, so you can no longer clearly hear the whispers of guests as they waited to enter in the **archway** below. Even today, however, if you stand in the archway itself with your nose to the corner, your whisper can be heard perfectly by someone in the corner diagonally opposite.

Oh, and Von Berg's image in the foyer cures eye diseases and madness – check with the stewards about the 30-day cure!

From that little spring on the slope of Little Munamägi begins the Emajõgi.

Sangaste "castle", symbol of Valgamaa.

NORTHERN VALGAMAA

Otepää has played an important role in Estonian history. It's also the national skiing capital and surrounded by gorgeous lakes and hills.

Otepää and the holy lake

Estonians flock to **Otepää** in northern Valgamaa summer and winter. Even in a mild winter, there's usually enough snow for cross-country skiing, and the Soviet team used to train here while staying at the nasty Pentagon sports centre. The town itself is small and clings to green hills. Otepää is dialect for "bear's head", reputedly taken from the shape of the old castle hill *(linnamägi)*. In the distant past there was a powerful fort here, mentioned in 1116 when Prince Mstislav of Novgorod besieged it while on a raid from Novgorod. Only recently has this fact been taught to Estonians. A raid from Russia? Never! It was later taken by the German Brethren of the Sword, the first foothold of the Order and feudalism in Estonia. On the castle hill you can find the **ruins*** of Estonia's first stone castle, built in 1224 for the Bishop of Tartu who ruled the region.

The **church** boasts the largest pipe organ in the country. See it only on

Here the Russo-Scottish general Barclay de Tolly rests in peace.

The Väike-Emajõgi cuts Valgamaa in half.

Sundays at services; singing every Sunday. Reliefs recently reinstalled on the church front celebrate a nationalist milestone – Estonia's flag, at the time the Estonian Students Union flag, was consecrated in the local pastorate by the ethnologist/pastor Jakob Hurt, who you'll find on the 10-kroon note. Otepää also has a semi-professional theatre company.

Lake heaven

The town's real treasure is its **landscape*****. There are about 130 lakes within a 20 km radius, the most renowned being the **Pühajärv***** ("holy lake"). Legend records that the lake formed from the tears of a mourning mother, whose five sons were killed in a war. The small islands are the tombs of the young warriors. Some 200 m from the road along the shore is a **Tibetan symbol** unveiled by the Dalai Lama when he visited in 1991. You can hire pedal boats a little further along. Other famous visitors to the region include Sartre and de Beauvoir, and Russian author Alexander Solzhenitsen, who wrote *The Gulag Archipelago* here. Perhaps

Sunset on the holy lake.

a cosmic force inspired them. By repute there are several **cosmic energy centres** in the area, the most positive being in town at the top of the hill on Mäe St, in the forest near the swings.

If you explore the Otepää region by car or on bike, you can discover all sorts of beauties – lakes nestling deep in woods, views from the tops of hills such as Kuutsemägi, traditional farms and concrete dormtowns. **Kuutsemägi,** with four lifts, is Estonia's downhill skiing capital. And from the tower on Hobusemägi ("horse hill") the **view of Pühajärv**** is as holy as the lake itself (unposted left turn from the Puka road 500 m before Saare farmstead). You might also like to take a single drop of water from the lover's spring *(Armuallikas)* at midnight on St John's Eve and divide it with your lover to ensure lifelong wedded bliss.

One Jaanus Raidal became mayor of Otepää in 1989 at the age of 26 and under his stewardship the area became one of the most politically interesting in the country. Whether building roads overnight or erecting the town's many swings, nothing seemed impossible. So instead of Valgamaa being the deprived distant province, this town at least took upon itself to lead for the whole country ... and maybe for the world.

Pühajärv holiday accommodation.

Can you make a bear's head out of Otepää's castle hill?

A bird's-eye view of the Pühajärv.

PRACTICAL DETAILS

ACCOMODATION

"Säde" hotel, 1. Jaama pst., Valga, tel 4 27 66
Valga's Hunter's House, 101. Kuperjanovi, Valga, tel 4 32 03
Pühajärve rest-home, Valga maakond, Pühajärve vald, tel 5 51 03, 55 051
"Otepää" hotel, Otepää, tel 5 54 31
Otepää hostel, Otepää, tel 5 59 34
Otepää ski-house, Otepää, tel 5 52 64
Ilmjärve guest-house, Pühajärve, tel 5 52 28
Sangaste castel, Sangaste, tel 9 13 35, 7 17 61
Aakre castel, Soontaga, tel 9 90 14
Saave Farm, Sihva, tel 5 62 17
Metsise hotel, 76. Kuperjanovi, Valga, tel 4 09 75
Kadajärve resont, Tõrva, tel 3 47 12
Kääriku sports centre, Kääriku, tel 5 72 31
Kuutsemägi guest-house, Otepää, tel 5 72 93
Mata sports centre, Sihva, tel 5 72 24
Mähajärve Chalet, Pühajärve, tel 5 40 03
Pühajärve resont, tel 5 54 30
Pentagon Sports Centre, Otepää, tel 5 54 30 Jaanikese hotel, Jaanikese

RESTAURANTS

"Mareta", 16. Kesk, Valga, tel 4 26 47
"Hämarik", 37. Vabaduse, Valga, tel 4 06 07
"Aure", Otepää, Tenniseväljak 1, tel 55 227
"Tõrvik", Tõrva, Valga 55, tel 3 34 90

BARS & CAFES

"Friis" bar, Lipuvälja 5, tel 5 59 06
Koidu, Valga, tel 4 10 14
"Mareta" bar, Valga
"Köie" bar, Tenniseväljak, tel 5 59 09
"Metsise" bar, Valga, Kuperjanovi 76, tel 4 09 75
"Manni" bar, Otepää, Virulombi 2

TRAVEL AGENCY

REAL REISID, 5. Lipuväljak, Otepää, tel 5 50 09
Otepää Reisibüroo, 11. Lipuväljak, Otepää, tel 5 40 60, fax (242)-55 293

MUSEUM

Otepää local museum, 59. Valga mnt, Otepää, tel 3 35 82
Helme Local Museum, Tõrva, Nooruse 2, tel 3 38 55 (U. Meil)
G.Wulff-Õis farm-museum, Nüpli, Otepää, Pühajärve vald

FILLING STATION

Valga, 1. Pikk, tel 4 15 84
Tõrva, 59. Valga mnt., tel 3 35 82
Otepää

CAR SERVICE

Valga, 47. Valli, tel 4 19 40
Valga, 21. Metse, tel 4 17 60
Otepää, 2. Tehase, tel 5 53 41
Tõrva, 7. Kangro, tel 3 38 97

TELEPHONE AREA CODE: 242

VILJANDIMAA

Area: 3589 km^2	**Capital: Viljandi**
Population: 65 030	**population 23 500**

Mulgimaa or Sakalamaa?

The leaders of Viljandi county have long played centre stage in Estonian history. In the 13th century, Estonians were fighting their first losing battles against a foreign force, in this case the knights of the German Orders. The warrior-hero Lembitu gathered tribal leaders around his fort in northern Viljandimaa, and the people made a last ditch attempt to regain their land. Alas, Lembitu was killed in 1217 in the St Matthew's Day Battle, the land was taken and the whole country fell into seven centuries of slavery.

It was also in Viljandimaa that the 19th century reawakening began. There are few luxurious manors in the county, because here the wealthiest people were not German feudal nobles with serfs, but free peasants. The first Estonians able to buy their farms from their German lords were south Viljandimaa peasants called *mulgid*, who earned their fortunes growing flax. Wealth gave the *mulgid* presumptions, and the county became the front line in the battle for education. Now the whole county is known as Viljandimaa, Mulgimaa, though technically this only applies to the southern half, or by the name of Sakalamaa. This last is the oldest of all. The Livonian Chronicles in the 13th century used this name for the region, and it was revived during the national awakening last century.

The natural axis of the district is the Sakala Highland, an area of rolling hills and rich farmland which extends southwards to Latvia. The Viljandi valley – the ancient waterway – divides the highland in two. At the edges of the highland there lie wide expanses of woods and swamps. In the bogs of north-west Viljandi county you can travel for kilometres without seeing any signs of human life. In the east lies a huge lake, the Võrtsjärv (270 km^2).

For hundreds of years southern Estonia and northern Latvia formed the land of Livonia, which was only

The ancient Estonians have gathered ... monument to a warrior-hero.

divided between the two modern nations in 1917. After World War II new settlements were founded on brand-new sites. The old centres were left alone, and thus rescued from demolition, reassignment or unsympathetic "renovation".

VILJANDI

The county centre is a picturesque town nestling on the valley slope of

a wide lake. Its ruined castle still impresses. The rest of the town is a lively mix of country-town and Soviet buildings.

The boatman of Viljandi

Viljandi*** was born beside an old Estonian hill-fort, later a German fortress, next to a fine large lake. A classic popular song tells about the boatman of Viljandi who sails across the lake dreaming about his darling and waiting for her. Every May the town is disturbed by runners, who've been coming here in their thousands since 1928 to race the 12 km around the lake.

A tour of the Old Town

Vabaduse väljak ("freedom square") is actually the carpark at the corner of Kauba and Tallinn Sts, next to the Iva restaurant and cultural centre. Heading north along Tallinn St, you pass the proud, rural **department store** and some other buildings from last century. Turn right into Tartu St, now the main shopping street in town. Here you can get a good idea of the rough 'n' ready mix of architectural styles that marks southern Estonian towns. The next right, at the little park and cinema, is Lossi ("castle") St, which leads to the castle ruins.

Before that, turn left from Lossi St and cross the park. The sharp statue of painter and politician **Johann Köler*** is a good spot to rendezvous. Because he worked in St Petersburg and had contacts in the court of the czar, Köler could carry the requests of Estonians to the highest level in the land. Through the park is Town Hall Square. Like most of the Old Town, the **town hall** dates from last century, though its spire clock is about 60, and so quite young. The **water tower*** is also young, about 80, but it's become one of Viljandi's symbols.

If you're feeling energetic, a flight of steps beside the town hall leads down **Trepimägi** ("step hill") past rambling old holiday homes to the beach. Sporting Viljandi is situated here – a ski-jump tower, tennis courts, stadium, pools and the Kalev sports complex. You can hire pedal-boats at the boatport. Otherwise, climb back up those steps and continue past the water tower along Kauba St.

There are several **neoclassical buildings** around Kindral Laidoner plats, the old market place. One, now a College of Culture, was the town's finest hotel at the turn of the century.

Castle ruins

Before you go to the castle, it's probably a good idea to visit the **Viljandi Museum*** on the corner of Lossi and Kauba Sts, in a venerable former pharmacy. This is one of those county museums with a little bit of everything: old photos of town, handicrafts, a heroic statue of Lembitu and a plaque showing the local people involved in last century's national reawakening.

In one of the rooms there's a **model of the castle** in its heyday, when it was one of the most powerful fortifications of the Livonian Order. You can see why. To capture it, soldiers had to breach two outer walls and three deep gullies before reaching the castle itself. In the north side of the main fortress were the gates, the church and the grand hall. To the west were storerooms, to the south the dining hall and kitchen, and to the east the sleeping quarters of the mercenaries. The Order had to resort to mercenaries, probably Germans,

Elements of Viljandi's castle.

From the castle to the castle park.

because they couldn't trust the locals, who after all they were busy oppressing. But mercenary loyalty is fickle, and at one stage the soldiers are reputed to have rebelled against the Order and let the Swedes.

Time to see **the castle*****. Walking along Lossi St you pass the back of St John's church (open for viewing Saturday and Sunday afternoons), one of the oldest buildings in Viljandi. Now you pass the castle's outer fortifications and cross its defensive gullies, lushly green with lake views. From the second knoll, crazy skiers practise their downhill technique in winter. You've reached the main castle. The fortress's beauty was legendary, for it was made of Saaremaa dolomite, and the Order Master himself often stayed here with his men.

You might try to find, on the front of the left **gatepost** about 2 m up, a stone with small notches in it. Stick your middle three fingers in here the first time you visit, and make a wish. In the south-west corner of the castle stands the remains of a tower, **"Villu's cell"**. In the 14th century the local Estonians revolted against their oppressors. Led by a man named Villu, they tried to capture the fortress. They cleverly hid in grain sacks and got inside, and would have taken the castle, liberated Estonia and the whole course of

Viljandi sits on a valley slope.

A gallant theatre for a small town.

human history would certainly have been altered – but the mother of one of the brave peasants betrayed them, thinking her own son's life would be spared. The soldiers pierced the sacks, discovered the men, and slaughtered all but Villu, who died a prisoner in the cell now named after him. The **view**** of the lake from the ruins is photogenic.

A gently swaying suspension bridge leads across a ravine from the ruins to the **castle park.** The bridge was built in 1879 and handed over to the town in 1931. The avenue of ancient lime trees in a gully is called the Philosopher's Boulevard, because when walking here one has the profoundest of thoughts.

Fountains to amuse the young.

Other attractions

If you follow the winding path and cross the song festival ground and the river, you come to a red-brick theatre, the home of **Ugala,** Viljandi's own theatre troupe. It was built with 599 seats, because 600-seat theatres came under central control. Behind the theatre 1400 old trees shade the overgrown **Riia St cemetery*.** The wrought-iron fences and headstones of granite and marble belong as much to the 18th

century as do the trees.
Head back to town along Vaksali St. St Paul's church appears on your left. On the same street, the **sports institute** is a Stalinist success. You're back at Freedom Square.
There's much more to see. Various buildings bear plaques declaring that they were once occupied by the office of the **newspaper *Sakala*.** During the Estonian national reawakening last century, *Sakala* was edited by Carl Robert Jakobson, whose face now adorns the 500-kroon note. Viljandi's attractions include artificial lakes and little parks decorated with pools and fountains. Many of the town's small houses are adorned with turrets, weather-vanes and gables. Some old farmhouses still look the part, though the town has swallowed them up. At the time of going to press, several buildings in the heart of town, including a German noblewomen's pension, were still occupied by the Red Army, adding a sense of darkness to the town's light atmosphere.

NORTHERN VILJANDIMAA

The northern part of the county aches with the pain of lost battles. Several affecting monuments are reminders of long years with only a faint hope of a better future.

Monuments round Suure-Jaani

If you leave Viljandi along the Tallinn highway, you enter a landscape of drumlins and greenery. To the left is the mental asylum of Jämejala, where the president of the first Estonian Republic, Konstantin Päts, was briefly imprisoned in 1954. Beyond it, like a vision from Kafka, the Viljandi hospital towers over a field.
Further north, a left from the Tallinn highway takes you to **Suure-Jaani***, centre of the war of independence in the 13th century, and the place for monuments. Near the indestructible church, a statue of 13th-century hero-warrior Lembitu serves as monument to the 20th-century war of independence. The cemetery is sumptuous as ever, and includes a fine headstone for the painter Köler.
The Navesti flows westward towards Vändra. On the left is the village of Lepakose, where people have lived for at least 7000 years. A **witch's "stockade"*** on the Vändra road is a monument to Estonian eccentricity. It's a bizarre construction like a schizophrenic stockade after a tornado.
The finest monument is east of Suure-Jaani. Following the road towards Olustvere, a sign points to *Lembitu linnus*, a mound in the mid-

The Navesti River.

These days, Olustvere manor houses a school.

dle of living forest. This was **Lembitu's fort, Lõhavere****. The grove of stone sculptures next to it represents the Estonians gathered under Lembitu to resist the German knights.

In **Olustvere*** there's an eclectic manor in a lovely park. Jaan Adamson, celebrated in a monument here, was born in the village and unsuccessfully tried to start an agricultural school for Estonians last century. Now there's one in the manor. **Võhma,** further north, is the home of slaughterhouses and meat factories. Foil-covered hot-water piping winds through the town above ground level; no doubt it makes repair easy.

Victims

Pilistvere lies in the direction of Põltsamaa from Võhma. The **spire*** of its gothic church (dating from about 1300) is one of the most outstanding examples among country churches in Estonia. Pilistvere was severely traumatised by the last war and by the deportations of Stalin's rule. In 1988 a simple **memorial cross*** was erected to the victims; many visitors bring stones to the cross, which is north of the village, the other side of the cemetery.

Of all the avenues in all the manor parks in all of Estonia, Olustvere's are the longest.

The militant pastor of Kolga-Jaani

Thousands of years ago, when the water level in the Võrtsjärv was higher, **Kolga-Jaani** was an archipelago on which fishermen lived. Now it's a small country town of historic wooden houses around a slim-steepled, 14th-century **church.** In this church there served a pastor who in 1917 encouraged Estonians to take up arms and go to war for their independence. Memorial days of celebration are now held in honour of Pastor Villem Reimann every May.

West of Kolga-Jaani, towards Viljandi, lies the district's biggest bog, the **Pilistvere swamp.** The road to Viljandi crosses it on a foundation of gathered trees and earth.

South of Kolga-Jaani on the road to Vaibla is the **glass factory in Meleski** (1792), the first industrial enterprise in Estonia. It was a giant for its time, with 538 workers at the beginning of the 19th century. Some buildings and a tiny museum remain.

Emajõgi and Võrtsjärv

South of Meleski you reach the **Võrtsjärv****, Estonia's second-largest lake. The sandy bottom gets deep only very gradually, and the water temperature is often over 20° in summertime. The lake is clean and rich in fish; local delicacies are bream and eel. **Kuradi** ("devil") island in the Võrtsjärv is a lay-up for yachters. There's a sandy beach and holiday bungalows at Vaibla, and several union holiday homes that will probably soon start taking foreign guests. But for now this beautiful lake is relatively undiscovered.

Just east of here, the **Emajõgi** ("mother river") begins its languorous journey to Lake Peipsi via Tartu.

From Vaibla going towards Viljandi you travel through a rural, rolling landscape. Some of the way you're following the bank of an ancient valley, 25 m deep, 800 m wide. On the right-hand side of the valley is the **home of Jaan Tõnisson,** a nationalist leader and representative of the oppositional "spirit of Tartu" who was at one time the head of state. He died in Siberia.

The lighter side of life in Kolga-Jaani.

Back to Viljandi

Just before Viljandi a lone oak appears 100 m to your right about the same time as Lake Viljandi appears. **Viiralt's oak*,** immortalised by the artist Eduard Viiralt, is a symbol of the whole of Viljandi county's magnificent countryside. Not far beyond, a pile of bricks is all that remains of the local synagogue. Careful if you're driving. The **view**** of the towered town of Viljandi may make you forget the wheel.

SOUTHERN VILJANDIMAA

The south is the heartland of the* mulgid. *Hidden amid the marvellous landscape are some hill-fort sites with unusual chapels, and a restored church at Halliste.

General Laidoner and pig dung

Leaving Viljandi on the Mustla road, there's a recent **monument** to the commander of the Estonian Republic's army, Johann Laidoner, on the right-hand side of the road.

He ended up in Siberia. Another symbol lurks nearby, one that celebrates the old Soviet love of gigantic production. At **Viiratsi pig factory**** 50 000 pigs produce 600 m^3 of liquid dung every day. Laidoner, who was born and raised in the neighbourhood, would never have dreamt of such a record-breaking production capacity.

Hilltops and riversides

You're deep in the world of **drumlins, small lakes and winding rivers.** At the **Pulleritsu schoolhouse** the people drafted an appeal to Czar Alexander asking for permission to open a secondary school for Estonians, to be named, diplomatically, the Alexander School. Though the appeal was unsuccessful, the campaign helped galvanise the national movement.

Mustla's church is through Mustla village, at Tarvastu. You can see the site of a **14th-century hill-fort*** by turning left at the little bridge below the church; keep going a kilometre beyond the end of the asphalt, turn left the other side of the old stone barns, and park by the 19th-century watermill. A **neoclassical crypt*** with a high hat stands on the stronghold hill.

The Tartu road continues to Suislepa. Below the town, on the riverside, you can see a small **sandstone exposure** with a couple of wee caves that locals associate with wartime hiding places or vile landlords. The plaque reads: "1695-1697, great famine in Suislepa".

From Suislepa to Kärstna the road begins to rise. From **Kabelimägi** ("chapel hill", 136 m) above Kärstna you have a **vista*** all the way to the Võrtsjärv lake. The tower is dangerous but near the ruined chapel in forest 100 m away there's a **boulder monument**** lionising Reinhold Anrek, a Baltic-German lieutenant-general of the Russian army killed fighting Napoleon in

What will the weather be like tomorrow in Karksi-Nuia?

Karksi's castle is in ruins but its church survives.

1807. On the hillslope stands **Kärstna manor** amid old boulevards.

The god of the purse

Just inside the town limits of **Karksi-Nuia,** head for the church on your left. The Halliste River carved out a magnificent place for a hill-fort here: reference was made to it in 1248. Two centuries later, the **fortress*** on the site defended itself with 2 heavy stone-throwers, 8 cannons, 2 barrels of gunpowder, 70 sets of armour, 25 bows and other arms. It's been in ruins ever since. There's a **stunning view**** from the castle hill to the valley. The road snakes its way down to the river valley and then snakes its way back up again into Karksi-Nuia itself.

The name of one of Karksi-Nuia's bars, **Kauka Bar,** is linked to the *mulgid,* the rich peasants of southern Viljandimaa who were the first Estonians to buy their farms in perpetuity. The totem of these reputedly stingy folk was the *kaugas* ("purse"). *The god of the purse* is a play on the theme by Estonia's greatest tragic playwright, August Kitzberg. Kitzberg was born in this town. The nearby village of **Karksi** is famous for its **beer.** One of Estonia's few breweries still pours it out today.

West of here, **Abja** was the capital of the land of the *mulgid,* as the fine buildings in the main street attest. It's now best known for the **valley of the Halliste River*** – here expanding into Lake Kariste – which runs through untouched forest and is perfect for a boat trip. The first 2 km of the road to Kanaküla offer some good views of the lake. Abja's **cemetery** has plenty of space for its dead and seating for the living.

In the south-west corner of the county is **Mõisaküla.** The Latvian border is one kilometre away. When historic Livonia split into north Latvia and south Estonia at the end of World War I, the border question was a ticklish one: this became one of the most heavily guarded borders in Europe.

Relentless hillscape

Going from Abja to Viljandi, you reach **Halliste church****, one of Estonia's most beautiful, just outside Kulla village. It's been rebuilt recently with voluntary contributions, and is often open for viewing. One of its pastors is legendary. During the Soviet period, Kalev Raave was a famous collective farm manager, but the wrath of the rulers fell on him because of his individual thinking: supposedly he used farm finances in

Kayaking on the Raudna River.

ways other than those prescribed in Moscow. After several years in prison, he dedicated himself to the church.

Õisu formed around a manor, now a dairy school, with a round stable. There's a lovely view from the mansion over Lake Õisu. You can visit a local **Põrguorg*** ("hell valley") of steep, layered sandstone ... on foot. Just plunge into the woods on the right at the river 200 m from the manor and follow the path up and down. Several trees have toppled as the sandstone walls have collapsed.

Beauty

The rolling landscape north of Õisu is earthily rural and dotted with **ancient vales****. The countryside is particularly attractive between Sultsi and Paistu. In **Paistu village,** Homer's *Odyssey* was translated into Estonian. Near Loodi village is **Paistu Põrguorg*** ("Paisu hell valley"): follow the road behind Loodi manor house past the former dairy and turn left at the apple tree; you'll have to go some of the way on foot.

Continuing north along Loodi valley a left at the Kondi busstop leads to an old hill-fort site on the shore of pretty **Lake Sinialliku.** If you just want to see the lake, follow the signs to Ramsi instead.

Before Viljandi, take a left to Heimtali. In the 30 m deep **Raudna valley** flowed the old waterway from Lake Viljandi to Pärnu. The land has risen since the ice age, and all that's left of the waterway is a rivulet in a ditch. **Heimtali**** itself is a gem. The extraordinary building on your left before the village is the restored 19th century **distillery****. The manor ensemble, surrounded by plunging green valley, includes a manor house, a stable with a courtyard, a wall around the baron's orchard and sundry other ruins.

WESTERN VILJANDIMAA

The western part of the county is swampy. You can travel for ages and only see wildlife and marshland.

Swampland

Instead of a waterway you can now follow a road to Pärnu. The river Kõpu marks the end of the drumlins and the beginning of great swamps and forests – central Estonia. **Kõpu** is the base for the distant farmhouses and isolated families who live in the area.

West of Kõpu you can travel only along muddy forest roads or serpentine rivers. The **bogs of Valgeraba, Öördi and Kikerpere** are large and rich in berries – they are also difficult to cross. In spring, the melting snows of the Sakala Highland turn this area into a vast lake. People sail boats in their backyards; the best way to visit then is by canoe or inflatable rubber boat.

PRACTICAL DETAILS

ACCOMODATION

"Viljandi" hotel, 11. Tartu, Viljandi, tel 5 38 52
KALEV sports base, 6. Ranna pst., Viljandi, tel 5 47 70
"Hotel", 38. Riia mnt., Viljandi, tel 5 28 15
Sammuli motel, Viiratsi, tel 9 47 13
Kolme Karu camping, Holstre-Nõmme, tel 2 97 77

RESTAURANTS

"Vikerkaar", 5. Roo, Viljandi, tel 5 29 09
"Viljandi", 11. Tartu, Viljandi, tel 5 47 95
"Iva", 2. Tasuja, Viljandi, tel 52 493
"Viljandi", 31. Lossi, Viljandi, tel 54 424
"Võhma", 2. Spordi, Võhma, tel 2 33 85
"Kaleva", 26. Tallinna, Võhma, tel 2 33 95
"Karksi", 2. Rahumäe, Nuia, tel 3 12 90
"Kungla", 34. Pärna, Mõisaküla, tel 6 41 44
"Lehola", 11. Pärnu, Suure-Jaani, tel 7 12 83

BARS & CAFES

"Draakon", 34.Tartu, Viljandi
"Marleen", 18. Jakobsoni, Viljandi
"Menu", 11. Jakobsoni, Viljandi
"Mulgi kelder", 5. Tartu, Viljandi
"Posti trahter", 18. Posti, Viljandi
"Koit", 6. Turu, Viljandi
"Kauka" bar, Nuia, tel 31 660
"Lambada", Mudiste

MUSEUMS

Viljandi regional museum, 12. Laidoneri plats, tel 5 26 63
Composer Mart Saar museum, Hüpassaare, Suure-Jaani, Vihi side
Composer's Kapp house-museum, Suure-Jaani, Tallinna mnt 30, tel 71 190
Mõisaküla local museum, Mõisaküla, Kiltre 1, tel 64 159
Meleski glass museum

TRAVEL BUREAUS

Viljandi Travel Agency, 6. Tallinna, Viljandi, tel 5 23 71

FILLING STATION & CAR SERVICE

Viljandi, 99a. Tallinna mnt., tel 5 50 50
Suure-Jaani, Oja 2, tel 71 186
Nuia station, EPT, tel 32 650
Abja station, Halliste, tel 62 240
Abja car service, Auto-Moto, tel 61 163

TELEPHONE AREA CODE: 243

PÄRNUMAA

Area: 4771 km²	**Capital: Pärnu**
Population (exc. Pärnu): 33 940	**population 52600**

Sun, sea and holidays are what Pärnu means to most Estonians, but they're only half the story. Pärnumaa, Estonia's largest county, includes boulder-strewn coasts and inland forests, marshes, ancient settlements and a modern capital. For centuries, traders from distant lands have used the seaport and Tallinn-Riga highway. Pärnu has known both prosperity and war. Today it's Estonia's most westernised town, prospering again, and with a bright future once the Via Baltica highway linking Germany with Poland and the Baltic states is finished.

The county's central artery is the Pärnu River; numerous tributaries stretch like veins into the remotest corners. The first people settled on the banks of the larger rivers: the settlement of Pulli, where the Pärnu River once met the sea, was founded 11 000 years ago, barely 4000 years after the glaciers receded. It's the oldest-known settlement in Estonia.

PÄRNU

Estonia's California is a large town full of trees, bars and festivals. The town is also steeped in history.

Pearl of the Baltic (slightly soiled)

Pärnu*** is summer city. Sun-worshippers fry themselves on long white beaches. Culturati catch plays at Estonia's only summer theatre, the Endla, or bop the nights away at music festivals. Fans of the mild sea air saunter along shaded avenues, or venture out onto the 2.5 km long pier that juts into the bay. Strollers ponder the sunset. The climate is gentle and refreshing. That's Pärnu's pretty face, the face tourists see. Sadly the sea is often dirty and the drinking water quite poor. However, the water is 25 times cleaner than it was 10 years ago. Warning signs go up when Pärnu Bay is unswimmable.

Parking spot outside town hall.

Ups and downs ...

For the last few kilometres of the river's course a high, sandy peninsula keeps the Pärnu River from the sea. A village on this strip of land was chronicled as early as 1154. In the Middle Ages Estonia's major river, the Emajõgi, ran to Pärnu and was the main link with Viljandi and Tartu. Since then the level of the Emajõgi has sunk and the connection has been severed.

Just before it finally does reach the

sea the Pärnu River meets the Sauga. These two rivers cut the town into three parts: Uus ("new") Pärnu, Ülejõe ("over-the-river") and Vana ("old") Pärnu. During the several wars fought over the area, all three Pärnus have changed hands many times and much has been destroyed. The Old Town is actually in Uus-Pärnu. As a Hanseatic port it played an important role in Livonian trade. The town boomed at the end of the Swedish era – Tartu's University even transferred here briefly in 1699. At the end of the 18th century Pärnu's harbour activity eclipsed Tallinn's. After the boom came the bust, a long period of stagnation. Prosperity only returned at the beginning of this century, when the largest paper mill in the Russian Empire was built here. By then the town was already a popular sea and health resort, offering mud cures and other thrills to those who could afford them. You can take a cure yourself, or maybe have a quick mud treatment, massage or water treatment. Pärnu's fate in World War II was typical. Even after the Germans had abandoned the place the Red Army kept shelling the Old Town, destroying many beautiful sights. Yet enough has survived to preserve the town's ambience.

Tour of the town

Today, **downtown Pärnu***** includes a heady mix of stone houses from the 18th century and more modern creations. The main square is near the bus station. Facing away from the Hotel Pärnu is a good way not to have to look at it. Ahead of you the main shopping street, **Rüütli*** ("knight"), teems with shoppers on weekdays. Several streets lead off Rüütli to various landmarks. There's a good **museum*** in Ringi St opposite the hotel, and the Orthodox Transfiguration church behind that. Pärnu's oldest building is hidden down an alley off Hommiku ("morning") St – the **red tower*** has a tiny exhibition about the Old Town and dates from the 14th century. In Nikolai St, the **town hall*** dates from the 17th century; concerts are held in its fine hall. **St Elizabeth church** is in the same street. Both it and exquisite **St Catherine's**** in Vee St were built during Pärnu's 18th-century baroque heyday.

Rüütli ("knight") St, hub of the town, has some well preserved shops.

The modern building in the park across from St Catherine's is the **Endla Theatre.** Endla are Estonia's only summertime theatre company, though that usually means they're impossible to see here in summer: they're too busy touring round the country. Through the park across the Pärnu River is Ülejõe ("over-the-river").

Staying on Rüütli St a little longer, directly ahead is the song-ground. Pärnu's summer highlight is an up-tempo festival each June, the Pärnu Fiesta. The opening night, *Tere Pärnu Suvi*, serves the whole country as an introduction to long warm days of parties and traditional celebrations.

Vana-Tallinna St behind the post office goes to another landmark, the old town gates known as **Tallinna väravad*.** You may be surprised to find the Tallinn Gates on the *south* side of town, but in medieval times traders from Tallinn came by sea and entered here. The Tallinn Gates and the section of moat next to them are remnants of Pärnu's medieval fortifications. There was once a town wall where now a ring of parks circles the centre, and a bastion atop a large mound, **Munamäe** ("egg-hill"), near the gates.

Lydia Koidula forever creating poetry in her own park.

Mole and sand

The Tallinn Gates are not far from the **Pärnu mole****. Ringi St leads to Muul St and thence past two beacon towers to the famous *muul* ("mole" or stone pier), a low boulder wall extending 2.5 km into the gulf, built to prevent the river mouth from choking on sea-sands. Another mole defends the other bank. Lovers, dreamers, families, all kinds of folk in a tranquil mood make their way to the end of the mole to watch the sun set. The **yacht harbour** is at the very end of Ringi St.

From the Tallinn Gates you can walk to the beach along Merepuiestee ("sea avenue"), a pleasant street lined with holiday homes and parkland. The art-nouveau **Amände Villa***, the town's finest, is in its own grounds on the right. The harmony and charm of **Pärnu's avenues**** is in the trees: in each avenue a single species of tree grows, maple, oak, pine and lime, to name a few. The town itself may take its name from the lime tree, *pärn* in Estonian.

The **beach*** itself is of white sand. In spring it vanishes – the spring thaw sometimes raises the level of the Gulf of Riga so much that parts of the town flood with icy-cold water. About 150 m to the right of the **Mud Institute** begins a women's beach, where many an all-round tan is earned. (No men, please!)

The poet who died of homesickness

Pärnu's first baths were founded in 1838 where Merepuistee meets Supeluse ("bath") St. In 1890 a mud cure institute opened on the same site, and one still stands there today. The villas and boarding houses, all the paraphernalia of seaside resorts, soon followed, and the **coast park** that separates the town from the sea. Notice the way the pines in the park bend, like most Pärnuvians, towards the sea. In the late 1930s, at the end

When summer's done, Pärnu calms down. The song stadium.

Pärnu is the capital of sea and sanatoria.

of the first spell of Estonian independence, two symbols of Pärnu were built here – the coast cafe *(Rannasalong)* and the coast hotel *(Rannahotell)* with its mushroom-shaped viewing platform.

Head back up Supeluse St, veering into Pühavaimu St. In pretty **Koidula Park**** a statue of Lydia Koidula, 19th-century poet and founder of Estonia's theatre, gazes into the distance. She led a tragic life. Her husband took her away from her beloved land and she died, they say, of a broken heart. There's a museum dedicated to her across the river in Ülejõe, and the Endla Theatre sometimes performs a play about her life. She's returned to fame on the 100-kroon note.

There's more to see: a couple of baroque buildings have been restored in Kuninga St. Around Koidula Park you can see fine old school buildings, the refurbished Victoria Hotel, and not far to the north-east, in Karja St, the bustling market. The town is full of parks and boulevards and circled by factories, which after all have their own charms, especially at sunset when you can see their smokestacks reflected in the slow waters of the Pärnu River. And there are **restaurants, cafes and bars**

The bay gets cleaner every year.

everywhere, some attractively located in cellars, or above the Tallinn Gates, or near the beach ... Pärnu leads Estonia in the number of bars per head of population.

NORTH-EAST ALONG THE PÄRNU RIVER

The meandering Pärnu River** is often beautiful. The road that follows its course sometimes glimpses or crosses it, though to see it properly you could take a boat trip. You can canoe almost all of the river from Paide to the sea: the full trip takes three days and you can hire boats and instructor from the Pärnu Rowing Club. The other highlight of a tour along the Pärnu is the home of Carl Robert Jakobson, now a model farm.

Misdirected stone

The Riga highway, part of Via Baltica, runs parallel to the seaside. On the left as you head out of Pärnu there are a couple of beautiful cemeteries and a modern **railway station***, one of Estonia's loveliest.

Paide road, left off the highway beyond the railway station, leads to **Sindi.** This is Pärnu's satellite city, an industrial town with a Soviet centre, a garden suburb and a textile mill founded 160 years ago.

Võnnukivi, the great boulder in the river near the Urumarja busstop, was hurled there by the legendary Kalevipoeg. He was actually aiming for Võnnu (Cesis) in Latvia, where brave Estonian troops were fighting. From here, the road runs parallel to the river to **Tori.** The stone buildings of a **horse stud*** give the town a historical odour. Tori has been renowned for its draught horses since 1856. To visit you should phone ahead. There's also a good wee museum. **Tori põrgu*** ("Tori hell") is a sandstone cave network by the river. Cave-ins have blocked most of the entrances, but you can still park at the cemetery and descend to hell on the riverbank. You get a wider view while crossing Tori bridge on the way to Vändra.

Bears and cultural nationalism

Vändra* has deep cultural traditions. Johann Voldemar Jannsen, the father of Estonian journalism, lived here. He was also father of the poet Lydia Koidula, she of the 100-kroon note. Mats Tõnisson, another famed Vändroid, was author of an Estonian-language almanac. Anger at the foreign overlords reached such a

Tori's famous draughthorses compete at their annual festival.

The people of Kurgja celebrating Carl Robert Jakobson's jubilee.

pitch that the 1913 edition sold over 150 000 copies – one Mats' calendar for every family! Tõnisson's home is right next to the well-organised **cemetery,** which is next to the church. One headstone is dedicated "To Lilli Suburg – from Estonian women". Lilli Suburg was the founder of an Estonian girls' school. You need to hit Vändra's side streets to see older wooden houses. **Lydia Koidula's birthplace** lies just out of town on the Viljandi road. She seems to have been born on a granite slab in a small paddock.

From Vändra, the Paide road continues north-east crossing a famous forest through which brown bears roam. Follow the signs to **Kurgja**,** to an idyllic model farm still run using 19th-century methods and equipment. You can see Estonian native breed cattle and Tori horses and pigs in the shed. In summertime, folk festivals and plays are held on the farm-museum's land.

The farm's previous master would have been well satisfied. **Carl Robert Jakobson** was a leader of the national movement at the end of last century, edited the radical newspaper *Sakala,* involved himself passionately in culture and education, and was, naturally, a leading farmer. The farmhouse is a museum

Vändra's old dairy is a bar, surprisingly.

A survivor in the Halliste Nature Reserve.

in his honour. At Kurgja begins the **"Sakala road"**, a 12 km forest path along which Jakobson used to travel part of the way to Viljandi. Today his birthday (26 July) and death (19 March) are commemorated with walking tours. He died at 40 in his sauna – it's still there. You can see his grave under oaks not far from the farm.

Continue from here to Suurejõe. The **old watermill** across the Pärnu River is rather photogenic.

Back to Pärnu

You can get back to Pärnu along the highway through Vändra. Or you can go via Kaansoo, along the right-hand shore of the **Navesti River,** though as usual the river can't be seen from the road. Large forests and abandoned homesteads dot the way. From an old suspension footbridge you can see the **confluence of the Navesti and Halliste Rivers***. It's 100 m left of the road by the Aesoo kool ("Aesoo school") busstop. As you approach Tori, you get another view of Tori hell by the Pärnu River.

SOUTH TOWARDS LATVIA

Along the coast road, you'll find several good beaches. Inland there's a rich marsh south of Kilingi-Nõmme.

The southern beaches

On the right of the Riga highway is **Tahkuranna,** birthplace of the first president of the Estonian Republic, Konstantin Päts. Päts was involved with the whole period of Estonian independence (1918-40). In 1989 his monument in Tahkuranna was restored, then destroyed again, then reopened a year later.

Häädemeeste at the turn of the century became famous for yacht-building. The port developed and a long

The pines of Pärnu Rannametsa.

log chute-canal, Timmkanal, was dug to bring logs from the nearby forests. It's on your left near the parking spot 4 km before the village. The old highway that follows the coast after Häädemeeste is more attractive than the new inland one. Most of the **beaches*** down to Latvia are of white sand. There are swimming spots at Kabli and Treimani. **Ikla** is the farthest Estonian point on the Riga highway.

The **swamp of Nigula*** is a protected reserve. To get there you turn inland at Häädemeeste to Tali, where you'll see a guidepost to the reserve. There's a lake, over 370 pools and many bog-islands. Rich "cranberry fields" have been planted on peat fields here – each hectare produces over 2 tonnes of cranberries.

Where vodka comes from

Kilingi-Nõmme is the main centre of south Pärnumaa. In the centre of town there's an old pine tree. A general, a victim of the Northern War, is buried under the tree. The church is by a lake and there's a ruined Orthodox church south of town.

Just before Tihemetsa there's a parking place at **Allikukivi*** ("sourcestone") which takes its name from the valley, where there are pure springs and large clay caverns. Legend notes that a prosperous wedding-house sank into the ground when an old wanderer was refused shelter. Since then, on midsummer eve the spring runs pure white vodka, especially if you've already had a bit yourself.

In **Tihemetsa*** there are old and new manors with parks. The new park is 150 years old, and for last 50 years has been the home of a family of white storks. The largest old-fashioned tavern in the Baltics is **Voltvet's Tavern,** just before Viljandi county. Gorbachev's temperance campaign halted restoration work on the tavern in the late 1980s.

WEST FROM PÄRNU

The western beaches tend to be isolated and difficult to get to, though often beautiful. It can also be an adventure getting to Soontagana, the site of an ancient hill-fort surrounded by swamps in the northwest of the county.

The nearest cleanish beach

The road from Pärnu towards Lihula crosses both of Pärnu's rivers and bypasses one excellent sandy beach, **Valgerand***, quite a popular place because the seawater is cleaner here. A right leads to *Kuld lõvi* ("golden lion"), a restored tavern.

Audru* is a mix, which some might describe as eclectic, of old buildings and collective farm architecture. The manor park is overgrown, bordered by a winding river, laced together with suspension bridges, and has a song stage and two crowd-control towers. You can buy a fox-stole at Audru's fox farm. From here heading towards Tõstamaa you travel along a seaside full of dunes covered with pinewood, inhabited mainly by fishing folk.

The western edge

At **Pootsi** a lane of trees announces an old manor. I'm told that every few years you can walk to Manilaid island from the tip of the peninsula to the south in midsummer, when the water only reaches as high as your neck. And in **Tõstamaa*** you can see an odd church, like a barn with buttresses and cement niches. Tõstamaa's beach is stony and the bay is full of little islands. From here you *could* keep going westwards, to **Varbla,** which has a pretty church, and to the western beaches such as the one at the lighthouse near **Saulepi*.** This is where you'll find lovely out-of-the-way corners.

Or you could head north. In the distant past Tõstamaa was an island, and in the basin behind the pine-covered dunes, now several km

Summer is berry-picking time.

Exploring Nigula swamp.

from the sea, are two large lakes rich in fish, **Tõhela and Ermestu.**

Defended by the swamps

The church at **Kalli** has seen better days: there are holes in the steeples and cracks in the walls. From here a side road leads to **Koonga,** a village of mostly white buildings, including the old manor house. Here, surrounded by enormous swamps, was **ancient Soontagana parish**.** Its centre is **Mihkli,** with a 13th-century church and 19th-century chapel. You are at the beginning of Estonian written history. Here the Latvian priest Hendryk wrote his *Livonian chronicle,* which contained what was in the 1230s the recent history of the region. This was the first time dozens of Estonian places were chronicled.

The biggest **oak forest*** in Estonia isn't far: head east at the shop and after 100 m you enter the *Keblaste tammik,* 300 ha of natural atmospherics.

Soontagana hill** is in the middle of Järve swamp. The German knights didn't find Soontagana easy to take in the 13th century, and built Mihkli church to celebrate and cement their victory. According to legend, a broken-hearted woman revealed to the Germans the secret log path submerged in the swamp. Boring conventional history says that they attacked in winter when the swamp was frozen over.

Valgerand means "white beach".

It's still an adventure to find the hill, and impossible in springtime when the ground is mush. Once through the oak forest turn left (north) at the Järve tee busstop. Follow the road, veering right once, through Järve village, and at the corner where the road suddenly becomes dead straight for some kilometres, turn left instead onto a forest track. If you're in a car, you'll soon need to park somewhere: the road is not maintained. Now you'll have to walk or cycle some 4 km. After the first kilometre you cross the river and the walk an avenue bordered by alders. Continue into the large clearing through ruined Kurese village. Until very recently, two families were still living here; one of them had been here for 22 generations. The stone walls that used to line village streets lead to the hill itself.

Back to Pärnu

Heading east you reach the market town of **Pärnu-Jaagupi,** which takes its name from the local church of St Jacob. Southwards, the highway passes through Are and crosses the Sauga River. You can see the ruins of an **old mill** from the bridge – Estonian roads generally crossed rivers in front of the mill weirs, where the water was low.

KIHNU AND MANILAID

Several islands lie off the coast of Pärnumaa. The most famous, Kihnu, is accessible by ferry from Pärnu leaving once every two days. To get to distant Ruhnu (see Saaremaa chapter), nearer Manilaid or any of the dozens of islets you'll need to hire a boat from Pärnu yacht port or persuade a fisherman to loan you a rowboat (though Ruhnu's too far to row to).

Return of an old salt

Only some twenty or thirty people live on **Manilaid*,** during summertime. Life on the island is traditional and modest, and the islanders got electricity only few years ago.

Kihnu*** was settled in the Middle Ages. Life before the Soviets arrived

Kihnu girls decked out.

was vivid. A legendary captain, Kihnu Jõnn, cruised all over the world at the turn of the century, and was only reburied on his home island in 1992. The bar Rock City (where you can sleep overnight) is not an attempt to go western, it's the name of his last ship, which he went down with in 1912. Legends abound. Because his ships were ancient as hell, he could only persuade landlubbing youths to sail with him. They say he plastered playing cards onto the various yardarms, sails etc because they were easier to remember than the real names. "Hoist the Queen of Spades!"

The old traditions and customs have survived better on Kihnu than on the mainland, and Estonians (who seem to be fascinated by the island) will often tell you that the women still wear their traditional costume every day. There are beaches, a small museum, a 19th-century lighthouse and an 18th-century church as well.

Stone for Estonians means limestone.

Karukose's suspension bridge succumbs to spring floods on the Raudna River.

PRACTICAL DETAILS

ACCOMODATION

HOTELS
PÄRNU
"Victoria" ****, 25. Kuninga, tel 4 34 12
"Pärnu", 44. Rüütli, tel 4 21 45
"Aisa", 39. Aisa, tel 4 31 86
"Emmi", 2. Laine, tel 2 20 43
"Leharu", 7. Sääse, tel 4 58 95
"Vesiroos", 42a. Esplanaadi, tel 4 35 34
"Terko", 1a. Ravi, tel 2 13 86
"Kajakas", 2. Seedri, tel 4 30 98
"Strand", 27b. Tammsaare, tel 2 52 05
"Villa del Mar", Esplanaadi 42a, tel 44 444, 43 534
GUEST HOUSE
"Estturist", 4. Seedri, tel 4 23 38
"Avangard", 12. Salme, tel 2 37 77
"EKE", Muru 1, tel 4 11 56
"Terko", 1a. Ravi, tel 2 13 86
"WEST", 33. Jannseni, tel 4 30 70
"Lepanina" motel, Kabli, tel 9 84 77
Uulu camping, tel 6 06 61
"Valgerand" camping, tel 6 42 31

"Jõekääru" motel, Sauga, tel 4 11 21

RESTAURANTS

"Rannahoone", 3. Ranna pst., Pärnu, tel 4 02 22
"Hermes", 74. Riia mnt., Pärnu, tel 4 26 81
"Postipoiss" (beer), 12. Vee, Pärnu, tel 4 02 04
"Vändra", Vändra, tel 9 57 42
"Kuldlõvi", Audru, tel 4 06 03
"Central", 6. Hospidali, tel 4 05 75
"Tallinn", 5 Akadeemia, tel 40 468

BARS & CAFES

"Bristol" bar, 45. Rüütli, Pärnu
"Vahtra" bar, 4. Kerese, Pärnu
"Florett", Lõuna, Pärnu
"Crown Marie", 8. Pühavaimu, Pärnu, tel 4 39 59
"Tallinna väravad", tel 4 50 73
"Viiking" bar, 7. Ranna pst., Pärnu
"Roosikelder", 18. Kuninga, Pärnu, tel 4 22 78
"Kadri", 12. Nikolai, Pärnu
"Vigor" bar, Pärnu jõel, tel 4 50 66
Kihnu (island) bar, tel 6 99 56

TRAVEL BUREAUS

Pärnu Tourist Service, 18b Supeluse, Pärnu, tel 4 55 33
FIESTA Tours, 10 Esplanaadi, Pärnu, tel 4 44 44
Pärnu Travel Bureau, 32 Kuninga, Pärnu, tel 4 27 50
Pärnu Yacht Club, 6 Lootsi, Pärnu, tel 4 19 48
Pärnu Rowing Club, 54 Suure-Jõe, Pärnu tel 4 41 88

MUSEUMS

Punane Torn-museum (Red Tower Museum), 11 Hommiku, Pärnu
Pärnu Regional Museum, 53 Rüütli, Pärnu, tel 4 34 64
Lydia Koidula Museum, 37 Jannseni, Pärnu, tel 4 16 63
C. R. Jakobsoni farm-museum, Vändra-Kurgja, tel 9 32 28
Tori agricultural museum, Tori, tel 6 69 97
Vändra local museum
Kihnu local museum

FILLING STATION

Pärnu, 2 Hommiku, tel 4 05 37
Riia mnt. (NESTE), tel 2 19 06
1 Niidu, tel 4 28 77

CAR SERVICE

Pärnu, 93 Tallinna mnt., tel 4 09 80
6 Karja, tel 4 27 67
89A Tallinna mnt., tel 4 22 43
Libatse, tel 9 45 94

TRANSPORT

BUS STATION, 3 Ringi, Pärnu, tel 4 15 54
HARBOUR, 2 Kalda, Pärnu, tel 4 04 42 (cruises to Kihnu, Ruhnu, Saaremaa)
AIRPORT, tel 4 07 52
TAXI, tel 4 12 40
RENT A CAR, 13 Haapsulu mnt., Pärnu, tel 4 10 51

TELEPHONE AREA CODE: 244

LÄÄNEMAA
WEST DISTRICT

Area: 2383 km^2	**Capital: Haapsalu,**
Population: 33 780	**population 14 930**

Every thousand years, Läänemaa ("west county") rises 1-2 m. Little by little the islands are united with the continent, and new islands rise from the sea. Virtsu and Noarootsi, large peninsulas today, were islands a few centuries ago. It's possible to walk through the sea to Tauksi island. As a result of the sea's withdrawal the "newborn" landscapes of Läänemaa are quite young compared with those of southern Estonia. Läänemaa's land is flat and low. There's a great deal of pastureland and meadows, swamps and forests. Young land is not very fertile, so the county has always been sparsely populated.

Ancient Läänemaa was called Maritima ("by the sea" in Latin) and Rotalia in the 13th century. There were sturdy fortifications at Lihula and Karuse, but the plain was not the best place to build forts. That's one of the reasons Läänemaa was weaker than its neighbouring districts. A railway was built here only because the court of the czar was swept by a fashion for the health resort and curative mud of Haapsalu. In the past Swedes lived on Vormsi island and Noarootsi peninsula. Though the people fled after World War II, they've still given those areas a subtly Swedish flavour.

HAAPSALU

Estonia's Venice lies in the bosom of peninsulas and coves. In the centre is the ruin of a powerful bishop's castle. The memories of the days when the town was a health resort for the Russian court also linger.

The White Lady

The Haapsalu inlet, cutting deep into the land, is still and shallow. In

Hot enough for a boat ride. Haapsalu harbour.

wintertime you can see fishermen in the frozen coves. Some of Haapsalu's ice-boat sailors are world champions. The inlet is the source of the town's curative mud, and thus of its prosperity. But the history of **Haapsalu***** is much older than that.

In the Middle Ages Haapsalu was a regular victim of war and conflagration, and from 1265 it became the seat of the Bishop of Saare-Lääne (the ancient bishopric of west Estonia and the islands). For the next 300 years the bishops ruled a vast section of Estonia from Haapsalu; their other major fortress, on Saaremaa, still stands today. The

ruins of the bishop's castle** dominate the town centre. The wall of the fortress was 805 m long and 10 m high. Standing in the inner courtyard or climbing on the ruins you get a powerful impression of the fortification. Of the original quadrangular palace, only the church has been preserved in the southern wing.

At full moon in August, you can see the White Lady at one of the church windows. She was the beloved of a priest and under the obscure impulse of love she dared to step over the castle threshold. As no female was allowed inside, the lady was punished by being immured alive into a wall of the church. You can see her once a year at the **central window of the large, curved baptistry****. Locals are not deceived by sceptics, who explain the appearance of the figure as merely moonlight reflected off the limed wall. Expecting the White Lady and a performance on the theme are the culmination of the White Lady Festival every August.

Glorious mud

Old Haapsalu is located on one of two thin strips of land poking into the bay. Between the two strips lies Väike-viik, a shallow inlet filled with miraculous mud. The first mud bath was founded in 1825, and suddenly the town became a resort. Czars and composers visited.

Today Haapsalu is a small, quiet holiday resort that's seen better days. With their lazily meandering streets, the wooden houses and gardens of the **Old Town**** are especially attractive in the summertime, when lilacs, jasmine and chestnut trees bloom. You can circle the town along the footpath by the shore, passing several monuments and resort buildings. Most amusing is **Tchaikovsky's bench***, where the great Russian composer used to sit and write music in 1867. Near the bench there's a monument to C A Hunnius, the sea-mud researcher who founded the first baths. The wooden pumproom and covered bandstand date back to the turn of the century. The old "cure room" *(kuursaal)*, an empty husk on the bay, echoes with memories.

The railway opened in 1906 and the station's **grand platform** really is worthy of a czar – it's the longest in Estonia. But like many of the old resort buildings, it needs a cash-and-love injection. Opposite the entrance to the castle you can visit the good little local **museum*** to find out more about the glory days.

VORMSI AND NORTHERN LÄÄNEMAA

Vormsi island and Noarootsi peninsula have retained some of their centuries-old Swedish charm.

Vormsi island

From the 13th century **Vormsi island**** ($93 km^2$) belonged to Swedes, who departed with over 10 000 Estonians in 1944, before the Soviet army invaded. Today its population is just an eighth of the pre-war population. A dozen years ago the houses were falling into ruin and Vormsi was an island of ghosts. Now holiday-makers are moving in from the city, and the Swedes are coming back to visit and reminisce.

The best way to discover the island is on bicycle, though it's not too big for walkers. There's much here for a peaceful weekend: **Saxby ligh-**

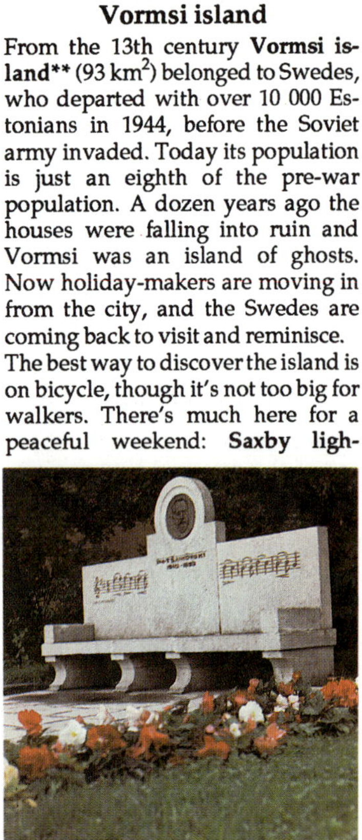

Tchaikovsky composed his "Haapsalu bibs 'n' bobs" here.

Lawnmower in the ruins of the bishop's castle. No concerts the day this was taken.

thouse; a 3 km long peninsula called **"Rumpo nose"** that's the world's only non-Arctic home for Arctic lichen; the 2.5 m high **Hoitburg coral reef;** the 5.8 m high **church-stone*** near Diiby village; the state farm with its derelict Orthodox church; as well as thick bushland, boulder-strewn coast, fishing and hunting. Vormsi's **14th-century church**** in Hullo village is one of the most pristine and inspirational in Estonia. There's a youngish thatcher on the island, so the traditional style farms are being revived.

You can smell the past in the local history museum, formerly Haapsalu town hall.

A ferry carries people and cars to Vormsi from Rohuküla harbour near Haapsalu in an hour (2-3 a day; try to be early; coming by car, they'll call out your number plate when it's your turn). You may have to pay a visitor's tax on arrival.

Noarootsi and the "birch law"

The distance from Haapsalu to **Noarootsi peninsula*** across the cove is about 1 km; by road it's 40 times further. Noarootsi is a peninsula of coastal meadows, juniper fields and pine woods. The coast is full of reeds, waiting to be turned into classic cane thatched roofs by

Junipers love Vormsi island.

the few Estonians who can still do it. The first reference to local Swedes dates back to 1294, the last to 1944. In the centre of the peninsula in **Pürksi*** you can find a beautiful manor park. Pürksi's name, from the Swedish word *björk*, a birch, is also related to Birka, an old trading town in Sweden. *Björk* happens to be the root of dozens of place names along the coast of Norway up to Karelia. These towns and villages were trading centres, where the so-called "Birka law" was in force. From **Österby** ("east village") there's a wonderful view of Haapsalu 2.5 km across the water. Noarootsi may strike you as a lonely place, whose past could tell us much but is keeping its mouth shut.

New land and pure lakes

The road from Noarootsi to Rigulda used to follow the coast. Passing by **Sutlepa village** you can find a subterranean river that disappears underground 2.5 km from the sea. The water spreads through numerous "graves" and only shows itself 1.5 km later. (Just ask for the *karsti rajoon.)*

The coast of Riguldi is the north-western edge of continental Estonia, and faces open sea. **Põõsaspea Cape**

Österby, a Swedish village on Noarootsi peninsula.

at the top, shaped by the sea into narrow limestone hills, fits in well with the wild scape. On a clear day you can glimpse **Osmussaar island** 10 km off the coast. When we went to press it was still occupied by the ex-Soviet army, which considers the island a "lock" to the Gulf of Finland. By 1994 it should be well and truly unlocked.

At the very north of Läänemaa, **around Nõva,** there are heaths, swamps and bogs. You'll only find villages and individual farms near roads and on some higher mounds. There are waterplants in three lakes here that are remarkably similar to those of the Scandinavian and Karelian lakes. The purest of them is the lovely **Veskijärv.**

The route returns southwards to Seljaküla and the Haapsalu-Keila road. A left turn at the pig stud in Linnamäe takes you to **Koela***, an old farming village with a farm museum. **Nigula's** 14th-century church is not much further; and its old cemetery is quite inviting. On the other side of Nigula you meet the Haapsalu-Tallinn highway.

"Sure I'll show you round. Do you speak Sheep?"

Shame of a Polish king

Läänemaa, long one of Estonia's poorest counties, has been linked from time to time with splendid legends of great people. In **Taebla,**

Pines grow on the old dunes.

A pure lake-spring at Nõva.

not far from Haapsalu on the Tallinn highway, there's a spring near the schoolhouse. It was by the spring that the locals noticed the King of Poland; His Majesty dropped a churchbell with a clang and blushingly fumbled for excuses. Old folk say he'd looked quite keen to take off with the bell.

Despite the legend, Taebla is better known for the **home of artist Ants Laikmaa*** (1866-1942), now a museum in his honour. A few kilometres from Taebla towards Haapsalu a signpost points the way. Laikmaa's home is as eccentric as the man himself. It's worth visiting for its thatched roof and unusual garret (an arrangement of triangular windows creates a harmonious mix of light and shadow), as well as works by the artist and other exhibits. His *cute* summer house is 100 m away. Ants Laikmaa was one of the first great ethnically Estonian painters. He walked 2000 km to Düsseldorf to study painting, and on his return began to treat the subject matter of Estonia on a new level. He founded a studio and school and gathered other Estonian artists round him. The place gives a taste of turn-of-the-century Bohemia.

SOUTHERN LÄÄNEMAA

Besides historical places lost and found, the south of the county includes two extraordinary natural treasures, Matsalu Bay and the Puhtu region.

Grave of a Swedish king

P'raps you can help the archaeologists while you're going south from Haapsalu. About 600 AD

Sweden's King Ingwar started a war against Estonians and razed a place called Adalsyla. The tenacious Estonians killed the king in their counter-attack. According to the saga, he was buried near the sea at "Stein". People have chosen to look for Ingwar's grave all over the **Ridala** district, though without result. Some clues point to the area. The old name of Ridala – Rotalia – once embraced the whole of Läänemaa, and the remains of a fortress wall south of the town indicate that an ancient settlement stood here. **Ridala church*** dates back to the 13th century.

As the hammer was descending ...

In the autumn of 1944, hordes of Estonians headed by road from Ridala south-west to the **coast of Puise peninsula.** They weren't going for the view: they were desperate to cross the sea before Soviet troops arrived. Tens of thousands of refugees, fleeing on those stormy September nights, escaped to establish their own communities in Sweden, Canada and Australia. By the roadside you can see **Põgari prayer-house** where the government of the Republic of Estonia, led by Prime Minister Otto Tief, held its last session. Not everyone managed to find room on the overloaded boats and not all the boats could get to them in time. (Tief has another monument in Raplamaa.)

Paradise of birds

Going due south-east from Ridala, a right turn goes to Haeska. If there's one world-famous place in Läänemaa, then it's the **Matsalu wildlife reserve**** – if not among people then certainly among birds. Tens of thousands of swans stop at Matsalu Bay for a couple of days in mid April. Although they're only passing through, they always choose Matsalu as their halt. The first arrive in February, but the real flocks come when the ice in the bay starts to melt. On the low coastal meadow there's a tower for those who want to observe the sea-birds.

The reserve's study centre and bird museum are at **Haeska estate***, a typical example of a neoclassical Estonian estate from the beginning of the 19th century. Today you can see slide-tape programs about Matsalu here. The wildlife reserve was instituted in 1958, and accorded inter-

Matsalu Bay takes on the tourists ...

... and keeps ducks safe in its care.

national status in 1971. The 400 km^2 area is administered at Penijõe, south-east of the bay.

Broad Kasari River empties into the bay carrying water thick with chemicals and fertilisers, and Matsalu is growing over. Every year the borderline of reeds extends a further 100 m. The flood plain of the Kasari is still Europe's richest sanctuary in birds. Some 68 species hatch their young here, and 103 species make their nests on the islands. A boat from Penijõe harbour takes you out to learn about the reeds and the bay (see below).

North-east of Haeska is **Martna,** a small country town. The 15th-century church was built in gothic style by the bishops of Saare-Lääne. You can see their coats-of-arms, resplendent with symbols of power õ a mitre, bishop's staffs, escutcheon and eagle.

Restorations near Kullamaa

Continuing south-east, at the Laiküla junction your choices are Tallinn and Virtsu. There are one or two places worth visiting in the direction of Tallinn. People have lived at **Kullamaa** since the earliest times. The local church was completed in the 13th century and, typically, changed its appearance over the next few centuries. The pulpit, the epitaph and the "Celtic" crosses date back to the 17th century. Kullamaa was one of the first villages to re-establish its monument to the War of Independence, something the Soviets forbade for decades.

A watermill on the Liivi River still has its old equipment and mill-dam with gates. Further north towards Tallinn, **Koluvere castle*** is a reconstruction of a 13th-century fortress. Several hundred years after the first building was completed, the river was diverted round it with the help of reservoirs and dams and so

Koluvere gained a moat. In 1905 the rebellious peasantry burnt the fortress down, but it has since been reconstructed. Risti is 12 km from Koluvere and Tallinn in its turn is about 50 km from Risti. But wait – you have yet to see the most southerly portion of Läänemaa.

View from a bridge

If instead you take the Virtsu turn at the Laiküla junction, you reach **Kasari bridge.** From this famous bridge there's a view over the **Kasari water-meadow*,** the 15 km long area of meadows up to Matsalu Bay. In the spring high water it's one great flood plain. A new bridge was built in 1990 but the old one – 308 m long, built in 1904 – has more charm. The Kasari is a mighty river, pouring 30 m^3 of water per second into the sea.

On the coastal plain, in the middle of **Kirbla village,** there's a late-gothic 15th-century church with a late-baroque altar and chandelier. The other local landmark is natural **Kirbla limestone scale.** This hill was born of sea sediments in the Silurian age. It's the site of an old settlement with six stone barrows (graves).

Lihula's attractive position

In 1220 the Swedish king landed with his army and conquered **Lihula*.** Less than a year later, the warlike people of Saaremaa island attacked the stronghold, slaughtered the Swedish garrison of 500 men and took Lihula back. The fortress's geographical position has attracted battles for centuries. Prosperity in the 15th century was followed by rough times after the Livonian War (1558-83). But the medieval castle's ruins, a manor house, old tavern and Russian Orthodox church remain.

These Kullamaa girls know what looks good.

The main roads from Lihula go to Pärnu and Virtsu. There's also a sideroad leading 3 km to the Matsalu centre in the manor at **Penijõe**.** In addition to boat excursions, a permanent exhibition and slide programs, Penijõe has a bird-ringing centre. Every year 120 000 birds are labelled for scientific research. On the southern coast of Matsalu Bay you can see hills formed of primordial coral and giant boulders. The biggest of them -- the **Näärikivid*** ("new-year stones") near Saastna at the mouth of the bay – were carried here by ice one long-gone new year's eve, or so the old people say.

Tuudi is 3 km from Lihula in the direction of Virtsu. The **classic west-Estonian landscape** of low plateaus, age-old forests and swamps is best seen from the small plateau where the Tuudi River meets the sea. **Karuse** and **Hanila** are old Estonian church villages. On the side of the road at **Kõmsi*,** not far from Hanila, you can see fenced barrows from the 1st-2nd centuries. And over 1000 finds have been excavated at a nearby 11th-12th-century crematorium.

The landscape changes to large juniper fields full of great boulders. As you approach Suur väin (the "great channel" between here and Saaremaa) and Virtsu peninsula, you can see **Uisu cliff.** The waves tear pyritic crystals from the cliff, which people like to collect on the beach. There's a particularly large number of boulders around **Kiireste hill.** The epic hero Kalevipoeg was bringing stones from the seaside for building, when the great bumbler's apron broke and the stones fell out. The people of Saaremaa island have

There was once a fort on Vatla hill, where Estonians fought battles in ancient times.

their own story about the stones. They say that their legendary hero, Suur Tõll ("Big Tõll"), tried to build a bridge of stones between the mainland and Saaremaa.

And here, at Kaseküla, they buried their dead.

An exotic peninsula

The sea and Virtsu harbour appear. The ruins of a vassal stronghold lie by the sea. From Virtsu you can take a ferry to Saaremaa, since Suur Tõll never finished his bridge.

Puhtulaid peninsula** is on the south-eastern side. Two centuries ago people began to build summer cottages and ornamental gardens here and the lush broadleaf forest was turned into a park. In 1813 a local councillor established a modest monument to Friedrich Schiller, the first monument to Schiller in the world. There's an exotic **broadleaf forest**** at Puhtu with a 600-year-old oak that's 23 m high and has a diameter of 1.38 m. The marine climate and soil rich in lime have created a small natural miracle. Birds (137 species!) live in the forest and 370 species of plants in **Laelatu's woody meadow.** The southern coastline starting from Virtsu is full of coves and islands. You can relax at some lovely isolated places and see coastal lakes that have only recently become separated from the sea.

Läänemaa's restrained landscape and long history are interwoven, and reshaping human hands have done little in the county. After all, as quickly as you remake everything, new land grows out of the sea!

PRACTICAL DETAILS

ACCOMODATION

"Haapsalu" hotel, 43. Posti, Haapsalu, tel 4 48 47
"Sporthotell", 3a. Ehitajate tee, Haapsalu, tel 5 67 73
"Pipi" pension, 37. Posti, Haapsalu, tel 4 51 74
Yachting Club, 5a. Holmi, Haapsalu, tel 9 71 72
Lihula guest-house, 10. Tallinna, Lihula, tel 7 55 27
Virtsu hostel, Virtsu, tel 7 55 27
Roosta camping, Noarootsi, tel 9 37 32
Silma camping, tel 4 55 82
Rumpo pension, Vormsi, tel 9 23 41
Suuremõisa pension, Vormsi, tel 9 23 09

RESTAURANTS

"Hubertus", 21. Männiku tee, Haapsalu
"Martima", 1. Tallinna mnt., Haapsalu, tel 4 44 45
"Paralepa", Haapsalu, tel 4 40 54
"TAMEN", 1a. Jaama, Palivere, tel 9 41 02
Peetri Pizza, 18. Karja, Haapsalu, tel 4 44 96

In Läänemaa ("western land") you can finally convince yourself that the sun sets in the west.

BARS & CAFES

"Greitz", 3. Karja, Haapsalu
"Wölvi", 4. Kalda, Haapsalu
Rootsituru cafe, 3. Karja, Haapsalu, tel 4 50 58
"Meririst" bar, 1. Tallinna, Haapsalu
"WESPO" bar, 10. Lihula mnt., Haapsalu
"Viigi" bar, 15. Suur-Lossi, Haapsalu
"R.E.J." bar, 22. Lihula mnt., Haapsalu
Count's Palace Cafe
GRILLBAAR, 14. Karja, Haapsalu
"Särts", Lihula, tel 7 82 62
"Mutionu", Virtsu
"Venta", 1a. Jalaka, Haapsalu, tel 5 57 66

TRAVEL BUREAU

WESRTA TRAVEL, 39. Posti, Haapsalu, tel 4 56 49
"WEST" Ltd., 14. Holmi, Haapsalu, tel 4 40 38
"WESTRA" Ltd., 6. Vaba, Haapsalu, tel 4 55 69
RETA Travel Agency, 39. Posti, Haapsalu, tel 4 52 57

MUSEUMS

Läänemaa regional museum, 2. Kooli, Haapsalu, tel 4 45 65
ANTS LAIKMAA MUSEUM, Taebla, tel 9 66 88
MATSALU NATURE RESERVE, Lihula, tel 7 84 13

FILLING STATIONS

Haapsalu, 11. Lihula mnt., tel 5 51 02
Tallinna mnt., tel 5 60 42

CAR SERVICE

Haapsalu, 73. Tallinna mnt., tel 5 58 84

TRANSPORT

ROHUKÜLA HARBOUR, tel 9 11 38 (ferry to Hiiumaa and Vormsi)
Haapsalu Yacht-Club, tel 4 55 82

TELEPHONE AREA CODE: 247

RAPLAMAA

Area: 2980 km^2	**Capital: Rapla**
Population: 39 900	**population 6390**

Raplamaa was founded only 40 years ago from the border regions of four ancient counties, and tends to be rather countrified, as the edges of counties usually are. Its flat landscape is unspectacular but perfect for farming. Don't expect small, quaint villages. This is the place for state farms, many of which have chosen to erect their concrete houses and oversized barns near old manors or fortresses. The pleasures of Raplamaa – its manors and restored inns and two good small museums – lie on either side of the trunk roads through the county, the Pärnu and Viljandi highways. The two tours here start at the county's northern edge.

SOUTH ALONG THE VILJANDI HIGHWAY

Manors and inns lie either side of the Viljandi highway, a real rural heartland.

Of oxen and lost Ifob watches

From Kernu on the *Pärnu* highway in Harjumaa, you can drive east along a pretty country road towards Kohila. When **Hageri church** was being built, devils kept wrecking the work each night. The builders, perhaps influenced by some spirit, put a load of stone on a wagon and let the oxen decide on a better site. Being oxen, they headed straight for a barn *(hager)*, which explains the town's name.

A detour 4 km south of Kohila takes you to **Lohu manor***, where 18th-century wallpapers with scenes from *Don Quixote* were discovered in the hallway. They're now in the history museum in Tallinn. Like the manor house itself, the glassed-in wooden balconies date from the late 18th century. Bridge, wall, balconies and roof form a dainty suite.

In **Angerja*** east of the highway are the ruins of a 15th-century vassal fortress. It's easy to get there from Kohila: head past the former mill, now a cafe, and Kohila's Orthodox church; take a left onto the highway and then the first right (sign says "Jägala"); keep going past the Juuru junction and turn right onto the little road just beyond the short bridge. You can still see remnants of the 6 m walls, and a typical collective farm nearby.

Even harder to locate is the biggest boulder in the area. You *may* find the huge stone in fir forest 3 km north of Angerja, if you walk around the perimeter of the military base. The baron of Pahkla lost his **gold fob-watch** in a crack in this boulder, and no one's found it yet.

Two Raplamaa theatres

Retrace your steps to the Juuru turn and head south. Follow the signs to **Järlepa,** for a while the home of August Kotzebue, Estonia's most

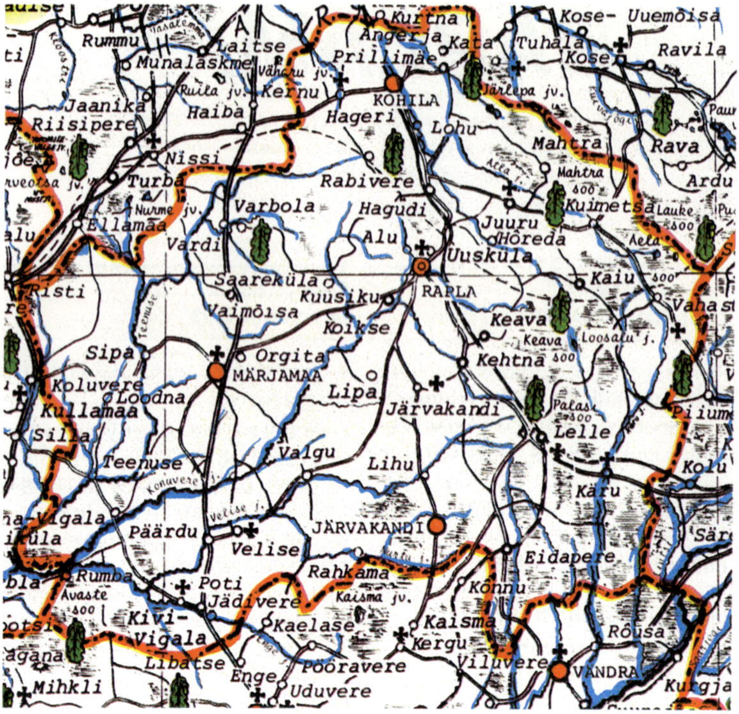

popular playwright last century. He organised a theatre here using nobles from nearby manors as actors. The courtyard-theatre existed for three years, then broke up when Kotzebue moved to Varbola after divorcing his wife. Now turkeys are bred at Järlepa. The long, tree-lined approach to the rather noble manor house would be splendid if it weren't for the small blockhouses on either side.

Back to the Juuru road, there's an attractive neoclassical manor on the Atla River by the roadside, hidden by trees. Take a left at the unsignposted asphalt road by the Pirgu busstop, then first left over the bridge. After World War II, the manor house in **Pirgu*** was designated to become a brickworks. Here's planning for you: the 20 m smokestack was already up before they realised there was no clay in the area. The project was abandoned and the manor fell derelict. Trees started to grow through the hallway. But in the mid 1980s a **centre for the development of country life** was founded here and the manor was restored, though a little clumsily. To see it, try the warden in the fenced house or ring Rapla 56908. The rambling old cellar is sometimes a bar, and you can see a photo of the ruin with chimneystack in the album in the ballroom. The oral history section is actually a theatre which performs the life stories of Estonians based on documentary materials, though currently they're suffering from the post-Soviet disease, lack of money.

The Mahtra war

The small manor of Mahtra and the featureless village in the forest would have remained quite unknown if there hadn't been an uprising against the landlords, the "War of Mahtra" on 14 June 1858. You can take a detour to **Mahtra** itself to see the monument, or cut to the chase in **Juuru,** at the fine **Mahtra Peasantry Museum*.** Many of the captions are in English. The first room gives you a feeling for the lives of peasants and barons in the middle of the 19th century. The second explains the war itself, and shows the sorts of crude weapons the 1000 peasants used against 50 well-armed soldiers sent by the central government in St Petersburg. The rebels were defeated and severely punished. The two main leaders received 1000 lashes and 20 years in prison, the other "ringleaders" a little less, while minor culprits were whipped. The Mahtra uprising was a revolt against unjust land laws – the powers in St Petersburg soon reformed them.

Both the church and the village of Juuru date back to the year 1238. The church was built on the site of a grove sacred to Estonians and the last roots of the grove-oak gave the place its name – Juuru ("of the root"). The **village inn**** at the end of the main street is the only well preserved village inn in the land. It's part of the Peasantry Museum, since it was the rebels' HQ, and you can ask at the museum about visiting.

A left (east) turn off the Viljandi highway at the railway crossing leads to 200-year-old **Nõmme inn**.** It's an inn again today, thoroughly spruced up, and a favourite local haunt.

PM for a day and his chimney

The dirt road just before the turn to Alu goes to a large memorial plaque on a small **chimneystand,** in the backyard of the first house. The chimney was part of the house where Otto Tief was born. In 1944, when the Germans had fled Tallinn and the Russians had not yet arrived, the underground Estonian government led by Tief declared an independent Estonian Republic. The Soviet occupation army came the next day and sent the one-day prime minister to Siberia for 10 years. The **Alu manor house** near Rapla resembles a fortified castle.

Not a town

Rapla was first chronicled in 1241. Half a century later a church dedicated to Mary Magdalene was built and Rapla became a parish centre. Though it's now county capital Rapla has never had town status, even during the Soviet years, when you could tell you were in a town by its statue of Lenin. Now the Lenins are disappearing everywhere and something new will have to be found to signify a town.

The approach from the north is more inspiring than the place itself. Rapla's is one of only two churches in Estonia with **two towers*;** the other is in Tallinn. Closer in, the buildings beneath the steeples resolve into a petrol station and shop, which speaks volumes. The church's altarpiece, pulpit and organ were made in Tallinn's best workshops. On the riverbank nearby stands the oldest building in Rapla, the pastorate from 1774. In front of this grows an oak commemorating the abolition of serfdom.

Despite being a parish centre, power was always in the hands of the landlord in Alu. When they were building the railway from Tallinn to Viljandi at the turn of the century the master of Alu refused to allow it onto his land for fear that the train whistle would send his horses wild. So the railway was built on the neighbouring manor and Rapla folk had to take a bus to their railway station. The town has since stretched up to the station.

Test your conscience

If you're in Rapla on midsummer's eve, you can put your purity to the test. On the Viljandi highway, halfway between the town centre and the station, near the Estoplast busstop, there's a **huge stone***, three-quarters buried. On 23 June everyone with a clear conscience can hear a bell ringing here. The bell is around the neck of a foal buried under the stone with a wolf. A man mowing hay 15 versts (about 16 km) away noticed the wolf hunting the foal, and hurled the closest thing to hand, his whetstone. He was of course the legendary hero Kalevipoeg helping a widow make hay in Ööre village. Unfortunately, the stone had a girth of 20 m, and both foal and wolf were trapped beneath it. And so the bell rings there every St John's Eve (though to tell the truth up till now nobody's heard it.)

The generous Keyserlings

You can go straight on through to Viljandi via **Kaerepere*** – one of the great collective farm towns – and Kehtna. Or you could take an attractive detour along the Järvakandi road, running south from Rapla's church, through Raikküla.

Nowadays **Raikküla manor*** is a fine ruin attached to a school for the mentally handicapped. For centuries it belonged to the Keyserling dynasty. A student at Berlin University and a good friend of Bismarck, Alexander Keyserling gained fame as a geologist. He was also loved by his peasants whose lives he tried to make much easier. He overdid it sometimes. Once he ordered chimneys to be built onto chimneyless

One of Märjamaa's churches.

Ruussalu's old stone bridge.

huts, paying for them himself. The huts now lost heat quickly, and the peasants had to fill the chimneys in again. Alexander's grandson, Hermann Keyserling, is a famous philosopher; Raikküla's intellectual atmosphere was not rarefied enough for him and he moved to Germany. His son Arnold Keyserling has decided to reverse the trend and since 1990 has organised philosophy summer schools here.
On the way from Raikküla to Kehtna you'll visit the windmill of **Põlma***. This centuries-old Dutch windmill is now a first-class restaurant and photo-stop.

From valet to horse-thief

Jüri Rumm worked as a valet in **Kehtna manor** at the end of last century. A legendary horse-thief who played tricks on the authorities and never got caught, "Rummu Jüri" is known all over Estonia. A popular operetta about him carries his fame from generation to generation. You can spend half an hour wandering beneath the tall trees in Kehtna **manor park**, craning your neck and looking for its 30 m high European larch, hundreds of years old. Clue: the larch is north-east of the manor house. Kehtna state farm is an important scientific centre. Here, for the first time in Estonia, pigs were artificially fertilised.

SOUTH ALONG THE PÄRNU HIGHWAY

While the manors along the Pärnu highway have decayed, Varbola hill-fort has survived to give you a good idea of how the ancient Estonians defended themselves. Sillaotsa Museum shows a (slightly) more recent side to Estonian life.

Cosy Ruunavere

Not far inside the northern border of the county, a motel sign indicates **Ruunavere** ("gelding blood"). Near the mill during a battle in the Livonian War, so much blood flowed that it reached up to the knees of a gelding. This was mainly the blood of 2000 Swedes killed here fighting the Poles on 3 February 1567. Last century when the Russian Empire built its network of post-roads, Ruunavere became a pleasant

Visiting Varbola hill-fort.

post-station on the Tallinn-Riga road, where geldings as well as people could put their feet up for a bit. Now the post-station has been restored as a spiffy restaurant and motel. The grave of notorious Vene Rubla is out the front.

The well at Varbola stronghold.

Ancient fortress

The owner of **Vardi manor** in Varbola was August von Kotzebue, the aforementioned playwright from Järlepa manor (see above). He was an impetuous enemy of Napoleon, and during the French campaign against Moscow the frightened baron kept a two-horse coach at the ready in case Napoleon came to Varbola. And he cleverly promoted potato cultivation among the peasants: by day he mounted an armed guard around the manor's potato field, which he conveniently forgot when night fell. He could have worked in advertising.

The **Varbola stronghold****, 4 km from the highway through Varbola village, is the most powerful surviving hill-fort from ancient Estonia. A walk along the top of the wall gives you an idea of the size. This half-a-million cartloads of stone was never taken by force. There were two gates, one of which has been reconstructed.

Märjamaa lies halfway between Tallinn and Pärnu on the highway. The local gothic Lutheran church has beautiful inner proportions. See it during Sunday services.

When wise folk could not build

Keep going through Märjamaa, then through Paeküla to Vana-Vigala. **Vana-Vigala manor** belonged to the oldest Baltic-German family, the Uexkülls. You can see the oldest works of art in Estonia on the walls of the mansion lobby – small, 2500-year-old, marble bas-reliefs from Pompeii – on weekdays when the school's open. The great **park*** out back is good for a ramble. Its grounds are well-treed and its several lakes well-algaed.

Kivi-Vigala ("stone Vigala") was the richest parish centre in old Läänemaa. For those with the know-how, the streaky clay soil of Vigala gives a good crop. Fertile clay opened the way to prosperity and gave wider opportunities to the people. Several important cultural and public figures come from the area. Two renowned sons of Vigala are Ants Laikmaa, a founding figure in Estonian art, and composer Veljo Tormis whose "runic" songs, based on ancient folk songs, are the most important contribution to Estonian music this century.

Yet for a long time Vigalans couldn't build houses that would stand up. Vigala manor house took only a few days to sink beneath the earth, and the Vigala church became the local tower of Pisa and had to be pulled down. Later it emerged that the wondrous clay, which extends down 20 metres, was responsible. *Viga* means "mistake". The locals say that the first stone building was a stone mistake, and thus Kivi-Vigala, and the second time round it was the old mistake again, thus Vana-Vigala. The nicest thing in town now is the current **church.** An oak out front was planted way back in 1989.

Collectors and the camel man

Take the road from Kivi-Vigala to Päärdu, cross the highway and head towards the village of **Velise,** which raises strong men. Georg Lurich is a synonym for athlete to Estonians. In one of his best turns, Lurich held his arms together and two horses were unable to pull them apart. On his tour of Central Asia he repeated the trick with two camels, which are much stronger than horses. The enthusiastic emir of Bukhara gave him the animals as a present and Lurich brought them to Velise. His nephew earned a good living exhibiting these "monsters" at fairs, until the next winter which they didn't survive. Evil minds suspect that the trick was more cunning than strength: old photos show that the ropes were tied round the camels' necks with slip-knots, so the harder the animals pulled, the more the ropes strangled. Lurich died of typhus in 1920 in North Caucasus. His fans are still searching for his bones for reburial in Estonia, but so far the commission of experts has certified none of the bones found as Lurich's.

Another powerful local was Tõnis Ervin. When the Orthodox church was being built in Velise he had a wee patriotic quarrel with the bricklayers. The court found him innocent as the judge couldn't believe that one man could beat up 50 bricklayers. So you can understand why during the disorders in 1905 the people of Velise were among the most eager to "nationalise" the property of the government and the barons. They were the first to

Memorial to the Mahtra War (1858).

declare a republic – the Republic of Velise which was in force inside the borders of the rural district. Eventually this cost many their lives, and they are remembered in the **memorial stone** in front of the Orthodox church.

One kilometre to the north is **Sillaotsa Farm Museum***, a treasure-trove for the farm machinery buff or anyone interested in the way of life of local people. You might have to visit the yellow house another 500 m further north to get the caretaker. The collection is based on the vision of a single dedicated individual, and everything on display was donated by locals ... many were built by locals too.

Highlights include: a photo of strongman Georg Lurich with his camels; the *hernesorteer* or "peasorter"; a locally made 4-horse corn mill which the caretaker might demonstrate for you; and various implements for making linen, once the lifeblood of the local economy – people had to work such machines as the treadle press all day long.

From here you can rock on back to the Pärnu highway, or head through Valgu and do a loop through the county along the Viljandi highway.

PRACTICAL DETAILS

ACCOMODATION

Hotel "Rapla", 1. Kuusiku tee, Rapla, tel 5 56 45
"Purila" motel, 14. Tallinna mnt., Rapla, tel 5 54 90
Pirgu estate, Pirgu, tel 4 12 13
"Tuur" motel, Hageri, tel 7 71 67
"Ruunavere" hotel (since summer 1993), Märjamaa

RESTAURANTS

RAPLA, 1. Kooli, Rapla, tel 5 60 96
JÄRVAKANDI, 33. Tallinna, Rapla, tel 7 76 39
RANGU, Märjamaa, tel 2 12 71
PÕLMA WINDMILL, Järvakandi, tel 6 30 09
RUUNAVERE, Märjamaa, tel 7 71 61

BARS & CAFES

Rapla, 19. Tallinna, tel 5 71 77
Rapla, 3. Hariduse, tel 5 78 37
Tohisoo bar, 37. Viljandi mnt., Kohila, tel 3 38 87
Alu bar, tel 6 83 16
"Koopa" bar, Märjamaa
"Suksu" bar, Kuusiku

Even in a small place like Rapla, there's no escaping the blockhouses.

MUSEUMS

MAHTRA RURAL HISTORY MUSEUM, Juuru, tel 4 41 99
SILLAOTSA, farm-museum, Velise, tel 2 87 13, 2 57 48

FILLING STATIONS

Rapla, 1. Tallinna, tel 5 53 35
Märjamaa, Orgita, tel 2 17 27

CAR SERVICE

Rapla, 19. Tallinna, tel 7 33 77
Rapla, tel 5 65 89
Märjamaa, 131-7 Pärnu mnt., tel 2 12 99
Kehtna, tel 7 55 98
Vana-Vigala, tel 2 45 80

TELEPHONE AREA CODE: 248

SAAREMAA

Area: 2922 km^2	**Capital: Kuressaare**
Population: 40 490	**population 16 570**

Saaremaa is Estonia's largest and most famous island. The county includes 500 smaller islands and islets. The largest of them, Muhu, is connected to Saaremaa by a stone causeway. The county's most distant responsibility is little Ruhnu, in the middle of the Gulf of Riga.

The ideal picture of Saaremaa contains flat juniper fields, windmills, ancient villages with thatched cottages and stone fences many centuries old. For a mainland Estonian the dream of Saaremaa has a powerful whiff of **pale, strong beer and dried flounder.** Many enjoy the dream so much that the next day they have swollen mouths and furry tongues.

Saaremaa attracts visitors of many interests and inclinations. The west coast is a bird paradise, especially the island of Vilsandi. Lake Kaali is one of the best-preserved meteorite craters in Europe. The sites of ancient Estonian forts, the bishop's castle in Kuressaare, old manor estates, medieval churches, dolomite mines – history has left some outstanding monuments in its wake.

The islanders form a people of their own. They have their own dialect, customs, songs, national clothing, tales, heroes, even their own special way of salting fish and cooking bread. Every year curiosity inveigles more and more visitors into making the journey here, and it can get touristy in summertime. A bus leaves for Kuressaare from Tallinn four times a day. From Virtsu a ferry leaves every half hour or thereabouts. There are fine yacht harbours in Nasva and Roomassaare, both within 6 km of Kuressaare.

There are times to avoid crossing – on Fridays from the mainland to the island and on Sundays coming back the queues of cars for the ferry can be insane. Visitors must pay a landing tax, though an invitation from an islander entitles you to a multiple-entry permit. It's worth it ... you may well want to stop by again!

Mustjala girls in costume.

MUHU

Muhu island's history and culture are closely linked to Saaremaa's. The undoubted highlight is the village of Koguva.

First stop, Muhu

After a mere 30 minutes on the ferry, you find yourself in the port of Kuivastu. You're not on Saaremaa yet: first the main road leads across Muhu island to a causeway over the Väike väin ("small strait").

At 200 km^2, **Muhu**** is the third-largest Estonian island. Over 6000 people once lived on it, and nine manors were built here. Apart from the barons, many free peasants also owned property. It may be in memory of their ancient liberty that Muhu women still wear traditional clothing to village parties and weddings. The Muhu costume is so well-known that it's sometimes considered Estonia's national costume, which is inaccurate, since every parish had its own costume.

The large colonnaded building on the left as you leave the port is the old 19th-century **Kuivastu inn.** A detour to the south coast takes you to a partly renovated manor, **Pädaste.** A detour to the north coast reaches **Üügu cliff.**

In the heart of the island, in Liiva village, **Muhu church*** dates from the 13th-14th centuries. There are fragments of 13th-century murals of the Last Judgment inside. The key is usually kept at the post office.

Just like the old days

The protected **village of Koguva***** is a living, working Estonian village. It's also an open-air museum, a record of the lives of Muhu's free peasants. Koguva was given its liberty in 1532, reputedly because a serf saved his master's life. All 105 buildings are protected. There are about 30 residents now, mostly older people, and plenty more in summertime. Many buildings are stone, and some of the homes and stables are surprisingly grand. Walk about the grassy lanes lined with mossy 200-year-old stone fences, past boats resting on walls... A boat was like a good friend. Old ones were retired to walls and could only be burnt on midsummer's eve.

Please don't disturb the villagers by camping, invading their homes, or picking their flowers and fruit. To see the village you have to buy a ticket at the farmhouse near the entrance. This is also the **Muhu Museum** and birthplace of writer Juhan Smuul. **A textile exhibition***, documenting the history of Muhu's costume, is in another building which staff will gladly open for you.

In summer, you can walk out to **Keinastu isle,** not far off the coast near Koguva.

Just before you leave the island you come to **Eemu windmill****, the only working trestle-windmill in the republic. You can buy flour milled right here.

TRAVELLING TO KURESSAARE

The road to Kuressaare leads past several historical centres and eerie Lake Kaali.

Strongholds and churches

Once across the 3.6 km causeway, turn off the main road towards Laimjala; another left the other side of the Levala busstop takes you to **one well-defended church***. Pöide church was in the centre of the lands of the German Order in the region. The castle next to it was destroyed in the St George's uprising in 1345, the last desperate attempt by Estonians to expel their German masters; you can see parts of the castle foundation north of the church. As punishment, the islanders had to build the Order a new castle at Maasilinn. A right at the same busstop passes the site of **Kahutsi stronghold,** which looks particularly effective from a distance and may have been a viking settlement. Continuing south you pass Pöide's beautiful **cemetery** with an interesting crypt decorated with skulls.

At Valjala are the remains of one of the island's most powerful ancient forts, **Valjala stronghold***. The **Valjala church** also dates from the

Muhu is small and so's its church.

Koguva village: a time machine to the past.

beginning of the 13th century, when the islanders were first conquered. It's the oldest stone country church in Estonia. On the church walls you can discern fragments of old paintings. Ask at the local pastorate/district house for the key.

The secret of Kaali

Some 18 km before Kuressaare a signpost indicates **Lake Kaali***** to the right. This circular lake, 110 m in diameter and surrounded by steep banks, has been a mystery to people since ancient times. Many a legend skirts it. In one, a church sank into the ground when a sister and brother were married. In confirmation of this version there's a tower-like stone formation at the bottom of the lake. Others explain that the lake was created when the earth swallowed up either some bride-stealers, or a landowner and his guests during an orgy.

Reality is more mundane. "A huge, terribly hot stone blew up in the sky; it was a treasure-laden goblin with seven heads and ten horns." After hearing this 17th-century version of the tale the Estonian geologist Reinwald came up with his own theory in 1927. Ten years later he salvaged ten pieces of meteorite from the lake, and his hypothesis was proved. Kaali was formed when a meteorite

Those mossy Koguva walls.

crashed to earth about 2700 years ago.

Unsurprisingly, ancient Estonians considered Lake Kaali sacred, and at one time had a settlement along its north edge: only a few metres of stone wall can be seen now.

Before Kuressaare, you can turn off towards Leisi to visit **Kaarma.** The stronghold is well-preserved, and the **church****, with two naves, some magnificent painted wooden reliefs and a fine pulpit, is splendid. Ask at the nearby pastorate for the key. The pastorate buildings are newly renovated. Saaremaa's baronic dynasties are buried in Kaarma's graveyard.

Junipers besiege the earthen stronghold at Valjala.

KURESSAARE

The island's capital, famous for its bishop's castle, is also one of Estonia's prettiest towns.

Kingissepa?

Poor Mr Kingissepp. Not only was the communist revolutionary shot in 1922, but the Soviets decided in their wisdom to rename the capital of Saaremaa after him, and so his name will always be linked with tyranny, pollution and appalling building methods. **Kuressaare***** got its old name back (literally "stork island") on midsummer's day, 1988.

The finely chiselled door of Valjala church.

The **Old Town***** is lovely, especially the central square. Here two lions guard the baroque **town hall.** Like the town hall, the **weighing house** in front of the old **market place** *(turg)* dates from the mid 17th century, a prosperous age that ended suddenly when plague and the Northern War reduced the town to poverty and a population of 11. From the end of the 18th century Kuressaare was reborn, and the midwife was Livonia's Lieutenant-Governor, von Campenhausen. His **grand home,** now a music school, lies north of **St Lawrence church.** A stroll through the Old Town reveals nobles' mansions and other old-timers still eking out an existence among the (thankfully few) concrete additions. A **windmill** transformed into a restaurant, the **gate** of the Orthodox St Nicholas church, and a **field-guard station** all recall a long history. Some of the newer buildings, including a bank and *some* blocks of flats, are surprisingly well designed. Much of Kuressaare deserves the label **garden town,** where private houses and holiday homes wear their manicured gardens with pride.

The childhood home of Johannes and Joosep Aavik draws visitors interested in language. Johannes Aavik put the Estonian language through one of the greatest reforms the world has seen. He invented new, Estonian-sounding words for new ideas and technologies; he added two new declensions of nouns to cope with new ways of thought. Joosep, his cousin, was a musician.

In the mid 19th century Kuressaare became a health resort. The most charming remnants of these times are on Pargi ("park") St. One is now a Citizen's Museum, with changing exhibits. Another lies in the park itself: the **Kuurhoone*** ("cure house") is as elegant as a well-phrased notion. Its restored assembly hall is now a restaurant. The park itself was laid out in 1861. Within its boundaries are two more wooden buildings – a hotel and the eclectic **Hunter's club*** – as well as Kuressaare's star tourist attraction ...

Saaremaa's power dwells in the Old Town of Kuressaare ...

The bishop sat in lordly state

From 1227 till 1559 much of Saaremaa and a great expanse of western Estonia were ruled in feudal fashion by the Bishop of Saare-Lääne. The **Kuressaare bishop's castle***** is the only medieval fortress in the Baltics preserved in all its essential parts. The great **keep** and the quadrangular **castle building** were erected

... and its secret in Lake Kaali.

The bishop's citadel of Kuressaare is a must-see.

over 40 years in the 14th century. Over the next two centuries the **wall** around the castle, 625 m long and 7 m high, and several **cannon towers** were added. One has been restored. Taller, slender Pikk Hermann tower was completed in the 16th century. The moat and various bastions and ramparts and reconstructions have been made by the Danes, Swedes and Russians who ruled the island since then.

The castle was built of dolomite limestone mined near Kaarma. The **basement rooms** are simple though still striking. The wood-munching **hypocaust** was a central heating system. Nine ducts channeled heat into the chapter house above. **The room of the immured knight** is interesting. The story goes that a skeleton was found seated in this bricked-up room when it was opened in 1785. According to legend, the skeleton was a loathed Roman-Catholic inquisitor from the early 16th century who'd been caught in the act with a nobleman's daughter and was punished by being bricked in with a glass of water and a loaf of bread.

Rooms on the **main floor** lead off a corridor designed as a monk's **cloister.** The gothic **chapter house** or grand refectory was sometimes used by the clergy for sessions of the bishop's government, and sometimes as a dining hall for feasts. In the small **chapel** next door you can see bishop's crests and other stonework, some as old as the 14th century. The pulpit dates from early this century. On the walls of the **bishop's living quarters** are some exceptional wooden epitaphs for nobles from the 17th century.

Don't forget to climb the mighty **keep** for the view. The **Pikk Hermann watchtower** can only be reached by a single entrance across a bridge. Rooms on many floors of the castle are now as galleries showcasing Estonian artists (bring your wallet). Others are home to the **Saaremaa Regional Museum****, a very good, comprehensive museum whose text is unfortunately not in

English. Objects date back to the earliest history of the island and include traditional costumes, war and independence memorabilia, and a collection of oddities Saaremaalians abroad have sent back home.
On the outskirts of Kuressaare you can find, towards Kihelkonna, the sundered ruin of the **"great bridge"** by the roadside. And towards Kuivastu there's **Kudjape cemetery***. Crypts, a chapel, tombstones and monuments in all shapes and sizes rest in peace 'neath shading boughs.

SÕRVE PENINSULA

Sõrve peninsula, once thickly populated, is now an empty, poignant place. Besides its lovely landscape, there are several reminders of World War II.

Beaches and blood

Head towards Sõrve peninsula. **Loode oak grove***, just outside town on the left, is ideal for an atmospheric stroll among individualistic oaks, some over 300 years old. The islanders' favourite beach is **Järverand.** In October 1944 at **Tehumardi***, a bloody night battle was fought between the retreating German army and an Estonian division of the Red Army. Legend says that in the pitch dark, soldiers decided which side someone was on by the presence or absence of a beard. A war grave and a monument in the shape of a huge stone sword recall a time when matters of loyalty and shaving were deadly.
Beyond Salme village you're driving down **Sõrve peninsula****, once the most densely populated countryside in Estonia. Now grass and trees grow wildly by the roadside, and all that remains of bustling communities are foundations hidden in the grass.
The peninsula ends with a lighthouse and a couple of islets. The islanders' legendary hero is Suur Tõll (Big Tõll), whose enemy was Old Heathen. These islets are rocks Tõll threw at Old Heathen when the latter was fleeing. On a clear day you can see Latvia's Kura coast over Irbe strait.
A couple of km from the lighthouse,

The belltower of Kihelkonna church.

Stebel's coast protection battery** was built by Soviet troops after the Molotov-Ribbentrop pact was signed in 1939, and wrecked before the Germans invaded in 1941. The battery north of the road includes a hole that contained the biggest gun on the island. Numerous communication tunnels linked it to the command centre, a tall stone structure in a forest clearing south of the road. The tunnels are now flooded.
On the way back along the Sääre-Kaugatuma-Lümanda route, you follow a **gorgeous coastline***, passing beaches and fecund forests. At **Ohesaare** there are foxholes near the edge of the bank, and several windmills. There's a splendid view of the Baltic Sea from **Kaugatuma rock.** A Greek cargo ship, now stripped, has been stuck off the coast since the early 1980s.

NORTHERN SAAREMAA

A precious nature reserve, steep cliffs, windmills and churches make the northern half of the island good for a long drive or cycle.

One man's kingdom

Lümanda is 18 km north-west of Salme, 31 km west of Kuressaare. Just north of the village beside the road lie **stone barrows***, an ancient burial ground. Further north a sign indicates **Viidumäe reserve****. Flora unique in the world grows here, thriving on the rare climate and springs in the swamp around the hill. From a lookout tower near the reserve's parking place there's a

view** of the west coast of Saaremaa.
Kihelkonna's church steeple is the highest in Saaremaa. Nearby in Viki village you can visit **Mihkli farmstead museum***, a 19th-century farm in working order. House with a kitchen still reeking of smoke, summer kitchen that doubled as a smithy, well, sauna and livestock runs represent one farmer's kingdom and devotion to tradition. Most of the items on display are from the one family.
On the left 9 km along the Kihelkonna-Pidula road you can see the **Odalätsi springs.** Suur Tõll was at blows with Old Heathen, and when Tõll broke his enemy's pike, the Old Heathen cried in dialect, *"Oda läts!"* ("the pike has gone!"). Well, that's one theory. Water from the Odalätsi sources flows through underground caverns to the sea. **Pidula manor** is a ruin. The "hill-fort site" in the attractive **manor park***, was actually built to order by the local noble who was also an amateur archaeologist.

Way up north

The area around **Võhma** is full of remnants of typical Saaremaa ancient landscape ... stone walls, old graves, the site of a viking fort. **Panga pank*** ("cliff cliff") north of Võhma is a limestone bluff over 21 m high with a beacon tower and a picnic table. It's a beautiful place to watch the sun set. Driving along the north coast you come to Leisi, and a few to the south is one of the most popular photo stops on the island – in the fields at **Angla****, five wooden windmills remain of an original nine.
The builders of **Karja church*** painted strange pagan designs on the ceiling, supposedly to ward off demons. This is one of the few Estonian churches that still contains medieval sculptures. (Usually open Wed-Sun during working hours in summer.) From here you can follow the coast road back to the causeway to complete your circle.

What a juniper!

SOME OTHER ISLES

Vilsandi bird sanctuary and distant Ruhnu are the best known of the many isles under the care of Saaremaa county. A summertime cruise around Saaremaa and its neighbouring islets is a great pleasure.

Nearby **Abruka island*** is now ruled by wild boars and some 30 people. Its small neighbours, **Vahase** and **Kasselaid,** are also worth a boat-trip.
Somewhat stronger efforts are required for a trip to **Ruhnu island**** (5km x 5km), situated in the middle of the Gulf of Riga 70 km from Kuressaare. Ruhnu's native inhabitants were Swedish. There are still many interesting cultural sights here, and the landscape and wildlife are quite unique. Some say the wooden church, from the 1640s, is the most beautiful in Estonia. Ask in Nasva or Roomassaare harbour about boats to Ruhnu ... or try in Pärnu harbour.
Rather closer to Saaremaa, **Vilsandi island**** is a bird sanctuary. Over 10 000 couples nest here. Since 1992 tourists have been allowed to visit but only under strict controls. Contact the park warden on Saaremaa 54-574 to make arrangements.

PRACTICAL DETAILS

ACCOMODATION

"Lossi" hotel, 27. Lossi, Kuressaare, tel 5 44 43
"Mardi" hotel, 5a. Vallimaa, Kuressaare, tel 5 74 36
"Tarsa" guest-house, 10. Kauba, Kuressaare, tel 5 72 93
"Panga" guest-house, 27. Tallinna, Kuressaare, tel 5 43 49
"Kuressaare" sanatorium-hotel, 20. Kastani, Kuressaare, tel 5 92 63
"Männikäbi" hotel, Mändjala, tel 5 56 80
"Merekivi" hotel, Kudjape, tel 5 77 44
Tahula motel, Tahula, tel 5 74 10
Tare motel, Pihtla, tel 9 01 25
Sõrve (J. Mitt tourist's farm), Torgu, tel 7 04 21
"Teo" motel, 8. km Kuressaarest
"Hobuturism", Muhu, Pärase, tel 7 87 50

RESTAURANTS

"Kuressaare", 1. Raekoja, Kuressaare, tel 5 51 36
"Tõllakuur", 12. Lossi, Kuressaare, tel 5 69 25
Orissaare, tel 9 56 53
"Tuulik", 19. Pärna, Kuressaare, tel 5 48 58, 5 77 35

BARS & CAFES

"Aed", 16. Tallinna, Kuressaare
"Grill", 2. Tallinna, Kuressaare, tel 5 52 39
"Kodulinn", 11. Tallinna, Kuressaare, tel 5 41 78
"Kuursaal", 2. Pargi, Kuressaare, tel 5 97 49
"Maiasmokk", 1. Raekoja, Kuressaare, tel 5 51 37
"Punane baar", 10. Tallinna, Kuressaare, tel 5 61 01
"Sateko", 11. Niidu, Kuressaare, tel 5 66 50
"Veski" cafe (windmill), 19. Pärna, Kuressaare, tel 5 48 58

TRAVEL BUREAUS

Saaremaa Travel Bureau, 2. Pärna, Kuressaare, tel 5 78 70
"MARDI", 4. Tallinna, Kuressaare, tel 5 48 75
"Arensburg Travel", Kudjape, tel 5 76 60
"COMPLEX Ltd., 3. Kitsas, Kuressaare, tel 5 46 61
"Thule", 1. Pargi, Kuressaare, tel 5 74 70
"VIISAM", 22. Uus, Kuressaare, tel 5 57 00

MUSEUMS

SAAREMAA MUSEUM, 3. Lossihoovi, Kuressaare, tel 5 75 42
Kuressaare citizens museum, art gallery, 5. Pargi, Kuressaare, tel 596 71
J. & J. Aavik's museum, 7. Vallimaa, Kuressaare
MUHU MUSEUM, Koguva, Muhu, tel 9 86 16
Mihkli Village Museum, Viki, tel 7 66 13
Viidumäe Nature Reserve, Lümanda, tel 7 63 21

FILLING STATIONS & CAR SERVICE

Kuressaare, 2. Kalevi, tel 5 74 57
89. Roomassaare, tel 5 55 75
Orissaare (car service), tel 9 56 37

TRANSPORT

Airport, 1. Roomassaare, tel 5 40 09
Airport Ticket-Office, 4. Pihtla, Kuressaare, tel 5 42 61
Roomassaare Port-Office, 12. Uus-Roomassaare, tel 5 55 74

TELEPHONE AREA CODE: 245

HIIUMAA

Area: 1023 km^2	Capital: Kärdla
Population: 11 540	population 4260

Hiiumaa is the second-largest island in Estonia, one-third the size of Saaremaa, and has a maximum width of nearly 60 km. It rose above the sea much later than other parts of Estonia, only a few thousand years ago. The people tend to live along the coast. The inland is swampy and forested.

By bike or car, you can see nearly everything in a couple of days. The landscape, the strong wind, the general island ambience and some unusual sites, mostly well signposted, make the island a moody, invigorating place to visit. The island is circled by beaches, at Malvaste, Luidja, Ristna, Kassari and Kärdla. The north-western beaches are the most beautiful, and those near Kassari the warmest. Lehtma and Orjaku are international yachting ports. Hiiumaa's tourist policy is to limit the number of tourists and to promote the island as a **biosphere reserve** to specialist groups, but for now no special permit is required beyond your Estonian visa.

What's in a name?

In times long past the trip from the mainland took a whole day, so Hiiumaa's Swedish people called the island Dagö ("day island"). The origin of the present Estonian version – Hiiumaa – is unknown. The literal meaning is "giant's land", reputedly because a giant lived here. The name may also come from the word *Hiis*, which refers to anything sacred for Estonians and suggests the island's intactness and naturalness.

Records from the 13th century call Hiiumaa *insula deserta*, empty island, though there were people here then. Swedes later moved onto the island, but its modern history really begins with the arrival of the barons – the de la Gardies, the Stenbocks and later one Otto Reinhold Ludwig **Ungern-Sternberg**, a gruesomely

Dressed up on Hiiumaa.

fascinating figure who ruled Hiiumaa like a king. The local people called him the Count of Ungru *(Ungru krahv)*, which sounds aptly demonic. You'll be hearing more about him and his descendants below.

The ferry trip from Rohuküla to Heltermaa is one of the two ways of getting here. The other one, by air, Tallinn-Kärdla, takes less than 30 minutes. The low flight gives you a wonderful view. On your right you can see Finland's skerries and coast on the horizon. On your left the Gulf of Riga stretches out of sight. Directly below lies Väinameri Strait (international name, Moonsund). This island sea, between the mainland and the west Estonian islands, is shallow and full of shoals and numerous islets. The plane trip to or from Saaremaa island is also convenient and cheap.

KÄRDLA

The capital is green, pretty and peaceful.

There's water underneath

In 1829 two of Ungern-Sternberg's descendants built a textile mill on the island. A port with fresh water from the river, the latest factory equipment and almost 500 workers by 1845 guaranteed success. By the time the factory was destroyed in 1941 the settlement around it had developed into an original garden city, a winner of prizes for its beauty in Paris and Liege exhibitions last century.

Today the green town of **Kärdla**** is Hiiumaa's capital. Alder trees and willow hedges, natural parkland, springs and overflowing wells, fountains in people's front gardens... Subsoil waters under pressure have helped form fine green areas and simplified the town's water management.

The old factory site in the northern part of town is now a square. Nearby is Kärdla church, which was built in 1861-63. The church only got its **organ** in 1904; before that the parish clerk had to ride 14 km to Reigi church to get the right tone for the Kärdla church choir and had to hum it all the way back. Or so the tale runs. Next to the church is a park and covered bandstand where song festivals, open-air concerts and plays have been performed since 1926.

At the south-eastern edge of Kärdla there's a **meteorite crater,** the largest in Estonia at 4 km across. The impact of the crater 400 million years ago trapped an underground lake. At the centre of the crater, Estonia's deepest bore-hole (800 m) has been drilled. You can see a sample of the deep rock in Kassari Museum. Kärdla mineral water, 400 million years old, is collected there now. The road rises and falls at the rim, but there's not much to see: the crater itself is too large and old.

WESTWARD HO

The coastal road circles the island. West are lighthouses, beaches and a dune of wild crosses with a story or two attached ...

Where's *your* cross?

In the western direction the road goes towards Kõrgessaare. **Ristimägi**** ("cross hill"), 10 km from Kärdla, is a small grassed sand hillock covered with rough, handmade crosses. By custom, anyone visiting the hill for the first time should make a cross from some available material and put it among the others.

The rude jumble is either heartening or touching depending on which story you believe. The **legend** says that two bridal wedding carriages, each refusing to give way to the other, crashed. One bride and the other groom were killed. The surviving pair married and lived happily ever after. If you want to believe this, then planting a cross guarantees lifelong happiness if you're married or a suitable partner if you're not.

The more sobering **historical story** says that the first crosses were put here more than 200 years ago by a local Swede. Unlike Estonians, the Swedes were free peasants and not serfs. They paid a high price for this freedom when, at the end of the 18th century, about a thousand Swedish peasants were deported by Catherine the Great from Hiiumaa to the Ukraine. Here, at the border between two parishes, they heard their last sermon on their home island. Placing a cross recalls this sombre moment. You can walk into the forest a couple of hundred metres along a sandy path before the crosses peter out.

A lyrical swerve to Tahkuna

A small detour off the Kõrgessaare road leads you to **Tahkuna lighthouse*.** This cast-iron lighthouse was made in Paris and erected here, at the tip of the peninsula, in 1875. It's in imperfect repair, but is still an elegant pointed landmark. The 42.6 m high light is visible for 18 nautical miles. Tahkuna peninsula has witnessed some violent battles. From the top of the lighthouse there's a good view of the coast and, directly below, some of the old World War I coastal batteries. You can enter one **battery*** next to the monument to the Russian "defenders" of 1941.

On the way to Tahkuna you might cast a glance at **Mihkli farmstead*** 500 m south of Malvaste village. The oldest buildings date back to the 18th century. After the deportation of Swedish peasants in 1781, Estonians settled in, and that's why the buildings bear stylistic features of both nations. One of the few original smoke saunas on Hiiumaa still works here.

Viscose town

Back on the Kõrgessaare road, ruins are all that remain of the inn in **Reigi,** across the road from the church. The sea reached right up to it and folk from the coastal villages could row to its door. The sturdy church was built about 1800. Reigi village was first recorded back in 1470 and was for centuries the cultural centre of Hiiumaa. Local pastors, as everywhere across Estonia, established parish schools and trained the first schoolmasters.

The oddly-named **Viskoosa** is a "suburb" of Kõrgessaare, by the port. In 1911-14 the Belgian company La Viscosa built a rayon factory on the land of the local manor. Everything was ideal: the forest was close by, there was fresh water and cheap sea transport. But World War I put an end to production just as it commenced, and today some of the

Kõpu's pines reach for the sky.

Kõpu lighthouse is old old old, but still saves ships.

buildings are used by an abattoir and a cannery. What you see is a jarring combination of model factory buildings from the 1910s made out of stone and designed to last, and Soviet-style piping and buildings, designed to fall apart.

Some drownings

In the waters to the northwest lurks a treacherous shoal, the Hiiumadal (Näckmansgrund), near one of the Baltic's most vital shipping routes. Near Viskoosa you can find Count Ungern-Sternberg's infamous **"wrong lighthouse",** a large stone with three holes in which a lantern was placed whose light could be seen through the forest from the sea. The light enticed ships onto the reef. According to maritime law, wrecked ships belonged to the local landowner, so by the count's connivance hundreds were wrecked. Nowadays fishing boats haul up several tonnes of flounder a year from the reef.

It's said that once at **Kurisu*** near Kõrgessaare a girl was ploughing a field with oxen, which tried to drink at the river and slipped in. Girl and oxen at once disappeared in a swirl of water. The girl's hairband was found later in a river 3 km away. Such "karst" areas of underground caverns and streams can be found in several places in Hiiumaa. You can watch the water plunge underground during the spring thaw, April and May.

Plenty of space in the villages on Kõpu peninsula.

Kõpu lighthouse

Besides its fine beach, **Luidja** has a spooky alder grove. You've reached **Kõpu peninsula** – the highest part of Hiiumaa (60 m). A road winds through pine forest and Kõpu's archaic villages. Hiiumaa's oldest-known settlement was situated here, as we know from archeological relics dating back to the Stone Age, when the rest of the island was still under water.

Andruse and Tornimägi hills are in the middle of the peninsula. On the top of Tornimägi stands the most interesting building on Hiiumaa. **Kõpu lighthouse****, the oldest maritime construction in the Baltic states, owes its existence to the notorious Hiiumadal reef just mentioned. As long ago as 1480 the Hanseatic League proposed building a lighthouse to direct traffic away from the reef. The lighthouse was built of granite, 20 m high, and a light has shone from it since 1531. At first, firewood was pulled up by winch. In 1845 a limestone extension was built and a staircase hewn inside. During reconstruction the height of the lighthouse was increased. Currently it's 37 m high (103 m above sea level) and can be seen 35 nautical miles away. You can get the key from the red house. Mind your head going up.

The **Ristna lighthouse*** dates from 1874, looks good, is climbable, and gives a view of the western tip of Kõpu peninsula. This was a Soviet frontier zone, and is relatively undiscovered by either tourists or locals.

The beach-rose is beautiful but thorny.

Cut from sand

From Kõpu the road leads back east and then south, towards Emmaste. The **Vanajõgi,** which flows into Mardihansu Bay, has eroded a gully from the sand, sometimes as deep as 10 m. At times the *Vanajõe org* is picturesque, but where the sand is most exposed, old pines stand with their roots clutching at the edge and the

Meat on the former Sõprus ("friendship") collective farm.

effect is darker. You feel that these trees, some of whose sisters have already fallen, stand a much smaller chance than the Estonian Republic or an infant's ice-cream on a hot day. You can find rare yew trees in the forest near the bay; they're relicts of a warmer climate in the past and are now protected.

There's little to see now at **Emmaste.** As far back as the 16th century there was a boat route from here to Saaremaa island, but in the last few decades travel has been done via the mainland. For 50 years Hiiumaa was an unappreciated outpost of the Soviet Empire and it'll be a long time before the glory days return. You can see some artillery positions at nearby **Tohvri,** and there's a view of Saaremaa from the coastal village of **Sõru.**

THE SOUTH-EAST

Continuing round the island, you can visit the special landscape of Kassari, an island right next to Hiiumaa. The Count of Ungru's manor at Suuremõisa and a strange formation of rocks speak of Hiiumaa's long and odd history.

A special landscape

Käina church was once an important centre for the Bishop of Saare-Lääne (the old episcopal realm of Läänemaa and Saaremaa), but was ruined in World War II. Rudolf Tobias, author of the first Estonian symphonic works, lived nearby. His home is now a museum.

Kassari island** (19 km^2) is joined to Hiiumaa by two causeways. Between them lies Käina Bay. The bay and the whole of Kassari are a migration stopover for birds. The island, blessed with a **landscape*** of low, wind-beaten junipers, is designated both a wildlife reserve and a landscape reserve. It also boasts curative sea mud and a yachting harbour, **Orjaku,** where you can hire boats. The southern tip of the is-

Aino Kallas's summer cottage.

Walking is the best way to see Kassari island.

land, **Sääre tirp****, is a 3 km walk through junipers. The last 500 m is a thin shingle strip into the sea.

Kassari and Hiiumaa have long been known as summer resorts; numerous celebrities spent their summers here. The Estonian-Finnish writer Aino Kallas passed 13 summers here (1924-38). Near her house you'll find the **Hiiumaa Local History Museum***. This little building houses a collection of ethnography, history and nature exhibits. Further west, at the unique **thatched stone chapel*** you can peer through the windows at unpolished wood railings and gloomy wreaths on the walls.

The very tip of Sääre tirp.

The Count of Ungru's palace

A lane of straight alders leads to **Suuremõisa manor house****, a palace from the mid 1700s in the late baroque style. You can see where the power resided on this island. At one time it had 64 symmetrically arranged rooms. Ceilings still flaunt their trompe l'oeil designs. Floors still wear their original parquetry. An imposing staircase leads to the large hall and guest rooms on the first floor.

The manor once belonged to Magnus Stenbock, who gambled away his manor at Kõrgessaare and sold the island's Swedes into slavery in the Ukraine on behalf of Catherine the Great. He eventually lost control

of Suuremõisa manor itself to the equally nasty "Count of Ungru", Baron von Ungern-Sternberg.
The Count (1744-1811) was a remarkable man. His friend the King of Poland made him Lord Chamberlain, and even though he left the king's service soon after, he insisted on being addressed as "lord chamberlain" and wore the uniform all his life. He landed on the island in 1781, intent on being ruler and much else besides. As well as wrecking ships for their salvage, he is said to have exercised the baron's "first night privilege" with local brides. The poor young woman was brought to the manor, washed and put to bed. The Count used a wardrobe, curved and black with a secret door, which you can still see today, to enter her room, inspect her and, if he desired, have his way with her. There's also a secret treasure store in a void between the two floors, and two secret tunnels once led from beneath the entrance to the river and the church.
One autumn one of his trading skippers, Captain Malm, arrived back a month late. Ungern-Sternberg suspected the man of secret trading and in fury killed him. Stenbock, still holding a grudge, turned the Count in, and all the vile stories came out during the trial. The Count spent his last days in Siberia.
The manor today is in poor condition. A school has moved into part of it, a bar elsewhere, and if you haven't hired a guide through the tourism firms you may be lucky to get in. Try anyway: best are weekday mornings when you might be able to find a teacher with the time and the key. Sometimes there are paintings from Tallinn's Art Museum in the school.

Põhilise leppe kivid

The 13th-century **church of Pühalepa*** is not far from Suuremõisa manor. It has a carved sandstone pulpit from the 17th century. One of Hiiumaa's former owners, Ebba Margaretha Stenbock, is buried in the old chapel beside the church.
About 350 m north of the church is an **enigmatic formation**** of granite stones splashed with lichen. The group is 16 m in diameter and 3 m high. Some say it's an ancient tumulus, others an unfinished model of an Egyptian pyramid, still others that gold is buried under the stones, and others a Swedish king. Certainly the place seems sombre, ancient and pagan. According to the folk tradition, these are the "main contract" stones *(põhilise leppe kivid):* every man who went to sea had to bring a stone here to guarantee protection against accident.

Stick to the coast

Along Hiiumaa's east coast you can look for fossils on a gravel beach on Sarve peninsula. There's a statue known locally as **Strand Ella Vulgaris** at the ferry port of Heltermaa. The road via Vahtrepa takes you past the **Kallaste escarpment,** where ocean waves have modelled a 9 m high, 400 m long limestone outcrop.
In summertime, if the owner's around, you can go inside the windmill at **Hagaste** and maybe see it working. He might sell you some honey and show you his smoke sauna and Finnish sleds, too. The island has some 30 windmills in working or near-working condition. A few, lacking sails, look like outhouses for a giant.

Rock in an alder grove

Back on your way to Kärdla, a road to the right heads past the **Soera farming life museum,** dedicated to island life in the 1930s. Hard times indeed. The road goes on to a parking place for the **Kukka kivi*,** 16.4 m long and the fourth biggest boulder in Estonia. More remarkable is the 500 m walk to the boulder. First you pass through a field, then clumps of junipers which quickly congregate into a juniper wood. This gives way to a stately pine wood. Single alders follow then a thick, eerie hazel wood. Last of all the rock itself appears.
So it's back to Kärdla. At the southwestern edge of town, you pass through the meteorite crater. To discover the **inland beauty,** you have to go on foot. The chance of seeing orchids and deer makes it well worth the trouble.

ABANDONED ISLETS

From Salinõmme port you can get to some protected islets. These are spe-

cially for the "greener" traveller, though you don't need to be an expert to enjoy virgin broadleaf forests or abandoned farmsteads.

Natural and military protection

To the south-west of Hiiumaa there's an **archipelago of protected islets**** which you may not visit alone. The islets are uninhabited, though the largest were inhabited until the middle of this century. The farmers on Saarnaki and Hanikatsi used to fish in summer and gave shelter to passers-by on the ice "road" in winter. But under the Soviets owning a boat and going to sea were prohibited; most beaches were even off-limits. Fishing folk had to give up their livelihoods and lifestyles in favour of the frontier defence of the great Soviet Imperium. Islets and coastal villages emptied and Estonians lost a centuries-old fishing culture.

Nowadays the islets are nature reserves. **Saarnaki** has a traditional farmstead and a landscape of junipers. On **Hanikatsi** there's a delicious deciduous forest and 600 species of plants. **Hanerahu** is a tiny shoal of limestone gravel. **Kõverlaid** often hosts seals. You can get to the islets (group size limit about 12) by calling the park warden, Tiit Leito, on Hiiumaa 94-299 or 91-663. Visits are only in May-September.

In summertime, when the Baltic is low, you can walk through the sea to **Vohilaid** off the east coast. This islet has no special protection, but still retains that special island ambience.

PRACTICAL DETAILS

ACCOMODATION

Kärdla hotel, 13. Vabaduse, Kärdla, phone 9 14 81
Malvaste camping, Lauka, phone 9 15 25
Kassari campinground, Sääre-tirp

RESTAURANTS, BARS & CAFES

Kärdla restaurant, 1. Vabriku väljak, phone 9 15 62
Rannapaargu, 5. Lubjaahju, Kärdla, phone 9 12 87
"Viinaköök", Viskoosa
Kärdla bar, Kalevipoja, Kärdla, phone 9 15 50
"Mõisa Pood", Kassari

MUSEUMS

HIIUMAA MUSEUM, Kassari, phone 9 71 21
Paul Kamm Museum, 40. Tiigi, Kärdla, phone 9 14 41
Rudolf Tobias Museum, Käina, phone 9 26 20

TRAVEL BUREAUS

DAGÖ, 1. Vabriku väljak, Kärdla, phone 9 12 41
Malvaste, Lauka-Malvaste, phone 9 15 25
ESTRESOR, Kärdla, phone 9 63 69

FILLING STATION & CAR SERVICE

Kärdla, 47. Kõrgessaare mnt., phone 9 13 59
Hellamaa (service), phone 9 46 72

TRANSPORT

AIRPORT Kärdla, phone 9 13 77
HELTERMAA HARBOUR phone 9 42 12
TAXIS phone 9 11 39

TELEPHONE AREA CODE: 246

FROM A NATION UNDER SLAVERY TO THE SOVIET "WEST" AND FINALLY TO A FREE PEOPLE IN A FREE LAND...

From the east they came, the Finno-Ugric peoples, from the Urals or perhaps even the north-eastern edge of Asia. For centuries they were moving westwards throough forests and across rivers until they reached the sea. Some of them pressed on still farther. They became Finns and Hungarians. The others – Estonians.
Here they lived for thousands of years, in relative peace, **taking root** in this land. They had no special name for themselves, except for "the people" or, if pressed, "people of the land". They owed their allegiances to their family, village, and to small groups of villages historians call "parishes". They buried their dead in stone graves or under burial mounds. If attacked they fled to forts with earthen defences, which were often on hills or deep in forests or swamps. This was pre-history: the sites of these forts are survivors from a time before there were any written records of this land. Then the peace ended ...

Giants stomped through

Estonia is a land formed by giants. The hero of the Estonian national epic, Kalevipoeg, bounded round the plain, dropping rocks, drinking lakes dry, ploughing hills out of marshes and generally "reforming" the landscape. In a similar though less generous way the giants of the region have invaded and ruled:

1220-1346, 1560-1629	the Danes
1220-1560, 1941-44	the Germans
1560-1645	the Poles
1220, 1561-1710	the Swedes
1710-1918, 1940-41, 1944-91	the Russians

For much of the time this wee land has been a **battlefield of great powers.** The first invaders, Germans and Danes, used the pretext of a crusade against paganism to build a bridgehead to the east ... yet there's evidence that much of the population had already been Christianised along the ancient trade routes. The invaders divided the land among the Bishops of Tartu and Saare-Lääne, and the Teutonic and Livonian Orders of Knights. They imposed a feudal society that had nothing to do with Christ's teachings. (And until 1920, against all cultural sense, northern Latvia and south Estonia formed a separate province known as Livonia.)
The indigenous people were kept to the lowest rung of the feudal hierarchy, while positions of power were taken by Germans and Scandinavians. Estonians were cut off from High Culture: this may explain why the **old peasant ways** survived for 700 years. Though folk customs were depleted by Christianity and other foreign forces, songs as rich as Norse or Irish sagas, village traditions, dances and of course the melodic language itself have come down to us today. The song festival grounds, swings and saunas you find in most villages are prisms of this old culture; while Hanseatic centres such as Tallinn, Pärnu and Tartu, ruined castles and hundreds of manor houses are remnants of the centuries when Balto-German families ruled the land from their manors.
The Swedes, keen to have a base for military expeditions in eastern Europe, took Estonia in the Livonian War (1558-83). Relatively, they were the best of Estonia's foreign rulers. They founded Tartu University, allowed Estonian language lessons, and even began to lessen the power of the old landowners. Upset, the barons invited the Russians in. Russia wanted a "window into Europe" and got it. After the devastating Northern War (1700-21) Estonia was ruled by a Russian czar who reinstalled the German landlords.

The provincial administrators were Balto-Germans in Tallinn. Estonians continued to serve at tables or plough the master's fields as if they were their own.

German? Russian? Wake up!

Industry arrived in the 19th century and the factories needed workers with a certain minimal education. Estonians were faced with a difficult choice: emulate the German upper class, or fight for an education in Estonian. Most Germans had a low opinion of the "rural language" and believed it would die out as the "natives" learnt more sophisticated ways... some Estonian intellectuals shared their view.

Yet the people chose the harder route: under the leadership of Carl Robert Jakobson, Jakob Hurt and others, the **national awakening** began. Estonians founded a system of village schools taught in Estonian, song societies and peasant unions; they published Estonian newspapers, wrote national poetry and romantically patriotic stories; they established a national theatre and began to collect traditional poetry. The Estonian epic poem, *Kalevipoeg,* was written at this time. Choirs and orchestras sprang up and song festivals became important expressions of national identity, as they still are today.

Thanks to its awakening, the Estonian nation had nearly rid itself of illiteracy by the beginning of this century. An intelligentsia and administrative class formed. But even as German influences diminished in the Baltics, Russian pressure grew. The czarists made Russian the language of education and officialdom. They built an Orthodox cathedral on Toompea in Tallinn as a symbol of Russian might.

War of Independence number 2, and after

At the end of World War I, a chance! The great powers were exhausted, the Bolsheviks ruled in the Kremlin. Estonia declared independence on 24 February 1918: immediately afterwards the Balto-Germans invaded from Latvia to retake "their" land, and the Russians invaded from the east. A 700-year-old hatred of the Germans meant commanders had a hard time keeping fighters at the eastern front. But the Estonians won (and helped found Latvia at the same time). There was even talk of taking St Petersburg! On 2 February 1920 in the **Treaty of Tartu** the Soviet Russia renounced all territorial claims to Estonia "for all time". Good-sized portions currently administered by Russia were in Estonia, including the east bank of the Narva River. The Setu people had their own Estonian county, centred on Petseri, south of Lake Peipsi.

The next 20 years of **sovereignty** gave Estonians a taste of freedom; without it, they may have gone the same way as other Finno-Ugric peoples such as the Maris, who are losing the battle against assimilation with Russians, and the Votyaks, who've already lost it. Estonia bloomed in the glittering 1920s. In the 1930s strident fascist and communist movements arose. The president, Konstantin Päts, declared martial law for six years. Elections of a sort were held in 1938, but cold winds were blowing from two directions.

50 years of World War II

Nazi Germany and the Soviet Union signed a non-aggression pact on 23 August 1939 that contained secret protocols giving the Baltic states to the USSR: the infamous **Molotov-Ribbentrop pact.** The Red Army occupied Estonia in June 1940 and deported 11 000 to Siberia. Two-thirds were women, children and the elderly. Most died. Not much later, the Germans took the country. In 1944 the Soviets reinvaded, blasting Old Towns to bits even after the Nazis had fled. This was the fate of Narva and of half of Tallinn. Estonians, drafted on both sides, were killing one another without any hope of controlling the land they were fighting over. Thousands fled, including the cream of the intelligentsia and most island and fishing folk.

The **occupation** lasted 45 years. The worst times were under Stalin. On 25-26 March 1949 tens of thousands of Estonians were spirited off to Siberia, 92% of them women, children and the aged. New, alien towns were built in Eastern Virumaa to serve oil-shale and phosphorite mines and a uranium treatment plant. A fierce wave of russification was imposed. Estonians who moved out of Narva, for example, weren't allowed to move back. By 1989 a third of the people in Estonia were immigrants; over half the population of Tallinn was Russian-speaking. Farms were "collectivised" and the inefficient grind of Soviet economics was installed. Pollution was horrific, though crime was low. Russian was made an official language and became the only language used in industry, navigation and many university subjects. Still, Estonians followed European ideas in fashion, homekeeping and leisure. Indeed, Russians labelled Estonia "the Soviet west".

Simmerings ...

Within the Soviet period there were times of discovery and achievement – as in the 1960s, when there was a **refocusing of national identity.** Several artists looked eastward, to Finno-Ugric relatives, and sometimes even further. Links were discovered with Siberian peoples, for example, and these explorations continue today. The writer, anthropologist and president Lennart Meri has researched Finno-Ugric and other minority peoples. Kaljo Põllu uses Finno-Ugric and Siberian cultural influences in his artworks. The composer Veljo Tormis has synthesised traditional Estonian music with his own ideas, and his extraordinary runic songs are world-renowned. Influenced by the Estonian philosopher Uku Masing, Jaan Tooming has tried to build an alternative Finno-Ugric theatre. Musicians like Arvo Pärt and Neeme Järvi, and painters like Raul Meel and Leo Lapin have carried the culture to the "outside" world. You may also recognise the names of the writers Jaan Kross and Jaan Kaplinski, conductor Eri Klas, opera singer Georg Ots ... and there are many more. These figures helped Estonian culture survive and even grow under communism.

... and breakthroughs

By accident, Mikhail Gorbachev gave the Baltic republics their chance. Estonians took the Soviet president at his word, and under the "openness" of glasnost formed a grass-roots protest movement when phosphorite miners threatened ancient Estonian sites. On the 50th anniversary of the Molotov-Ribbentrop pact, people linked hands in a Baltic Chain 650 km long, from Tallinn to Vilnius. Singing together was still a crucial way of gathering as a nation, and one in three Estonians attended the 1988 of Estonia Day Song. Thus the latest revolution has been called the **Singing Revolution.**

In 1991 the hardliners in Moscow tried to reassume leadership of the Soviet Union. The Baltics rebelled. Estonia reasserted independence on 20 August 1991. Almost immediately the most powerful western nations recognised the reborn country. A year later – so fast! – Estonians introduced their own currency and held free elections. The flag flies again over Toompea: blue for the sky, black for the earth, white for the soul. The problem of the Russian minority remains thorny: Russians were 50% of Tallinn's population but most weren't allowed to vote in the 1992 elections. (On the other hand, they are entitled to become citizens if they can pass an Estonian language test and have been resident here for two years, and they can vote in local elections. What are the citizenship laws in *your* country?)

Now a **new giant** has arrived, the "benign" giant of Anglo-American mass culture. At the same time the nation fears that the dinosaur has legs: that the mighty Red Army will never accept Estonian independence. As we went to press there were still 10 000 uninvited troops in the country and certain rabid military elements in Russia were talking about retaking the Baltics. Estonia is facing tough economic times and is caught between cultures. But the people have their land back, and in a spirit of freedom anything is possible.

For more history, see the individual chapters, especially the Tallinn and Tartu chapters.

MINI PARLEUR

How do you do	–	Tere
Good bye	–	Head aega
Yes, No	–	Jah, ei
Thank you	–	Tänan
Please	–	Palun
How much?	–	Kui palju maksab?
Cheep	–	Odav
Expensive	–	Kallis
Open	–	Lahti
Shut	–	Kinni
Hairdresser, barber	–	Juuksur
Toilet: men's, women's	-	Tualett: meeste, naiste
Envelope	–	Ümbrik
Stamp	–	Mark
Postcard	–	Postkaart
One, two	–	Üks, kaks
Three, four	–	Kolm, neli
Five, six	–	Viis, kuus
Seven	–	Seitse
Eight	–	Kaheksa
Nine	–	Üheksa
Ten	–	Kümme
Money	–	Jootraha
Ticket	–	Pilet
Excursion	–	Ekskursioon
Restaurant	–	Restoran
Menu	–	Menüü
Coffee, tea	–	Kohv, tee
Beer, milk	–	Õlu, piim
Water	–	Vesi
Salt, sugar	–	Sool, suhkur
Bill/check	–	Arve
Car service	–	Autoteenindus
Post office	–	Postkontor
Railway station	–	Raudteejaam
Hotel, motel	–	Hotell, motell
Camping site	–	Kämping
Doctor	–	Arst
Pharmacy	–	Apteek
Hospital	–	Haigla
Customs office	–	Tollipunkt
Police station	–	Politsei
Harbour	–	Sadam
Airplane	–	Lennuk
Steamer, ship	–	Laev, praam
Train	–	Rong
Bus/coach	–	Buss
Airport	–	Lennujaam
Travel agency	–	Turismibüroo
Telephone	–	Telefon

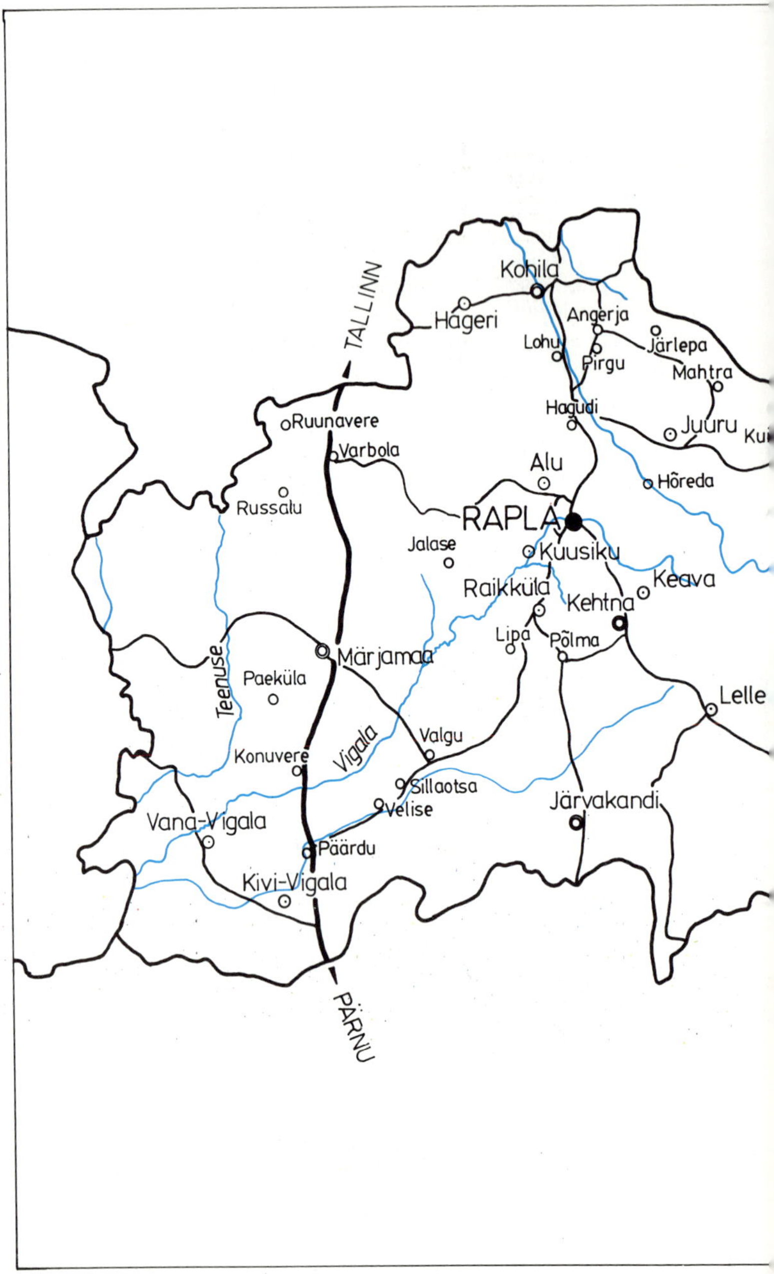
TALLINN
Kohila
Hageri
Angerja
Järlepa
Lohu
Pirgu
Mahtra
Hagudi
Juuru
Kui
Ruunavere
Varbola
Alu
Hõreda
Russalu
RAPLA
Jalase
Kuusiku
Raikküla
Keava
Kehtna
Lipa
Põlma
Märjamaa
Teenuse
Paeküla
Lelle
Vigala
Valgu
Konuvere
Sillaotsa
Velise
Järvakandi
Vana-Vigala
Päärdu
Kivi-Vigala
PÄRNU

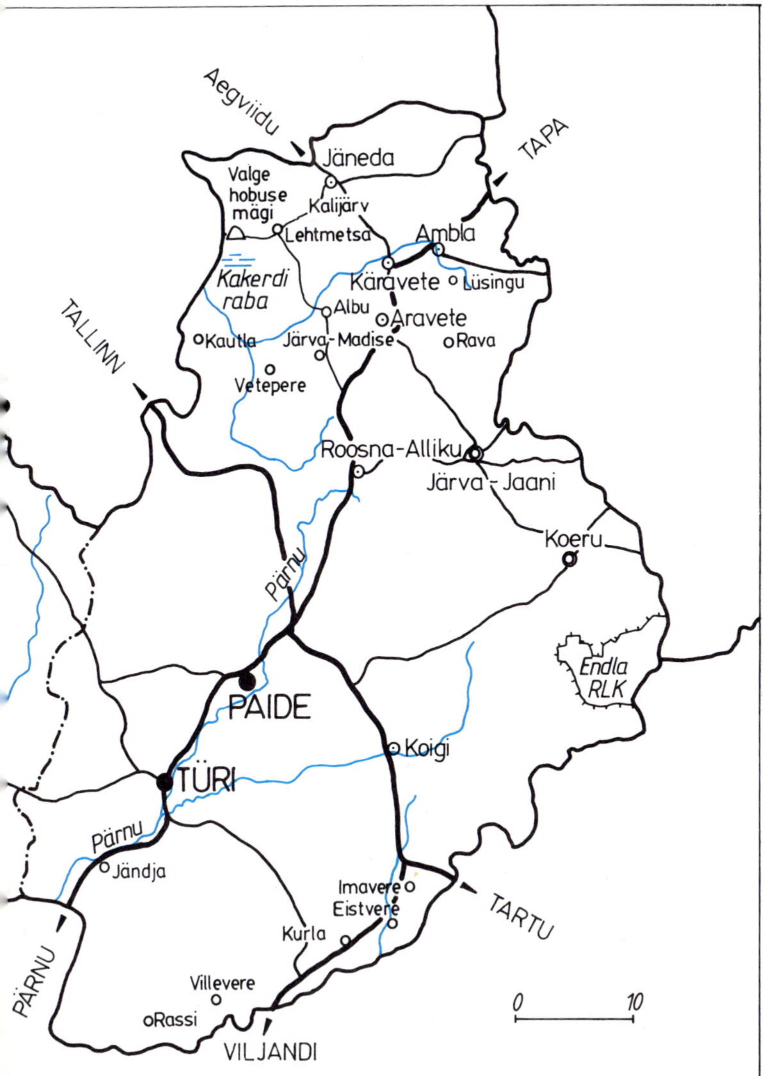

JÄRVA - JA RAPLAMAA

SOO
Vainupea
Altja
Võsu
Vihula
Sagadi
Karepa
Toolse
Letipea
KUNDA
Lammasmägi
Ilumäe
Joaveski
Palmse
Viitna
Viru Nigula
Kalvi
Aseri
Pada
Hiiemägi
Purtse
Lüganuse
TALLINN
RAKVERE
KIVIÕLI
Sonda
Kadrina
Torma
Rägavere
Maidla
Neeruti
Mõdriku
Vinni
TAPA
Lasila
Assamalla
Viru-Jaagupi
Küti
Kullenga
Porkuni
PAIDE
Tudu
Roela
Tamsalu
Väike-Maarja
Muraka raba
Vao
Kiltsi
Ebavere
Muuga
Äntu
Avanduse
Simuna
Laekvere
Rakke
Avinurme
Salla
Edru
Lohusuu
Emumäe
JÕGEVA
Kalmaküla
TARTU

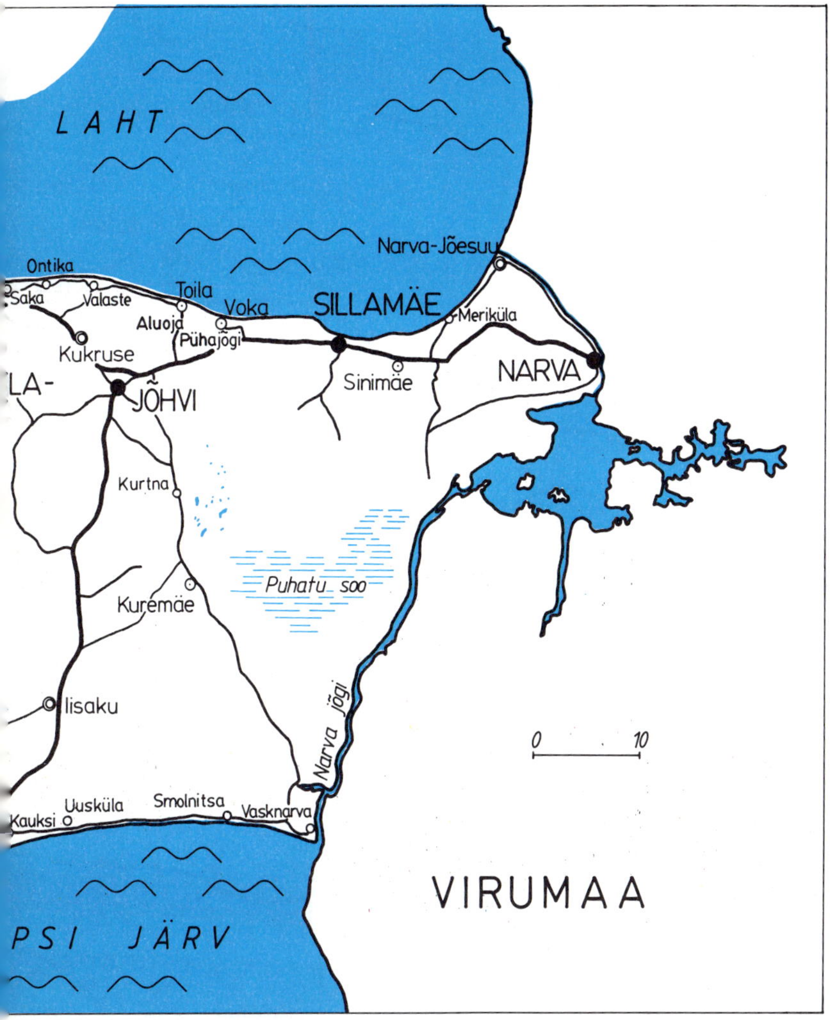

LAHT
Narva-Jõesuu
Ontika
Saka
Valaste
Toila
Voka
SILLAMÄE
Merikūla
Aluoja
Pühajõgi
Kukruse
NARVA
Sinimäe
LA-
JÕHVI
Kurtna
Puhatu soo
Kuremäe
Iisaku
Narva jõgi
0
10
Uusküla
Smolnitsa
Kauksi
Vasknarva
VIRUMAA
PSI JÄRV

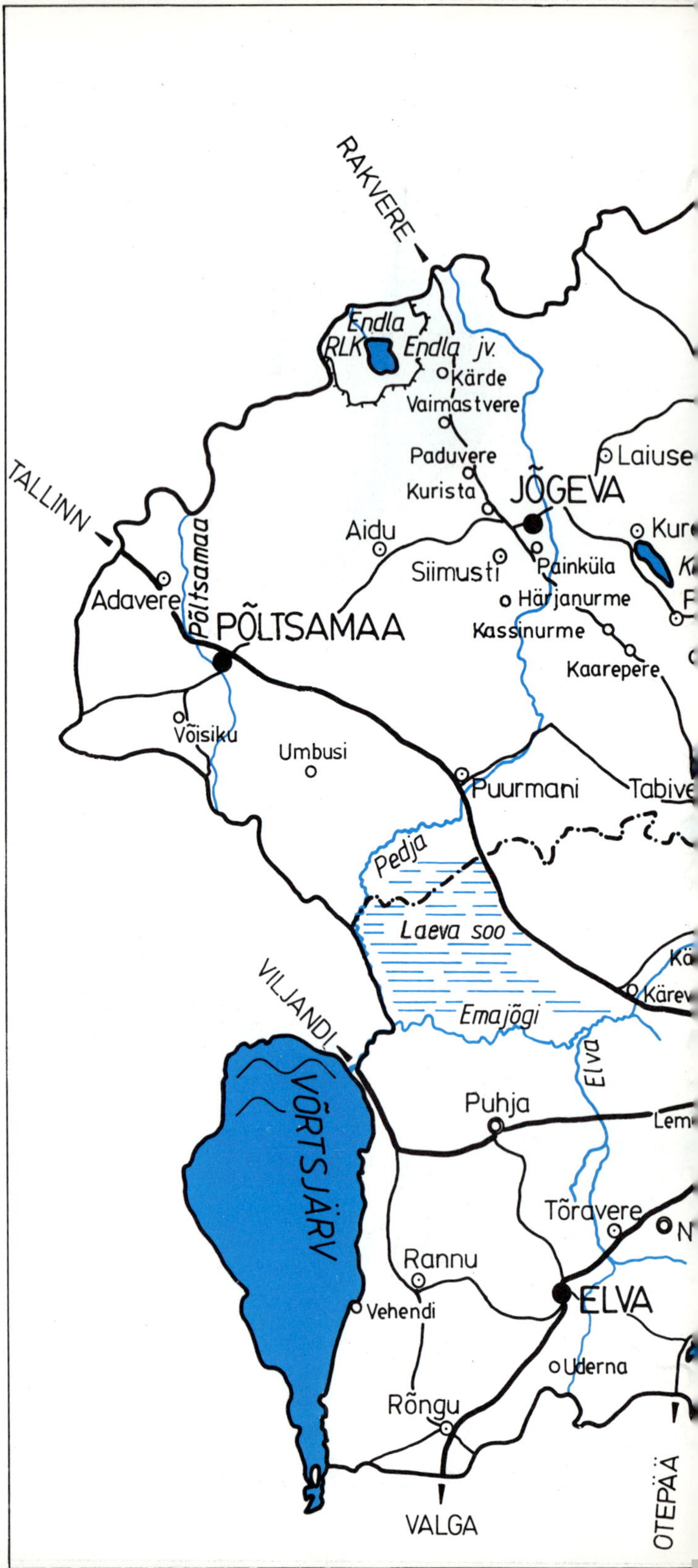

RAKVERE
Endla RLK
Endla jv.
Kärde
Vaimastvere
Paduvere
Kurista
JÕGEVA
Laiuse
TALLINN
Aidu
Siimusti
Painküla
Härjanurme
Kassinurme
Kaarepere
Adavere
Põltsamaa
PÕLTSAMAA
Võisiku
Umbusi
Puurmani
Pedja
Laeva soo
VILJANDI
Emajõgi
Elva
VÕRTSJÄRV
Puhja
Tõravere
Rannu
ELVA
Vehendi
Uderna
Rõngu
VALGA
OTEPÄÄ

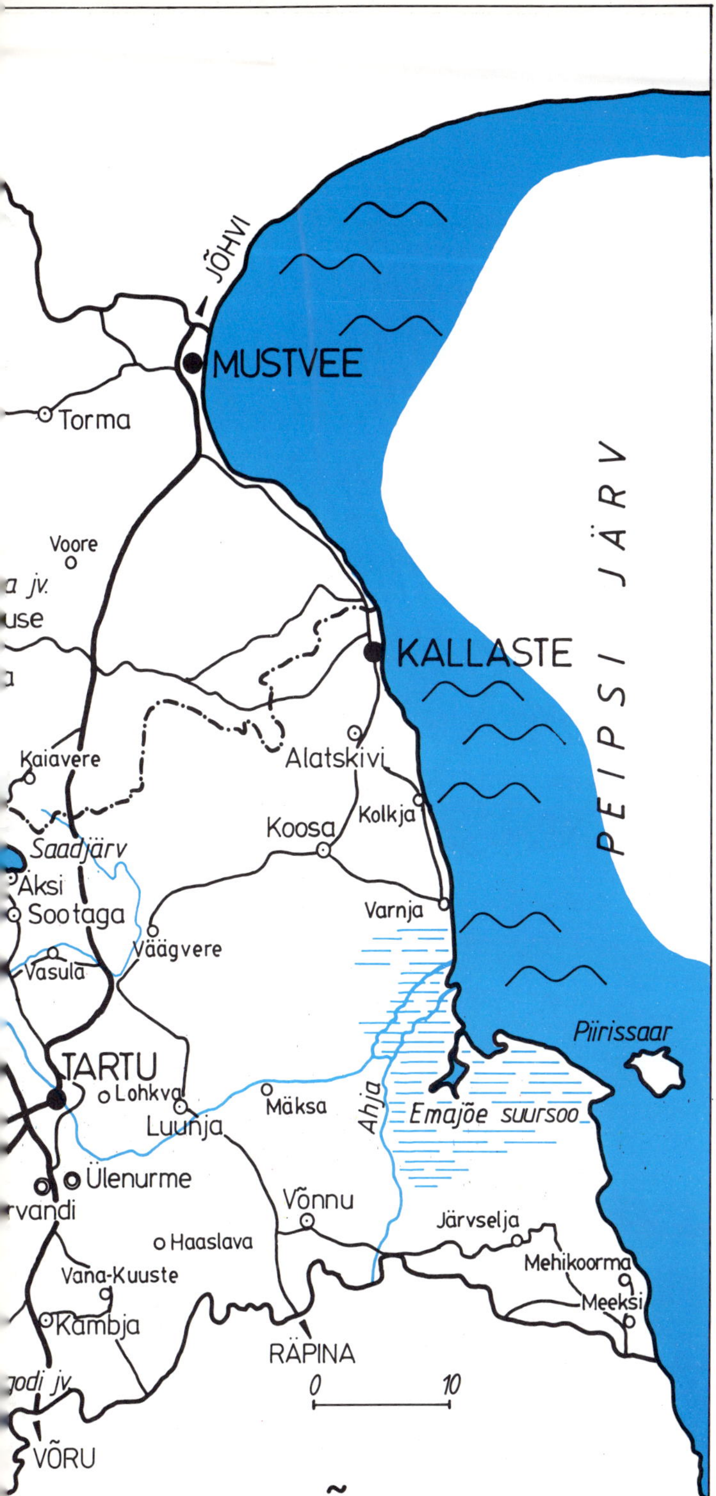

TARTU - JA JÕGEVAMAA

VÕRTSJÄRV
TARTU
TARTU
PÄRNU
Õhne j.
Väike Emajõgi
Puka
OTEPÄÄ
Sihva
Pühajärv
Helme
Kääriku
Hobusemägi
TÕRVA
Jõgeveste
Koorküla
Sangaste
Urvaste
Hummuli
Tsirguliina
Piiri
Laatre
Antsla
Lõõdla
LATVIA
VALGA
Kaagjärve
Karula
Kaika
RIIA
Ähijärv
Hargla
Saru
Mõniste
Kuutsi
Naha
talu
Valgjärv
Must
Tsoor

VÕRU -, VALGA - JA PÕLVAMAA

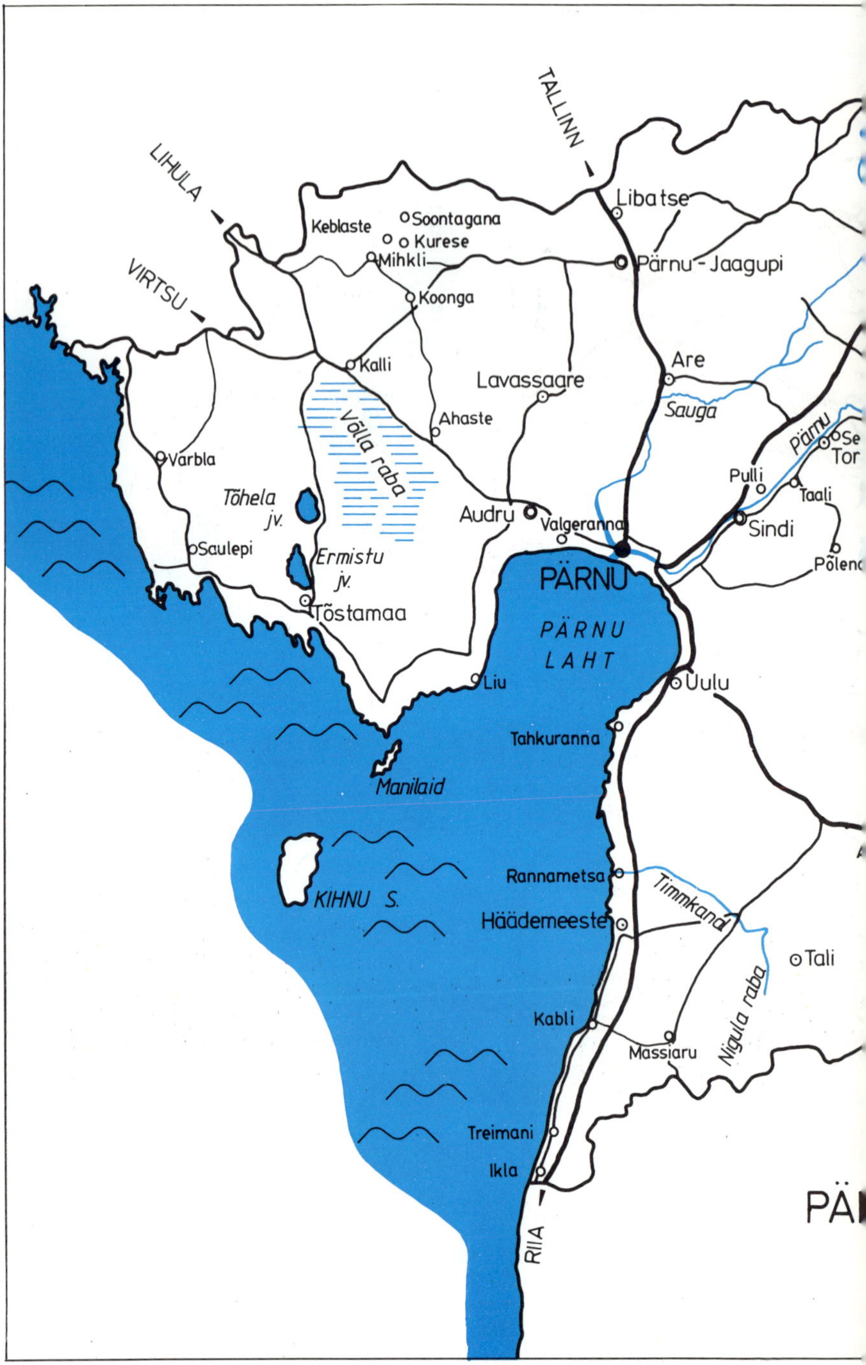
TALLINN
LIHULA
VIRTSU
Libatse
Keblaste
Soontagana
Kurese
Mihkli
Pärnu-Jaagupi
Koonga
Kalli
Are
Lavassaare
Sauga
Ahaste
Vätla raba
Pärnu
Varbla
Tõhela jv.
Pulli
Taali
Audru
Valgeranna
Sindi
Saulepi
Ermistu jv.
Põlen
PÄRNU
Tõstamaa
PÄRNU LAHT
Liu
Uulu
Tahkuranna
Manilaid
Rannametsa
KIHNU S.
Timmkanal
Häädemeeste
Tali
Nigula raba
Kabli
Massiaru
Treimani
Ikla
RIIA
PÄ

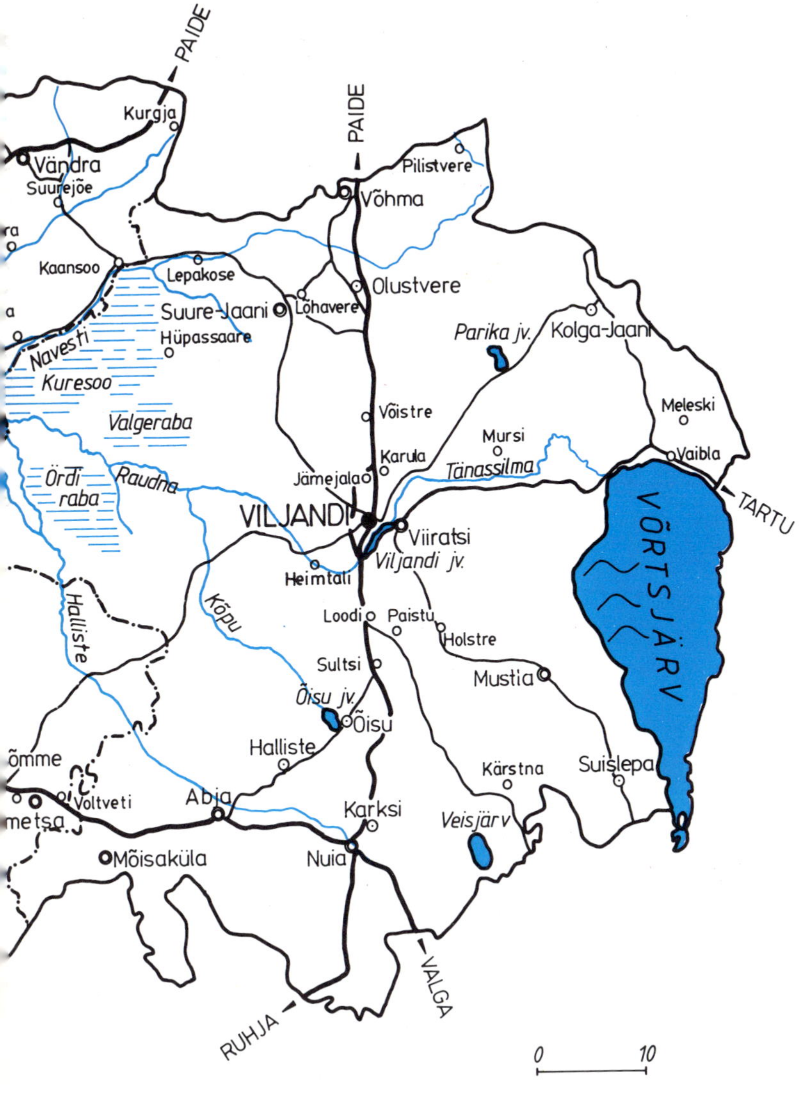

- JA VILJANDIMAA

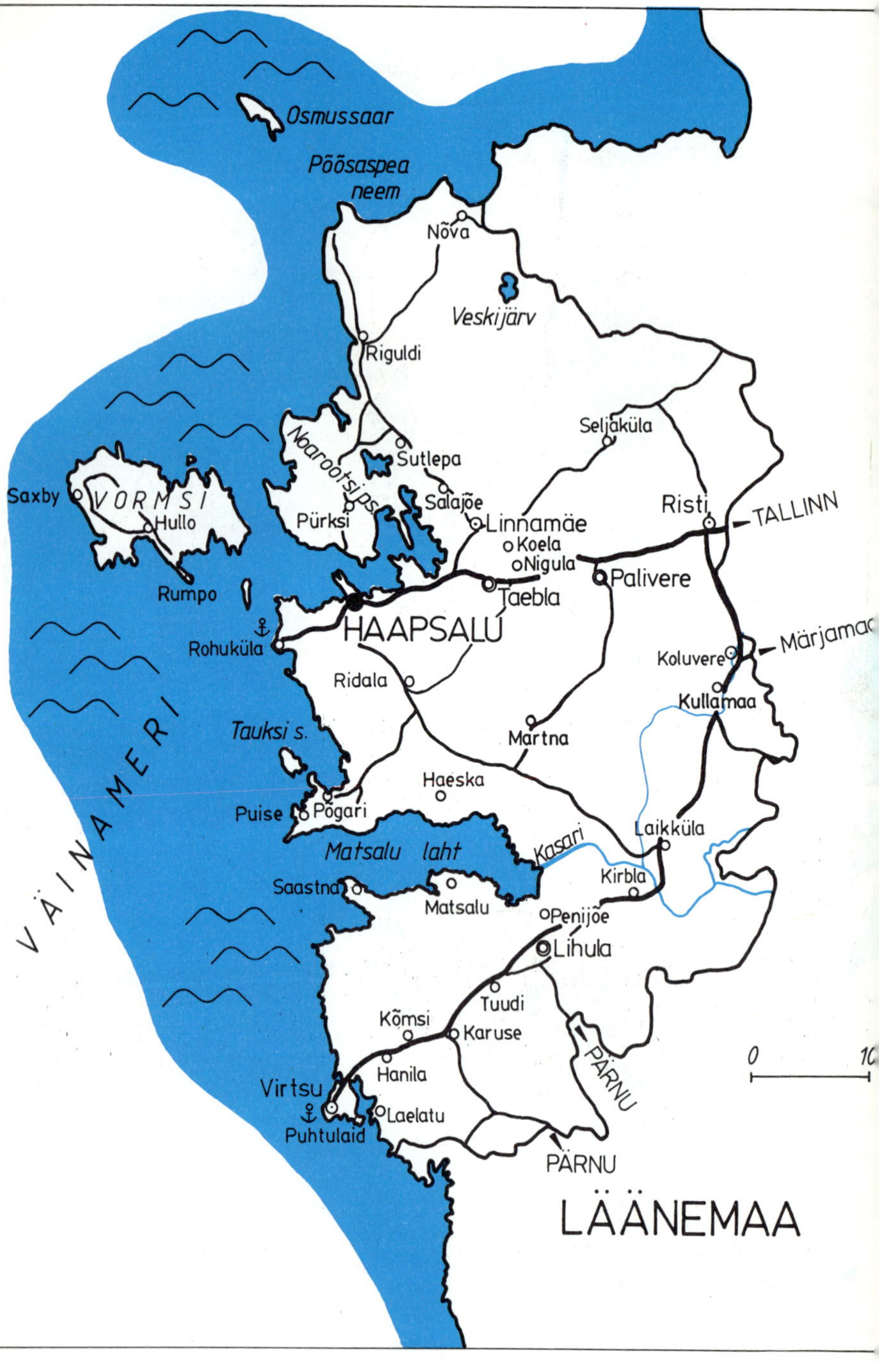
Osmussaar
Põõsaspea neem
Nõva
Veskijärv
Riguldi
Noarootsi ps.
Sutlepa
Seljaküla
Saxby
VORMSI
Hullo
Salajõe
Pürksi
Linnamäe
Risti
TALLINN
Koela
Nigula
Palivere
Rumpo
Taebla
HAAPSALU
Rohuküla
Märjamaa
Koluvere
Ridala
Kullamaa
Tauksi s.
Martna
VÄINAMERI
Haeska
Puise
Põgari
Laikküla
Matsalu laht
Kasari
Kirbla
Saastna
Matsalu
Penijõe
Lihula
Tuudi
Kõmsi
Karuse
PÄRNU
0
10
Hanila
Virtsu
Laelatu
Puhtulaid
PÄRNU
LÄÄNEMAA

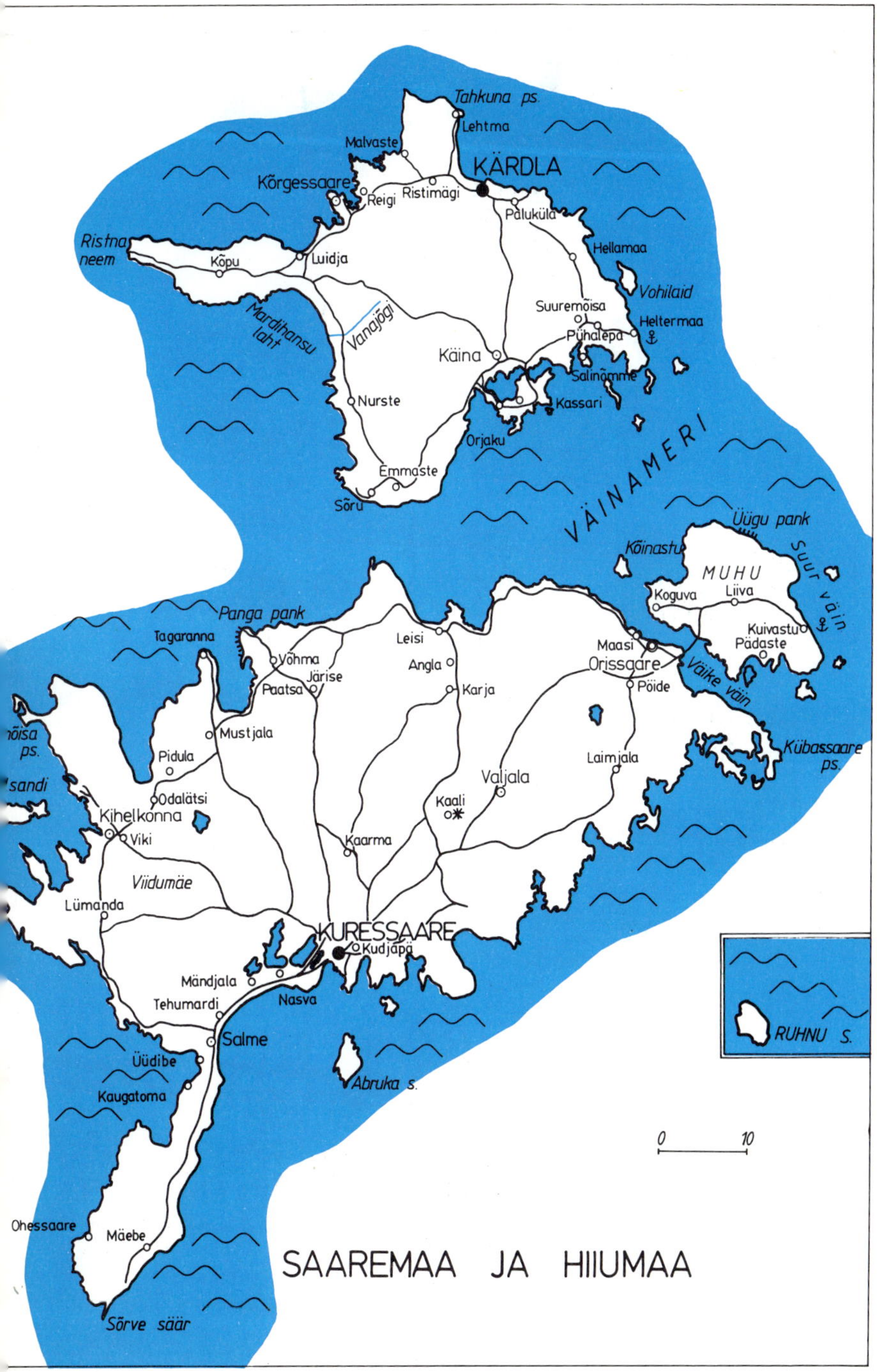
Tahkuna ps.
Lehtma
Malvaste
KÄRDLA
Kõrgessaare
Reigi
Ristimägi
Paluküla
Hellamaa
Ristna neem
Kõpu
Luidja
Vohilaid
Mardihansu laht
Vanajõgi
Suuremõisa
Heltermaa
Pühalepa
Käina
Salinõmme
Nurste
Kassari
Orjaku
Emmaste
Sõru
VÄINAMERI
Üügu pank
Kõinastu
MUHU
Suur väin
Koguva
Liiva
Kuivastu
Pädaste
Panga pank
Tagaranna
Leisi
Võhma
Järise
Angla
Maasi
Orissaare
Paatsa
Karja
Pöide
Väike väin
Mustjala
Pidula
Laimjala
Kübassaare ps.
Valjala
Odalätsi
Kaali
Kihelkonna
Viki
Kaarma
Viidumäe
Lümanda
KURESSAARE
Kudjapä
Mändjala
Tehumardi
Nasva
Salme
Üüdibe
Kaugatoma
Abruka s.
RUHNU S.
0
10
Ohessaare
Mäebe
SAAREMAA JA HIIUMAA
Sõrve säär

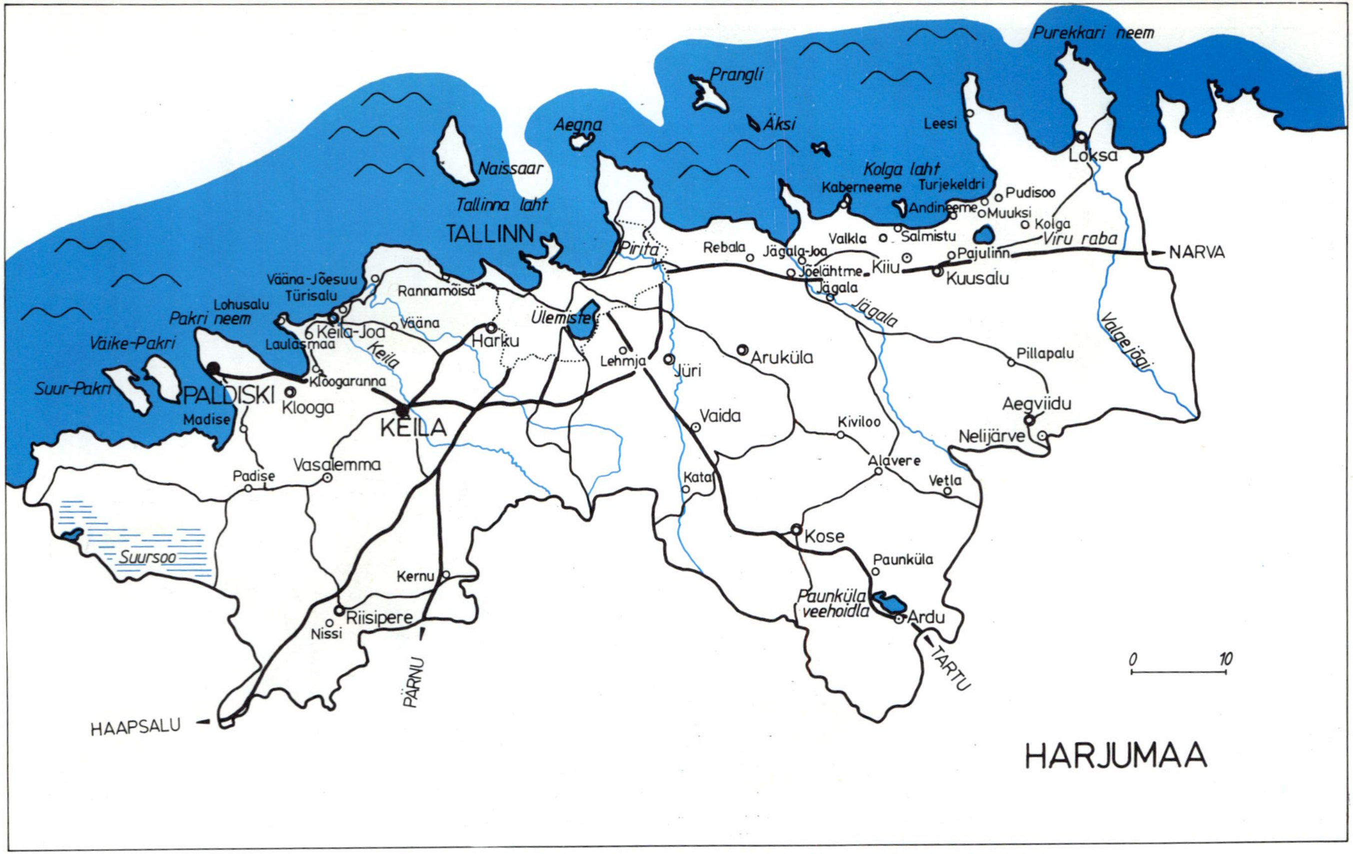
Purekkari neem
Prangli
Äksi
Aegna
Naissaar
Tallinna laht
TALLINN
Leesi
Loksa
Kolga laht
Kaberneeme
Turjekeldri
Pudisoo
Andineeme
Muuksi
Kolga
Viru raba
NARVA
Pirita
Rebala
Jägala-Joa
Valkla
Salmistu
Kiiu
Pajulinn
Joelähtme
Kuusalu
Jägala
Vääna-Jõesuu
Türisalu
Lohusalu
Pakri neem
Väike-Pakri
Suur-Pakri
Rannamõisa
Keila-Joa
Vääna
Laulasmaa
Ülemiste
Harku
Keila
Kloogaranna
PALDISKI
Klooga
Madise
KEILA
Lehmja
Jüri
Aruküla
Pillapalu
Valgejõgi
Aegviidu
Nelijärve
Vaida
Kiviloo
Alavere
Vetla
Vasalemma
Padise
Kata
Suursoo
Kose
Paunküla
Kernu
Paunküla veehoidla
Ardu
Riisipere
Nissi
PÄRNU
TARTU
HAAPSALU
0
10
HARJUMAA

NARVA

Paju
prospekt
I.Fedjuninski
V.Dejevi
Õhu
NARVA
Tallinna mnt.
4. Roheline
3 Roheline
Kangelaste
Kevade
A.Puškini
Vabaduse
Komsomoli
Pimeaia
Hariduse
Hariduse
O. Koševoi
PEETRI
EESLINN
Nõukogude
Kommunaaride
E.Vilde
J. Mahmastali
L.Koidula
Tallinna mnt.
V.Kingissepa
prospekt
Võidu
Kreenholmi
Energia
Tuleviku
VANALINN
Peetri plats
L.Koidula mnt.
Leningradi
J. Anveldi
M. Kalinini
JAANILINN
Kosmonaudi
Linda
A.Puškini
Raja
Malmi
Suur-Aguli
Oru
A.Bastrakovi
A.Puškini
I.Grafovi
JOAORU
Uusküla
1. Mai
J. Tombi
Vaksali
Oktoobri
K. Orgini
Vaivara
UUSKÜLA
prospekt
Raudtee
Kanepi
KREENHOLM
26. Juuli
V.Gerassimovi
Lenini
Turu
Kooli põik
Puuvilla
Proletarskaja
Kreenholmi
Kalda
Haigla
NARVA
Mängu
Palli
Ak.Maslovi
Savi
Spordi
Kose
prospekt
Beregovaja
Kulgu
Pionerskaja
Pastorovi
Lenini
NARVA
N
Kotovski
200 0 200 400 m
© REGIO

TALLINN

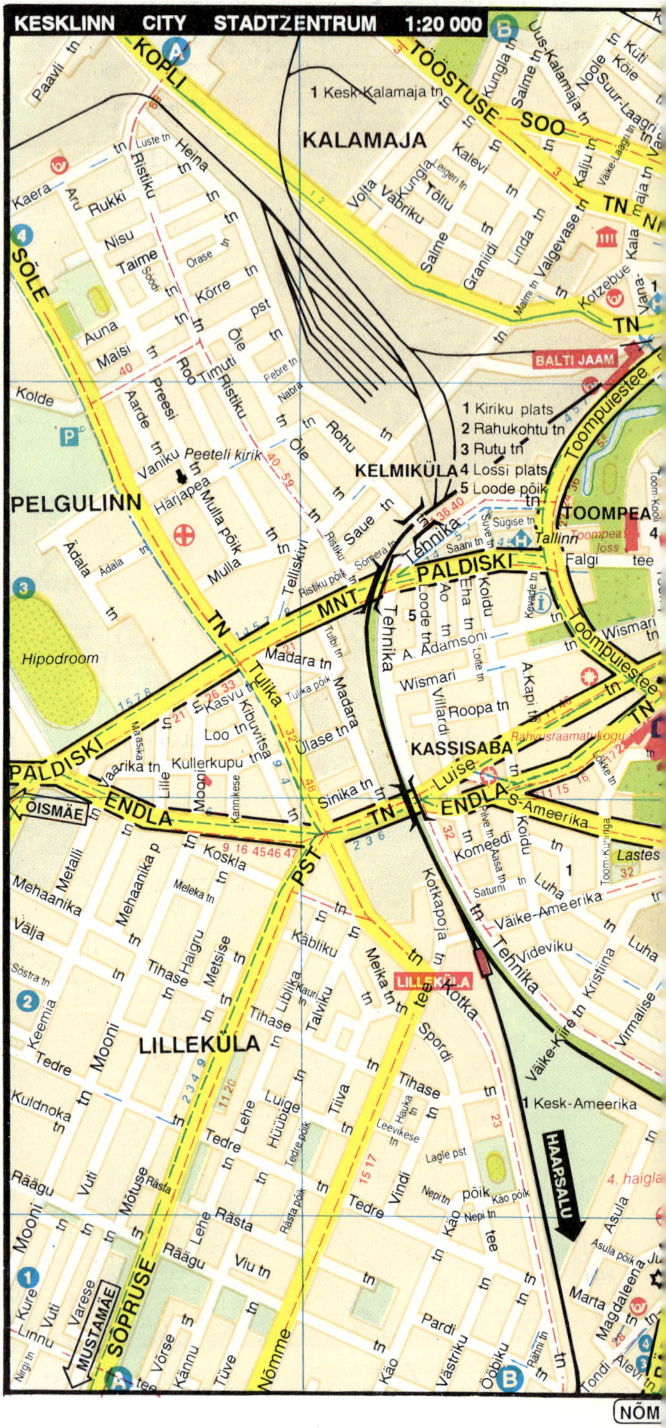
KESKLINN CITY STADTZENTRUM 1:20 000
KOPLI
TÖÖSTUSE
SOO TN
KALAMAJA
1 Kesk-Kalamaja tn
Paavli tn
Luste tn
Heina tn
Ristiku
Kaera
Aru
Rukki
Nisu
Taime
Orase
Kõrre tn
Auna
Maisi
Sõle
Kalevi
Volta
Vabriku
Kungla
Tõllu
Salme
Graniidi
Linda tn
Valgevase tn
Kotzebue
Vana-
BALTI JAAM
Toompuiestee
1 Kiriku plats
2 Rahukohtu tn
3 Rutu tn
4 Lossi plats
5 Loode põik
KELMIKÜLA
TOOMPEA
Toompea loss
Falgi tee
Tallinn
Sügise tn
Saani tn
Peeteli kirik
Kolde
Preesi
Aarde
Vaniku
Härjapea
Mulla põik
Mulla
Rohu
Pebre tn
Nabra
Timuti
Roo
PELGULINN
Ädala
Telliskivi
Saue tn
Sõmera tn
Tehnika
PALDISKI MNT
Hipodroom
Madara tn
Tulika
Kasvu tn
Kibuvitsa
Loo tn
Ülase tn
Kullerkupu tn
Vaarika tn
Lille
Mooni
Kannikese
Sinika tn
A. Adamsoni
Wismari
Villardi
Roopa tn
A.Kapi tn
KASSISABA
Rahvusraamatukogu
Luise
ENDLA TN
S-Ameerika
PALDISKI
ÕISMÄE
ENDLA
Koskla
PST
Metalli
Mehaanika
Mehaanika p
Meleka tn
Välja
Söstra tn
Haigru
Tihase
Metsise
Käbliku
Meika tn
LILLEKÜLA
Kotkapoja tn
Kotka
Komeedi
Saturni
Luha
Väike-Ameerika
Videviku
Kristiina
Virmalise
Väike-Kiire
Lastes
Keemia
Tedre
LILLEKÜLA
Liblika
Talviku
Spordi
Kuldnoka tn
Luige
Hüübi
Tiiva
Tihase
Leevikese
1 Kesk-Ameerika
HAAPSALU
4. haigla
Lagle pst
Nepi tn
Käo põik
Rääga
Vuti
Mõtuse
Rästa
Lehe
Rästa põik
Vindi
Tedre
Asula
Asula põik
Marta
Magdaleena
Mooni
Rääga
Viu tn
Kure
Vuti
Varese
Linnu
Nirgi tn
MUSTAMÄE
SÕPRUSE
Võrse
Kännu
Tüve
Nõmme
Käo
Pardi
Västriku
Ööbiku
Rähni tn
Kondi
Alevi
NÕM

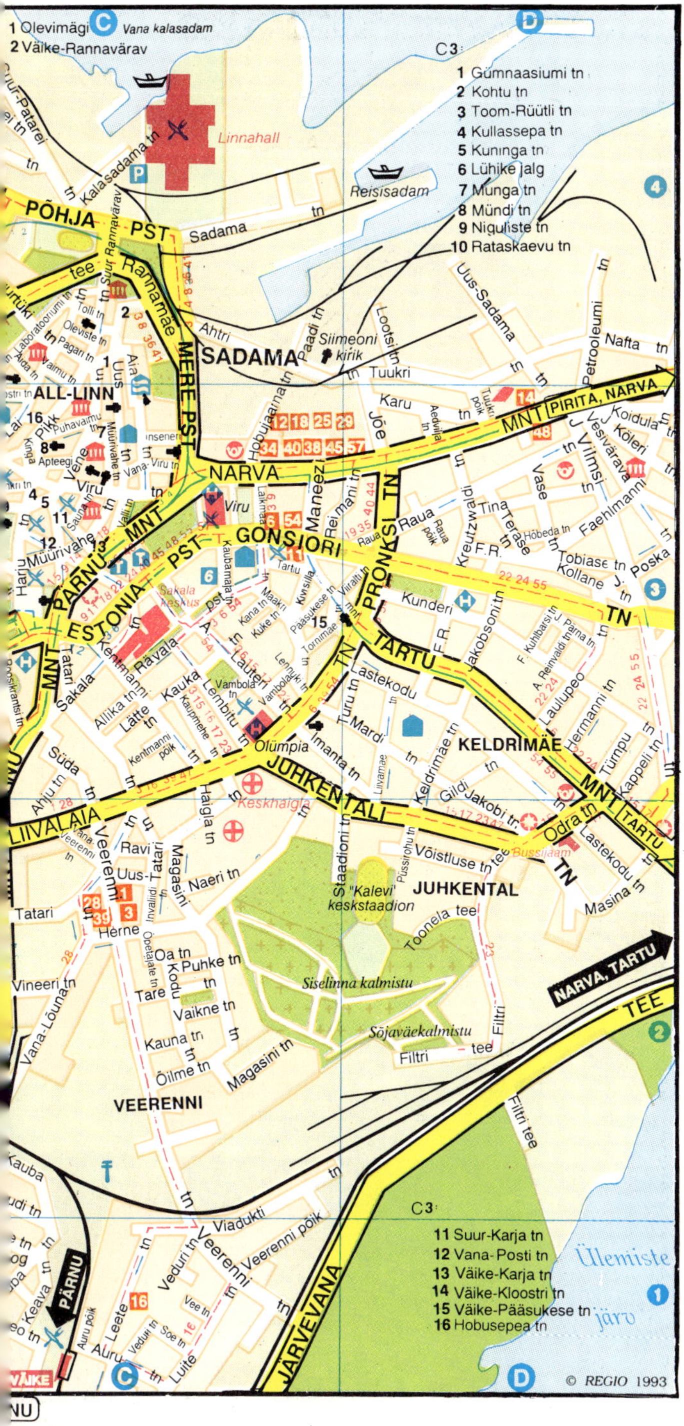
1 Olevimägi
2 Väike-Rannavärav
Vana kalasadam
C3:
1 Gümnaasiumi tn
2 Kohtu tn
3 Toom-Rüütli tn
4 Kullassepa tn
5 Kuninga tn
6 Lühike jalg
7 Munga tn
8 Mündi tn
9 Niguliste tn
10 Rataskaevu tn
Linnahall
Reisisadam
Kalasadama tn
PÕHJA PST
Sadama tn
Rannamäe tee
Suur Rannavärav
MERE PST
SADAMA
Siimeoni kirik
Ahtri
Paadi tn
Lootsi tn
Uus-Sadama
Petrooleumi
Nafta tn
Tuukri
Karu
Jõe
Aedvilja tn
PIRITA, NARVA
MNT
Koidula tn
Köleri
Vesivärava
J. Vilmsi tn
Vase tn
Faehlmanni
Tina
Terase
Hõbeda tn
Tobiase tn
Kollane
Poska
ALL-LINN
Pikk
Puhavaimu tn
Müürivahe tn
Vene
Viru
Vana-Viru tn
Apteegi
Laboratooriumi tn
Tolli tn
Oleviste tn
Pagari tn
Vaimu tn
Aia
Uus
Inseneri
NARVA
Viru
Laikmaa
Maneeži
Reimani tn
PRONKSI TN
Raua
Raua põik
Kreutzwaldi
F.R.
GONSIORI
Tartu
Kivisilla
Paasukese tn
Tornimae
Kunderi
Jakobsoni tn
Müürivahe
Sauna
Valli tn
PÄRNU
MNT
ESTONIA PST
Sakala keskus
Kaubamaja
Kana tn
Maakri
Kuke tn
Lauteri
Tatari
Sakala
Kentmanni
Räväla
Allika tn
Lätte tn
Kauka
Kaupmehe tn
Lembitu
Vambola tn
Vambola
Kentmanni põik
Olümpia
TARTU
Lastekodu
Turu tn
Mardi
Imanta tn
Liivamäe
Keldrimäe tn
Gildi
Jakobi tn
KELDRIMÄE
A. Reinvaldi
Kuhlbarsi tn
J. Pärna tn
Laulupeo
Hermanni tn
Türnpu
Kappeli tn
Odra tn
Lastekodu tn
TARTU
Süda
Ahju tn
LIIVALAIA
JUHKENTALI
Haigla tn
Keskhaigla
Vana-Veerenni tn
Veerenni
Ravi
Uus-Tatari
Magasini
Naeri tn
Staadioni tn
"Kalevi" keskstaadion
Võistluse tn
Püssirohu tn
Bussijaam
JUHKENTAL
Masina tn
Tatari
Invaliidi
Herne
Õpetajate tn
Oa tn
Puhke tn
Kodu
Tare
Vaikne tn
Kauna tn
Õilme tn
Magasini tn
Toonela tee
Siselinna kalmistu
Sõjaväekalmistu
Filtri tee
NARVA, TARTU
TEE
Vineeri tn
Vana-Lõuna
VEERENNI
Kauba
Viadukti
Veerenni
Veerenni põik
Veduri tn
Vee tn
Soe tn
Leete
Auru põik
Auru
Luite
Keava
PÄRNU
JÄRVEVANA
Filtri tee
C3:
11 Suur-Karja tn
12 Vana-Posti tn
13 Väike-Karja tn
14 Väike-Kloostri tn
15 Väike-Pääsukese tn
16 Hobusepea tn
Ülemiste järv
© REGIO 1993

TARTU

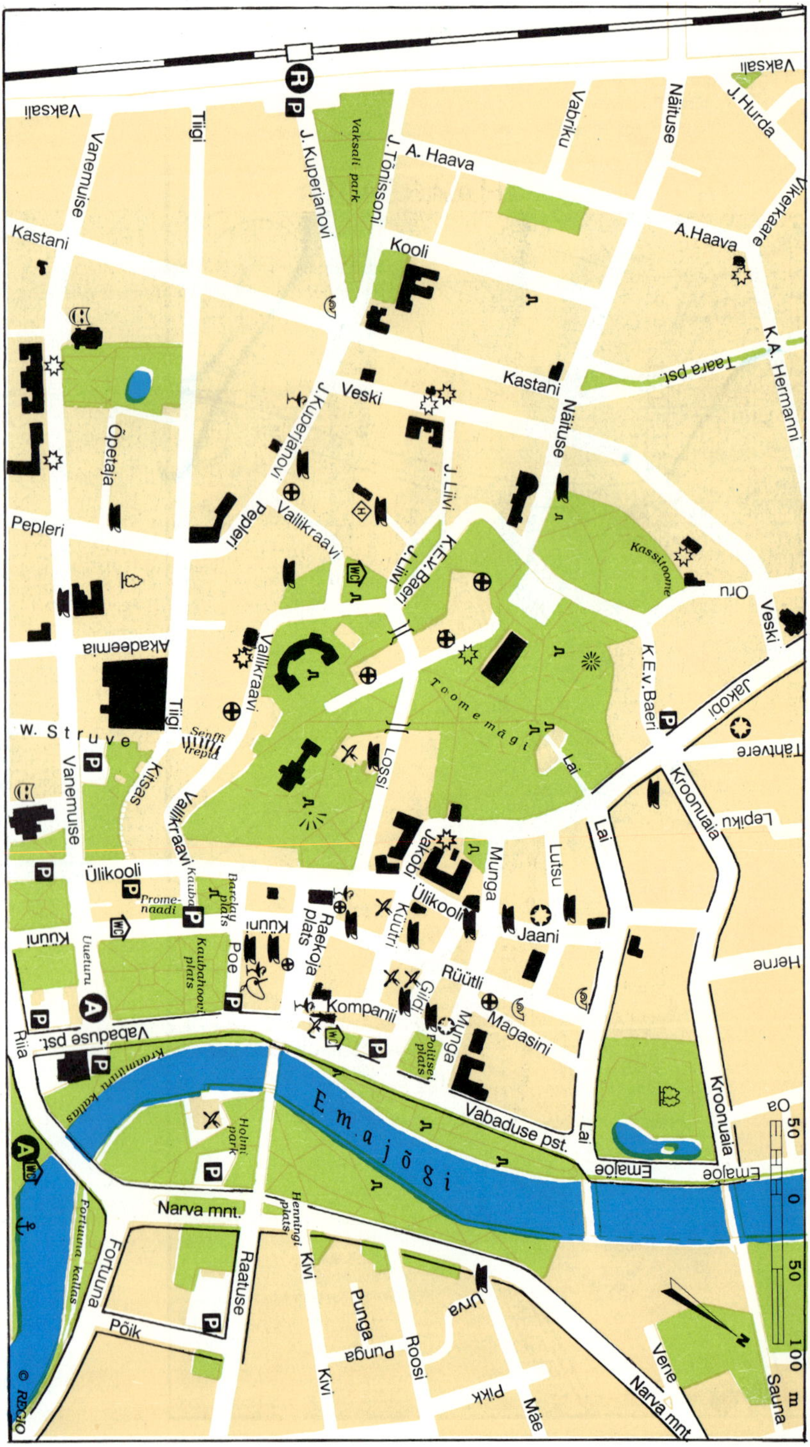
Vaksali
Tiigi
J. Kuperjanovi
Vaksali park
J. Tõnissoni
A. Haava
Vabriku
Näituse
J. Hurda
Vanemuise
Kastani
Kooli
Vikerkaare
A.Haava
K.A. Hermanni
Taara pst.
Veski
Kastani
Näituse
Õpetaja
J. Kuperjanovi
J. Liivi
Pepleri
Pepleri
Vallikraavi
K.E.v.Baeri
J. Liivi
Kassitoome
Oru
Veski
Akadeemia
Vallikraavi
Toomemägi
K.E.v.Baeri
Jakobi
W. Struve
Tiigi
Senffi trepid
Lossi
Lai
Tähtvere
Kitsas
Vallikraavi
Vanemuise
Kroonuaia
Lepiku
Lai
Lutsu
Munga
Jakobi
Ülikooli
Promenaadi
Kauba
Barclay plats
Raekoja plats
Küüni
Küütri
Ülikooli
Jaani
Küüni
Uueturu
Kaubahoovi plats
Poe
Rüütli
Herne
Kompanii
Gildi
Munga
Magasini
Riia
Vabaduse pst.
Politsei plats
Kroonuaia
Kroonuaia kallas
Emajõgi
Holmi park
Vabaduse pst.
Lai
Oa
Emajõe
Emajõe
Narva mnt.
Henningi plats
Fortuuna kallas
Fortuuna
Raatuse
Kivi
Punga
Punga
Roosi
Pikk
Mäe
Una
Narva mnt.
Vene
Sauna
Põik
Kivi
50
0
50
100 m
N
© REGIO

HAAPSALU

EESLAHT
TAGALAHT
Väike Viik
N
Holmi
Kalúri
Uus-
Sadama
Lahe
Väike-Viigi
Sadama
Sadama
Suur-Liiva
Lembitu
Lahe
V.-Liiva
Laia
Kalda
Wiedemanni
Rüütli
Kalda
Kärja
Õhtu
Mihkli tn
Vaba tn
Vee
Kopli
Korkja
Roo
Eha
Koidula
Endla
Vonnu
Posti
Koidula
Metsa
Aia
Kalda
Kreutzwaldi
Uus
Turu
Luha
Põllu
Aiavilja
Kalevi
Surnuaia
Nurme
Potissepa
Ungru tee
Jaama
Haava
Metsa
Haava
põik
Mulla
Niine
Jalaka
Raudtee
Õpetaja
Staadioni
Kuuse
Pärna
Sambla
Lille
Kiltsi tee
Niine
Toominga
Tallinna mnt.
Lepa
Tedre
Kauba
Lihula mnt.
Sireli
Paju
Jalaka
Kase
Raudtee
Pihlaka
Kadaka
Lehise
Räägu
Tiigi
Saare
Vahtra
Männi
Tamme
Männiku tee
Kastani
Kuuse
© REGIO

KURESSAARE

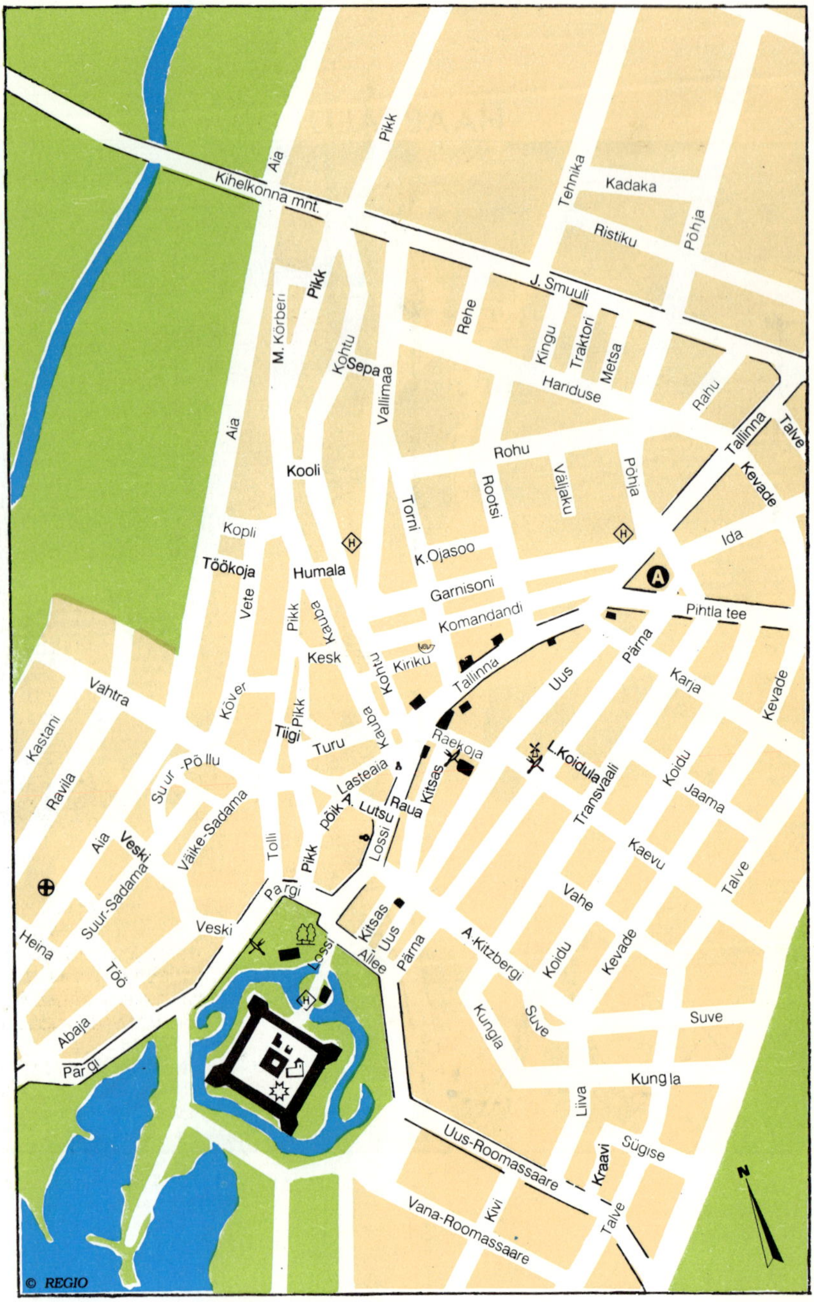

Aia
Pikk
Kihelkonna mnt.
Tehnika
Kadaka
Ristiku
Põhja
J. Smuuli
Pikk
M. Körberi
Rehe
Kingu
Traktori
Metsa
Kohtu
Sepa
Vallimaa
Hariduse
Rahu
Tallinna
Talve
Aia
Rohu
Kooli
Rootsi
Väljaku
Põhja
Kevade
Torni
Kopli
Ida
K.Ojasoo
Töökoja
Humala
A
Garnisoni
Pihtla tee
Vete
Pikk
Kauba
Komandandi
Pärna
Kesk
Kohtu
Kiriku
Tallinna
Uus
Karja
Vahtra
Kõver
Kevade
Kastani
Tiigi
Pikk
Kauba
Turu
Raekoja
L.Koidula
Suur-Põllu
Lasteaia
Koidu
Transvaali
Ravila
põik
A. Lutsu
Raua
Kitsas
Jaama
Väike-Sadama
Aia
Veski
Tolli
Pikk
Lossi
Kaevu
Suur-Sadama
Pargi
Talve
Vahe
Veski
Kitsas
Uus
Heina
Lossi
Allee
Pärna
A.Kitzbergi
Koidu
Kevade
Töö
Kungla
Suve
Suve
Abaja
Pargi
Kungla
Liiva
Uus-Roomassaare
Sügise
Kraavi
Kivi
Talve
Vana-Roomassaare
N
© REGIO